Innovation in Open & Distance Learning

Successful Development of Online and Web-Based Learning

edited by
Fred Lockwood
Anne Gooley

**KOGAN
PAGE**

First published in 2001 by Kogan Page Limited

Kogan Page Limited
120 Pentonville Road
London
N1 9JN
UK

Stylus Publishing
22883 Quicksilver Drive
Sterling
VA 20166-2012
USA

British Library Cataloguing in Publication Data

A CIP record for this book is available from the British Library.

ISBN 0 7494 3476 7 (paperback)
ISBN 0 7494 3477 5 (hardback)

May 14, 2001

Typeset by Jean Cussons Typesetting, Diss, Norfolk
Printed and bound by Creative Print and Design (Wales), Ebbw Vale

Contents

List of contributors

Professor Ulrich Bernath
Carl von Ossietzky Universitaet, Oldenburg
26111 Oldenburg, Germany
e-mail: bernath@zef.uni-oldenburg.de

Professor Stephen Brown
Head of Learning Technologies
Director of International Institute of Electronic Library Research
De Montfort University
The Gateway
Leicester LE1 9BH
UK
e-mail: sbrown@dmu.ac.uk

Yvonne Brunetto
Queensland Open Learning Network
PO box 3165
South Brisbane, Qld 4101
Australia
e-mail: y.brunetto@mailbox.uq.edu.au

Dr Edward Peter Errington
Formerly University of Leeds

Dr Rod Farr-Wharton
Queensland Open Learning Network
PO Box 3165
South Brisbane, Qld 4101
Australia
e-mail: r.farr-wharton@mailbox.uq.edu.au

Anne Gooley
Chief Executive
Queensland Open Learning Network
PO box 3165
South Brisbane, Qld 4101
Australia
e-mail: a.gooley@qoln.net

Mike Green
Open University Business School
Open University
Walton Hall MK7 6AA
UK
e-mail: m.green@open.ac.uk

Dr Cathy Gunn
Centre for Professional Development
University of Auckland
Private Bag 92019
Auckland
New Zealand
e-mail: ca.gunn@auckland.ac.nz

Lindsay Hewson
Faculty of Arts and Social Sciences
University of New South Wales
Sydney, NSW 2052
Australia
e-mail: l.hewson@unsw.edu.au

Chris Hughes
Faculty of Medicine
University of New South Wales
Sydney, NSW 2052
Australia
e-mail: c.hughes@unsw.edu.au

Dr Alistair Inglis
ITAP – Bundoora Campus
RMIT University
GPO Box 2476V Melbourne 3001, Vic.
Australia
e-mail: alistair.inglis@rmit.edu.au

Dr Tapan Jena
Reader
School of Health Sciences
Indira Gandhi National Open University
New Delhi 110 068
India
e-mail: ignusohs@ndf.vsnl.net.in

Associate Professor Bruce King
Director: Flexible Learning Centre
University of South Australia
Underdale
Adelaide, SA 5032
Australia
e-mail: bruce.king@unisa.edu.au

Dr Fred Lockwood
Open University
Walton Hall
Milton Keynes MK7 6AA
UK
e-mail: F.G.Lockwood@open.ac.uk

Associate Professor Ric Lowe
Instructional Design and Educational Technology
Faculty of Education
Curtin University of Technology, WA
Australia
e-mail: r.lowe@educ.curtin.edu.au

Dr Patrick McGhee
Dean of Learning Support and Development
Bolton Institute
Dean Campus
Dean Road
Bolton BL3 5AB
UK
e-mail: p.mcghee@bolton.ac.uk

Dr Claire McLachlan-Smith
Centre for Professional Development
University of Auckland
Private Bag 92019
Auckland
New Zealand
e-mail: c.mclachlansmith@auckland.ac.nz

Dr Catherine McLoughlin
Teaching and Learning Centre
The University of New England
Armidale, NSW 2351
Australia
e-mail: mcloughlin@metz.une.edu.au

Chris Morgan
Teaching & Learning Centre
Southern Cross University
PO Box 157
Lismore, NSW 2480
Australia
e-mail: cmorgan@scu.edu.au

Todd C Y Ng
Open University of Hong Kong
30 Good Shepherd Street
Kowloon
Hong Kong
PRC
e-mail: tng@ouhk.edu.hk

Professor Christopher O'Hagan
Dean of Learning Development
Centre for Educational Development and Media
University of Derby
Kedleston Road
Derby DE22 1GB
UK
e-mail: c.m.ohagan@derby.ac.uk

Associate Professor Ron Oliver
Coordinator of Interactive Multimedia
School of Communications and Multimedia
Edith Cowan University
2 Bradford St
Mt Lawley, 6050 WA
Australia
e-mail: r.oliver@cowan.edu.au

Meg O'Reilly
Teaching & Learning Centre
Southern Cross University
PO Box 157
Lismore, NSW 2480
Australia
e-mail: moreilly@scu.edu.au

Professor Santosh Panda,
Director, Staff Training and Research
Institute of Distance Education, Indira Gandhi National Open University
New Delhi 110 068
India
e-mail: pandasantosh@hotmail.com

Bernadette Robinson
Special Professor of Comparative Education
School of Continuing Education
University of Nottingham
UK
e-mail: b.robinson@open.ac.uk

Professor Eugene Rubin
Associate Dean – Distance Education
Graduate School of Management and Technology
University of Maryland, University College
College Park
Maryland, 20742–1616
USA
e-mail: erubin@nova.umuc.edu

Claire Simpson
Open University Business School
Open University
Walton Hall
Milton Keynes MK7 6AA
UK
e-mail: c.a.simpson@open.ac.uk

Peter Skippington
Queensland Open Learning Network
PO Box 3165
South Brisbane, Qld 4101
Australia
e-mail: p.skippington@qoln.net

Andre Smit
School of Social and Workplace Development
Southern Cross University
PO Box 157
Lismore, NSW 2480
Australia
e-mail: asmit@scu.edu.au

Dr Stephen Towers
Queensland Open Learning Network
PO box 3165
South Brisbane, Qld 4101
Australia
e-mail: s.towers@qoln.net

Dr Sheila Tyler
Open University Business School
Open University
Walton Hall
Milton Keynes MK7 6AA
UK
e-mail: s.tyler@open.ac.uk

Professor Danny S N Wong
Open University of Hong Kong
30 Good Shepherd Street
Kowloon
Hong Kong
PRC
e-mail: dwong@ouhk.edu.hk

Series editor's foreword

We are in the midst of a teaching and technological revolution. Increasing numbers of teachers and trainers are experimenting with, and embracing, student-centred learning approaches and basing their teaching on constructivist models of learning. The *Sage on the Stage*, the expositional form of teaching, is being increasingly replaced by the *Guide on the Side*, an approach where the teachers act as a facilitator of learning.

The potential of Information and Communication Technologies (ICT) is being explored across all academic levels and in all teaching and training areas. There are Virtual Schools with thousands of young learners as well as eUniversities serving international clients. Academic staff are innovating; they are exploring the implications of changes in methods of teaching and in the use of the new technologies. The basis for our assumptions are being questioned as are the practices we have used to develop course materials, to support learners and assess them. For example, the provision of synchronous and asynchronous computer mediated communication has transformed the ways in which we can interact with learners and how they can interact between themselves. Until recent years we could only simulate such interaction – today, as a result of the work of innovators and *early adopters* we can engage in actual interaction.

The driving force(s) for such innovation are many: reduced per capita funding for teaching and training, increasing competition and a desire in increase access to disadvantaged groups as well as providing the most valuable learning experience possible. Whatever the reasons, without colleagues who are prepared to take risks, and innovate, these twin revolutions will stall and opportunities for your learners may be lost. Furthermore, unless we encourage these innovators and *early adopters* to record their experiences and research findings there is a real danger of duplication and wasted effort.

This collection of chapters cannot provide a full picture of the work in progress nor that which is becoming influential in current teaching and training – but it can give a snap shot. The book *Innovation in Open and Distance Learning* draws together accounts from innovators and *early adopters* from around the world and provides a record of their experience and findings. Collectively they illuminate both the teaching revolution and the technology of which they are a part.

I hope you enjoy the different chapters, that you become another *early adopter* and are encouraged to become an innovator.

Fred Lockwood
November 2000

Acknowledgements

This book would not be possible without the contributors from around the world who have been generous in sharing their knowledge and expertise. They have highlighted the challenges ahead for all of us who are involved in open and distance learning and who are concerned about the need for long term thinking, openness and cooperation in addressing the needs of the life long learner.

We would also like to express our gratitude to Jessica Lambert, who assembled the manuscript. Her attention to detail, diligence and ability to keep smiling when meeting the deadline has made this book possible.

Fred Lockwood and Anne Gooley
November 2000

Chapter 1

Innovation in distributed learning: creating the environment

Fred Lockwood

Introduction

The past 30 years have witnessed an amazing revolution in teaching and training around the world. Whilst forms of correspondence teaching have been practised for thousands of years, and refined during the last century in various correspondence courses, it was the creation of the Open University in 1969 that signalled a major change in the way teaching and learning was organized and practised (Perry, 1976). Since the creation of the Open University, Open, Distance, Flexible, Resource Based – and now Distributed Learning (DL) – have expanded dramatically around the world. Today 11 mega-universities currently enrol about 3 million undergraduates with hundreds of thousands following other, non-degree courses (Daniel, 2000). However, this number is dwarfed by those in industry, commerce and the public services who study using self-instructional material in the workplace and at home.

At the present time we are poised on the threshold of another revolution, one involving Communication and Information Technology and the Knowledge Media, which will have a profound effect on teaching and learning for all of us (Ryan *et al*, 2000; Inglis *et al*, 1999). The challenge facing us is to learn from the experience of others, to encourage and evaluate educational innovation, so that all of us can achieve our full potential. This book is offered as a modest contribution to this goal and this opening chapter as an orientation to the rest of the contributions.

The above phrase, 'Open, Distance, Flexible, Resource Based – and now Distributed Learning', is cumbersome and I am reluctant here to become embroiled in defining this terminology. If my esteemed colleague, Derek Rowntree, is not unduly concerned I feel in good company: 'Open learning? Distance learning? Flexible learning? Which are you concerned with? Maybe some combination of the three. Or perhaps your form of learning goes under another name. No matter' (Rowntree, 1994: 2).

However, elsewhere I do offer a discussion on the difference between open, distance and flexible learning (Lockwood, 1998) but will use the term Distributed Learning (DL) below, a term that Inglis (Chapter 8) comments upon.

Distributed learning in the new millennium

A decision by individuals and organizations to embrace DL methods, and the new technologies, will require changes to the way we teach and how we manage that change; this is not an easy task. Chapter 5 by King describes how the University of South Australia succeeded in instituting a low-cost communication platform, UnivSAnet, that focused on teaching and learning, spanned the entire university, provided support and allowed academic staff to focus on the content and not technical intricacies; it reads like a success story and is endorsed by the independent evaluator. The case study by Tyler *et al* (Chapter 6) is slightly different. It focuses upon the evaluation of Lotus LearningSpace within a large multinational corporation and reveals that the transfer from conventional to online teaching was not unproblematic:

> The future is not merely a matter of revisiting the social learning and resource-based course models of the past... It offers the possibilities of new methods of working consistent with re-engineering of processes (e-commerce), distributed industry and sustainable development. The future is exciting, but how do we proceed? The Lotus project shows that the gradualist approach (addition and adaptation) are unlikely to work: it is necessary to break out of text-heavy courses geared to individualist approaches to learning.
>
> (Tyler *et al*, Chapter 6, p 73)

However, the account by Hewson and Hughes (Chapter 7) offers an alternative; a Web-based environment that builds upon conventional teaching methods and bridges the gap between the traditional face-to-face and emerging online teaching. The above chapters describe how the particular Web-based environments were used in their respective institutions. The contribution by Inglis provides a framework, checklists and pointers to how you can decide which of these 'electronic learning environments' will satisfy your needs. It offers invaluable Web sites to existing systems and discusses, amongst other aspects, the cost, scalability and compatibility of such systems and notes: 'If the intention is to make the transition from face-to-face delivery or more traditional modes of distance education delivery to delivery via the knowledge media, then one of the tasks involved in making that transition is putting in place the appropriate delivery infrastructure'(Inglis, Chapter 8, p 88).

This is precisely what the Australian National Training Authority (ANTA) Multimedia Toolbox Initiative was intended to do and is described by Oliver *et al* (Chapter 9): 'The concept of a software toolbox carries the forms of flexibility and functionality required for scalable and sustainable software developments. A software toolbox is essentially a package that has been designed with flexible use in mind. The toolbox represents a product that can be used in a variety of ways to achieve essentially the same end' (Oliver *et al*, Chapter 9, p 102).

They note the high costs associated with online development and the benefits offered by collaboration or ease with which existing resources and systems can be customized. The ANTA project, which provided A$3.8M in support funds, sought to limit localized 'cottage industry' and to enable maximum use (customization) of materials and systems created.

The process illustrated by the above chapters, and others, may be aided by a consideration of the context within which such innovation in DL can flourish and how examples of such innovations have been realized. In Chapter 2 Robinson reviews the experience of a large number of colleagues involved in innovation in DL, from a variety of contexts and cultures, and flags several key features that influence the success, or otherwise, of particular innovations. She termed these *Resource availability, Organizational issues, Human resource capacity* and *Use of technology*. Her account is valuable because it both identifies the frustrating events many of us have experienced, alerts us to other pitfalls, and contributes to our understanding of the context within which innovations in DL take place. However, the four features Robinson identifies are not self-contained or mutually exclusive – they merge with their effect being compounded. The chapters in this book, to different degrees, illustrate, refine and extend these four features.

Funds and resources

The provision of adequate funds and resources is not only vital to any innovative task but needs to be agreed at the highest level of the organization; this is evident in the chapters from all the contributors.

Robinson summarizes the experience of many practitioners who struggled with inadequate resources. Perhaps, like me, you will be able to recall enthusiasts who committed themselves to an innovative course development task with an inadequate budget, experienced an inappropriate flow of funds or resources for completion and who adopted an unrealistic time frame. Or even worse, colleagues who undertook the task with no budget, support that was dependent upon 'calling in favours' or doing it themselves and which resulted in an increased workload that extended over a receding time-scale that drained those involved. Perhaps you will be able to recall managers who naively believed that the innovation would readily prove to be cost effective or who had unrealistic expectations of its take-up in wider markets or in general applications. Or even worse, those who through neglect or a desire to maintain control allowed projects to flounder, thus maintaining the status quo.

McLachlan-Smith and Gunn (Chapter 4) provide two case studies from within a traditional university that professes to be changing its methods of teaching and becoming a more flexible learning institution. However, as you will read, they conclude that funds, resources and support were inadequate and adversely affected the resultant learning experience. In persevering and completing the projects the innovators may not have done themselves any favours:

> these flexible courses have been successful essentially against the odds: due in part because they met the needs of their niche market and in part to the time and dedication of the 'early adopters' who coordinated them... as so much of the work [and costs] of developing these courses is hidden [the university] could look upon the success of these courses as an indication that further resourcing and support is unnecessary.
>
> (McLachlan-Smith and Gunn, Chapter 4, p 50)

However, the account by McLachlan-Smith and Gunn of life at the University of Auckland is in stark contrast to the positions adopted by another traditional university, De Montfort University, the Open University of Hong Kong and two dual mode universities – the University of South Australia and University of New South Wales which have created their own university-wide teaching and learning environments. At De Montfort, pump-priming funds, development funds and a range of resources were made available to innovative projects within the *Electronic Campus*; the procedures adopted are business-like: 'The goal of the Electronic Campus is to ensure a maximum and rapid return on investment of resources through integration of previously disparate strands of activity' (Brown, Chapter 11, p 125).

The goal of the Open University of Hong Kong (Wong and Ng, Chapter 12) is to prosper as a self-financing institution when it has unpredictable student demand and intense competition from subsidized local institutions as well as over 100 institutions overseas deploying DL. In their account of student recruitment and retention they depict an institution that: 'Just like a commercial operation, it has to work on its revenue strategies – how to recruit and retain more students, how to improve its courses and how to get more income' (Wong and Ng, Chapter 12, p 133).

They describe various strategies that in only seven years have resulted in the steady growth in the university, increased retention rates and the cost of their unsubsidized courses becoming 20 per cent cheaper than those offered in Hong Kong by other providers. However, they stress this is not at the expense of quality but rather because 'cost control is on the agenda from day one. It believes that successful pricing strategies must be accompanied by good cost strategies. It must keep the cost down to stay competitive at the pricing level' (Wong and Ng, Chapter 12, p 141).

Brown (Chapter 11) stresses that the De Montfort innovation is not designed to create a DL institution but rather one committed to mixed mode delivery and one that encourages peer interaction as well as interaction between staff and students – regardless of geographical location. The innovation with the University of South Australia is remarkably similar. King makes it clear that whilst UnivSAnet is part of a DL initiative it was designed to ensure teaching was learner centred and 'to bring a degree of rationalization to a range of exciting but uncoordinated activities' (King, Chapter 5, p 56).

He notes how internal Grants for Innovative Teaching & Learning are used to encourage and support these innovative projects.

Their descriptions support the observations of both Robinson and McLachlan-Smith and Gunn in describing how central funding for the production of DL courses and innovative projects is needed if they are to have any chance of success and are not to be one-off events completed 'against the odds'. However, in evidence from the Lotus Experiment described by Tyler *et al*, it is evident that *Espoused Theory* differs from *Theories in Use* (Argyris and Schön, 1974). The sponsors of the learning package, the multinational company, wished to 'accelerate culture change, create new leadership and build a learning organization capable of sustaining adaptability and flexibility among managers... [it] was keen to enhance teamwork and action learning' (Tyler *et al*, Chapter 6, p 63).

However, the subsequent evaluation revealed that it failed to support its learners in several ways. The mismatch between assertion and reality was not lost on the learners who maintained the company 'should provide time and opportunity for students to apply their learning'.

Organizational issues

Robinson (Chapter 2) and Errington (Chapter 3) note the problems encountered by innovators when faced with procedures and practices designed for a conventional teaching system but which are inappropriate for one involving DL methods. This is demonstrated in the two case studies provided by McLachlan-Smith and Gunn. I suspect the following observation they make could be applied to many institutions: 'The university at present can be seen to be strong on rhetoric and gestures, but weak on implementation through revision of infrastructure, resources, training, support and quality assurance of materials' (McLachlan-Smith and Gunn, Chapter 4, p 49).

Robinson notes how those she surveyed found it extremely difficult to change or amend existing systems, how a lack of coordination often resulted in inefficient 'cottage industries' being created, how cosmetic changes to the systems in operation were insufficient and radical change was needed. Her point is reinforced by McLachlan–Smith and Gunn who quote 'structural and political reasons' for not instituting change. In such a context change must be based on a collective institutional vision as expressed in policies and realized in institutional strategies. Brown and King describe how senior staff created such a vision and assembled policies that allowed the organization to be 're-engineered' so as to enable it to respond meaningfully to changing circumstances. The accounts, from institutions literally from opposite sides of the world, describe some of the mechanisms that have enabled the vision to be shared and realized.

King, like Hewson and Hughes, identifies that the critical change was to be a student-centred learning environment that was significantly technologically mediated adequately resourced and supported by appropriate professional development of staff (King, Chapter 5, pp 52–53).

Gooley et al (Chapter 10), in describing the efforts of the Queensland Open Learning Network, reinforce this point. Furthermore, they note the importance of providing core skills, and competencies associated with computer literacy, if learners are to have a chance of success. Indeed, the potential barriers they identify are applicable to many learning communities – whether in vocational, further or higher education: '(1) low self-confidence related to previous educational experience; (2) high costs associated with telecommunications, travel and distance; (3) the availability of relevant learning programmes and services for rural and remote client groups; and (4) limited access to information and communications technologies' (Gooley et al, Chapter 10, p 113).

Brown specifically identifies the need for project management and describes the role of Learning Development Managers, indicating that those assembling the innovative learning materials 'have the benefit of professional advice and guidance when considering issues such as teaching methods, assessment strategies, learning support methods, learning resource requirements (eg library provision, IT facilities), teaching resource requirements (eg AV/IT provision, videoconferencing) and staff development needs (eg media production and acquisition skills)' (Brown, Chapter 11, p 130).

This point is reinforced by Oliver et al who note that without advice and assistance from instructional designers 'text formed the basis for online materials with accompanying media being a secondary consideration' (Oliver et al, Chapter 9, p 106).

The materials were presented in a format that resembled conventional paper-based teaching.

At this time it is noteworthy that in summarizing the success of the Open University, the Vice Chancellor spoke of the four contributory factors:

One: very high quality multi-media learning materials produced by multi-skilled academic teams. Study materials must be excellent and varied to make the campus in the home or workplace a congenial experience. Two: dedicated personal academic support... their own tutor for each course... [to] comment and mark the student's assignments, hold group meetings and give support by phone, email and computer conferencing. Three: slick logistics. Each individual student must receive the right material and information at the right time... Four: a strong research base.

(Daniel, 1998: 26–27).

Without organizational support (or slick logistics) Robinson describes how innovators can become marginalized; McLachlan-Smith and Gunn describe how evidence from evaluations that indicate how improvements can be made are not acted upon because they have resource and workload implications. Tyler *et al* describe how the evaluation identified many aspects in need of revision as well as resistance to change from both students and tutors; a consequence of change noted by King who comments:

the potential of the new technologies to alter power relationships in the teacher-learner interaction, and even tensions between traditional views of the role and function of a university and an emerging organizational culture that accommodates more specific notions of social accountability, customer service and accommodation of student diversity.

(King, Chapter 5, p 52)

Tyler *et al* also reveal how a desire to provide an extensive, detailed and stimulating resource can result in over-length material – the effects being counterproductive as student comments revealed:

'There's so much reading to do for the course, I don't have enough time to think about it properly'. A large majority of students (78.6 per cent) agreed with the statement; almost the same proportion (76.7 per cent) said that to get through the course they do only what's necessary although many (61.2 per cent) were unhappy about this way of studying...

'Our aim is to reduce the material we have to read; anything on top of that is disregarded'.

(Tyler *et al*, Chapter 6, pp 70, 72)

The *Action Centred Learning Activities*, the vehicle by which group work and collaboration was to be encouraged, were not attempted by the majority of learners.

Evidence of innovative, online activities generating large amounts of work is illustrated by Bernath and Rubin (Chapter 19). In their evaluation they discuss two unexpected outcomes – one being the sheer number and volume of messages created by participants, the other being the perceived learning benefits by apparently 'non-active' participants or 'witness learners'. Over the seminar period, with about 50 per cent of participants contributing, the participants and experts together generated material equivalent to about 120,000 words – equivalent to a substantial book. They remark: 'This data clearly shows how the sheer volume of online activity can be overwhelming to both the teacher and the student, and why the workload of online faculty is often reported as significantly higher than face-to-face teaching' (Bernath and Rubin, Chapter 19, p 221).

One solution to this problem is offered by Oliver and McLoughlin (Chapter 13) who describe how a supportive Web environment can be created; one that provides access, support and opportunity to collaborate but which is not continually dependent upon the teacher. They observe how there is a tendency for teachers to design online environments in ways that increase student–teacher communication. The implementation of this form of dialogue may result in volumes of communication which become time consuming and unproductive (Oliver and McLoughlin, Chapter 13, p 158).

Their description of WebFAQ, WebURL and RonSub may encourage you to explore similar Web-based tools to save you from being 'overwhelmed'.

In addition to workload, a second factor typically dominates the lives of learners in DL contexts; demands of assessment. Morgan and O'Reilly (Chapter 16) note how assessment demands 'drive and shape' learning and, in general, how conservative DL assessment methods appear. In contrast they describe and illustrate how online assessment, involving problem solving and teamwork, can be employed to create 'a learning community'. They present case studies which demonstrate how interactive online learning can 'encourage purposeful dialogue, multiple discourses, collaboration, peer and self-evaluation, and contribute to a sense of community and shared purpose amongst distance learners' (Morgan and O'Reilly, Chapter 16, p 185).

Similar constructivist approaches to teaching and learning, of collaboration and negotiation, are illustrated amongst teachers, trainers, administrators and managers by Bernath and Rubin. They talk about a 'knowledge building community' where 'participants met, talked, agreed, sometimes strongly disagreed, sympathized, empathized, and formed relationships (several of which have lasted beyond the end of the seminars)' (Bernath and Rubin, Chapter 19, p 218).

The Web tools described by Oliver and McLoughlin involve the searching/sharing of information, articulation of problems, sharing solutions and collaborative work, supporting learning communities, contributing to an environment based on access, support and communication and the social, collaborative and interactive nature of learning.

The satisfaction associated with the creation and delivery of some course or product can be substantial. However, Errington comments how teachers and trainers need rewards or incentives to modify and sustain the innovation and change. Sometimes modest resource provision can have a disproportionate benefit to those working on an innovation; it signifies that the institution recognizes and values the work being undertaken. Brown recognizes that the rewards open to staff are limited but describes a series of initiatives in his own institution, including a Teacher Fellowship Scheme which formally recognizes and rewards innovation and excellence in teaching.

A common belief that runs through many of the following chapters is that a teaching and learning climate has to be created in which innovation and change is encouraged and supported. Elsewhere (Abdullah, 1998) it is reported that teachers need to know that any innovation and change carries with it the risk of failure – but that there is no disgrace in failing – only in not even trying. It is evident in the chapters in this book that whilst creating and maintaining this climate is the responsibility of all, senior staff carry a major responsibility. In this context Brown states categorically that creating the *Electronic Campus* is a management-led and not a 'grass roots' innovation; like UnivSAnet, it was a university-wide initiative promoted by the Vice Chancellor and not a local trial. If, as reported by Robinson and by McLachlan-Smith and Gunn, the innovation is regarded as a local trial, teachers may resort to absorbing administrative tasks into their teaching roles so that the innovation can be realized, and as a result its chances of being sustained are slim.

Human resources

Many who have reported on research and development in DL have identified the key role of innovators or *champions*; those who have perceived a need, an application and alternative way of teaching or communicating and who have strived to realize it. However, not all of us can be the *champions* and there is a lot the *early majority* and *late majority* (Rogers, 1995) can contribute to teaching and learning. Indeed, if an innovation is to be successful it is vital that these two groups are not only involved but committed if the innovation or change is to be sustained; if it is to reach a *critical mass* and be self-sustaining. In this context Errington argues that the educational developer can play a significant role in a traditional teaching organization that is moving towards DL methods and in aiding innovation and managing change. He argues that a fundamental determinant of the success of an innovation is the teachers' belief system; how they perceive their role in teaching and learning. In his chapter he argues that these beliefs (and fears) must be addressed, and how they map on to the proposed teaching and learning system explored, if any change is to be more than transitory. If differences between teachers' beliefs and the intended operation of the innovation or change are not reconciled, practices will revert or be suborned.

However, without the resources and institutional support many such *champions* have been frustrated and sometimes defeated. Robinson identifies continuing professional development as a major factor in supporting those associated with innovative projects in general and open and distance learning in particular. The series of Virtual Seminars described and evaluated by Bernath and Rubin indicates how this need was met. Indeed, its success has resulted in the creation of a master's degree in Distance Education – taught at a distance. The success of similar staff development activities is noted elsewhere (Latchem and Lockwood,

1998), with many contributors asserting that such activities should be regarded as an investment rather than a cost. In this context Robinson notes that poor planning, weak pedagogic skills and superficial awareness of the techniques and procedures associated with self-instructional material can detract from the innovative projects. The case studies presented by McLachlan-Smith and Gunn illustrate the result of inadequate staff development, the VESOL innovation (McGhee and O'Hagan, Chapter 17) provides opportunities for staff to practise their presentation and data integration skills, and formal staff development and problem-based learning described by Brown goes a long way to reducing potential problems. Indeed, the decision by the University of South Australia to commit itself to a single electronic environment (common across three regional institutions) was to aid briefing, training and support for both staff and students. As Inglis notes, it also eases equipment and software maintenance.

Many of the chapters acknowledge the contribution that support staff – tutors, mentors and online moderators – made to the innovation. Wong and Ng stress the importance of tutor support within the Open University of Hong Kong; elsewhere (Salmon, 2000; Simpson, 2000) detailed accounts are provided about how tutors in a DL context and E-moderators respectively can contribute to innovative programmes and projects. Simpson also describes how other supporters – friends, relatives, neighbours, work colleagues and fellow students – can provide a support network. Morgan and Smit (Chapter 14) describe how one such support mechanism, that of mentors, can 'enhance student interactions and well-being'. They note the widespread use of mentors in industry, commerce and the public services but its limited use in education. Oliver and McLoughlin and Panda and Jena (Chapter 15) also describe how students successfully fulfilled a mentoring role and contributed to a supportive learning environment. In this context Morgan and Smit argue that the traditional conception of a hierarchical relationship is being replaced by a network of cooperative individuals; an environment similar to the learning community described by Morgan and O'Reilly and by Bernath and Rubin. The three-dimensional mentoring model that Morgan and Smit describe, and case studies they illustrate, may encourage you to explore this form of student support as a way to enhance learning.

Use of appropriate media

Adopting a medium that is readily available or convenient because it is under-used at the present time, one with which one is familiar or one that may attract support from colleagues or funds is common in many course development proposals. However, evidence from learners, those who will spend perhaps hundreds of hours interacting with the media selected, can reveal their preferences and needs, as the case studies presented by McLachlan-Smith and Gunn reveal.

However, despite ample evidence and a detailed account of the ACTIONS model to inform media selection:

Access: how accessible is a particular technology for learners?
Costs: what is the cost structure of each technology?
Teaching functions: what are the best teaching applications for this technology?
Interactivity and user friendliness: how easy is it to use?
Organizational issues: what changes in organization need to be made?
Novelty: how new is this technology?
Speed: how quickly can courses be mounted with this technology?

(Bates, 1995: i)

The inappropriate use of media in teaching and learning tasks is all too common. Robinson notes that careful consideration of the media to be used, of the technical support needed and evidence to indicate its contribution to the teaching task is a vital prerequisite. This point is echoed by McLachlan-Smith and Gunn: 'Although technology offers much potential, both staff and students need additional training and support to fully realize this' (McLachlan-Smith and Gunn, Chapter 4, 47).

Gooley et al stress the importance of the 'key foundations for continuous learning' – which include Information and Communication Technology literacy.

In their evaluation of the ANTA multimedia Toolbox Initiative, Oliver et al note that variations in hardware specification and variety of software systems complicate distribution and the training that needs to be provided. It is a point echoed by Inglis who, in the context of selecting an 'electronic learning environment', notes: 'Once the selection decision is made, users will have to live with the consequences of that decision for some considerable time. Also, when the time comes to review the choice that has been made, there will be a cost involved in switching to a new system. Therefore, the price of making an inappropriate decision can be high' (Inglis, Chapter 8, p 99).

It should be added that this caution is not restricted to the new information technologies but to other communication media, like the use of visual representations, that we take for granted. Indeed, Lowe (Chapter 18) challenges our current thinking about the role of pictorial representations and their 'intuitive' interpretation. With the increasing ease by which static and dynamic displays can be included in DL materials, and dramatic reductions in cost, there is urgent need to understand how students learn from them and how we can assist in the process of learning. When Tony Bates argued many years ago that students had to learn how to use television in their study, initial scepticism soon gave way to a grudging acceptance and a whole research area was opened. In a similar way Lowe illustrates how one can work from the perceptual characteristics of learners and build on these to develop sophisticated learning involving pictorial displays.

In terms of technical competence it is noteworthy that despite assumptions by Tyler *et al* that learners, using computers and communication media on a daily basis within the large multinational company, would be technically competent, two-thirds experienced technical problems. This apparently sophisticated audience had problems which directly affected their subsequent use of Lotus LearningSpace. The technical problems and excessive workload resulted in few attempting the *Action Centred Learning Activities* that had been specially designed to facilitate group work/collaboration and to blur the distinction between formal learning and the workplace. Morgan and O'Reilly reinforce this point about the barriers to learning that technical complexity can create. The success of many of the innovative online assessment methods they describe was based on their simplicity in use: ' "low-tech" application of computer-mediated communication ensures a low level of technical frustration for end-users and consequently a high level of learner control, collaboration and negotiation' (Morgan and O'Reilly, Chapter 16, p 183).

Robinson also notes that many Information Technology innovations failed to live up to the expectations of general and widespread application within and beyond the organization; they were often limited to applications by the original developer. In contrast, the Electronic Campus described by Brown, UnivSAnet described by King, WebTeach described by Hewson and Hughes and experiments with Lotus LearningSpace described by Tyler *et al* restricted the delivery platforms and software used and achieved both economies of scale and standardization that have reduced or eliminated incompatibility problems. The creation of new Web-based learning environments, such as WebTeach and customizing from available authoring tools like UniSAnet, are substantial undertakings. The chapters by Hewson and Hughes and by King respectively illustrate how the participation of both teachers and learners in their development and their user-friendly nature are vital. They also reveal how such Web-based environments can be a stepping stone from conventional teaching to online teaching and how they can gain rapid acceptance: 'WebTeach is designed to facilitate discussion and the use of familiar classroom teaching strategies within a virtual classroom' (Hewson and Hughes, Chapter 7, p 79).

In a similar way the description of VESOL, by McGhee and O'Hagan, illustrates the benefits afforded by a low-cost, online video editing system – a system that 'maximizes academic autonomy' and which gives the learner control of when and how to use the resource. The system, which can combine video recordings of lectures, can also incorporate other visual, textual and computer-generated information which the academic controls (edits) via a series of buttons. It illustrates, in a similar way to Hewson and Hughes, how the benefits and skills of conventional teaching can be captured, transformed into DL, and quality of learning maximized.

In achieving their goals De Montfort University employed Learning Development Managers and a newly created Centre for Teaching and Learning that were charged with leading and supporting organizational change and making the innovation a mainstream activity. This is mirrored within the

University of South Australia, University of Derby and the Open University where the Flexible Learning Centre, Centre for Educational Development and Media and the Institute of Educational Technology respectively provides advice and assistance across the whole institution. If such innovations are to become mainstream, and to be extended, the evidence they provide will need to be obtained and shared with others; the 'strong research base' identified by Daniel.

Conclusion

A brief review of the literature will indicate ongoing interest in innovation in DL. The International Centre for Distance Learning (ICDL) database [http://www-icdl.open.ac.uk] notes two recent conferences devoted to innovations in distance and open learning (AAOU, 1996) and universities in the digital era (Szucs and Wagner, 1998); others are likely. Recent years have seen the growth in online journals such as the *Journal of Asynchronous Learning Networks* and the *Journal of Interactive Media in Education*, of online magazines and virtual seminars [see http:///www.iet.open.ac.uk]. Indeed, in terms of actual implementation I suspect such interest will be driven as much by learners, and the fees they pay, as by enthusiastic teachers and trainers. In an increasingly competitive teaching and training environment, with a recognition of the needs for lifelong learning, increasing numbers of educational and training institutions will embrace DL. What is more, other organizations, currently associated with leisure, entertainment and mass media, will also embrace DL. Indeed, the evidence is around us. In January 2000 Time Warner and AOL merged to become the fifth-biggest company in the world. In the same month, in the UK, yet another high street electrical retailer offered its own free Internet service and ownership of microcomputers increased even further. In Japan mobile video phones became available and from an online order Amazon.com could deliver a book halfway round the world in a few days. In February 2000 the British mobile telephone company Vodofone announced a massive takeover of the German company Mannesmann to become the largest mobile telephone operator in the world, with 54 million customers in Britain, Germany and the USA. In announcing this takeover the Chief Executive commented upon the role of mobile telephones in providing access to the Internet and to worldwide communication – in the hands of the user. With resources like these, the potential of the knowledge media to create learning environments, and talented teachers, the next few years will see many more innovations in DL.

References

Abdullah, S (1998) Helping faculty to make the paradigm shift from on-campus teaching to distance education at the Institut Teknologi Mara, in *Staff Development in Open and Flexible Learning*, ed C Latchem and F Lockwood, Routledge, London

Argyris, C and Schön, D A (1974) *Theory in Practice. Increasing professional effectiveness*, Jossey-Bass, San Francisco

Asian Association of Open Universities (1996) *Innovations in Distance and Open Learning*, Proceedings of the 10th Annual Conference, Payame Noor University, Tehran Islamic Republic of Iran, 14–16 November

Bates, T (1995) *Technology, Open Learning and Distance Education*, Routledge, London

Daniel, J S (1998) Can you get my hard nose in focus? Universities, mass education and appropriate technology, in *The Knowledge Web: Learning and collaborating on the Net*, ed M Eisenstadt and T Vincent, Kogan Page, London

Daniel, J S (2000) *Mega-Universities & Knowledge Media*, Kogan Page, London

Inglis, A, Ling, P and Joosten, V (1999) *Delivering Digitally: Managing the transition to the knowledge media*, Kogan Page, London

Latchem, C and Lockwood, F (eds) (1998) *Staff Development in Open and Flexible Learning*, Routledge, London

Lockwood, F (1998) *The Design and Production of Self-Instructional Material*, Kogan Page, London

Perry, W (1976) *Open University: A personal account by the first vice-chancellor*, Open University Press, Buckingham

Rogers, E D (1995) *Diffusion of Innovations*, The Free Press, New York

Rowntree, D (1994) *Preparing Materials for Open, Distance and Flexible Learning*, Kogan Page, London

Ryan, S, Scott, B, Freeman, H and Patel, D (2000) *The Virtual University: The Internet and resource-based learning*, Kogan Page, London

Salmon, G K (2000) *E-moderating: the key to teaching and learning online*, Kogan Page, London

Simpson, O (2000) *Supporting Open and Distance Learners*, Kogan Page, London

Szucs, A and Wagner, A (eds) (1998) *Universities in a digital era – transformation, innovation and tradition: roles and perspectives of open and distance learning*, Proceedings of the 7th European Distance Education Network Conference, University of Bologna, Italy, 24–26 June

Chapter 2

Innovation in open and distance learning: some lessons from experience and research

Bernadette Robinson

> There is nothing more difficult to plan, more doubtful of success,
> nor more dangerous to manage than the creation of a new order
> of things.
>
> *Niccolò Machiavelli,* The Prince *(16th century)*

Introduction

Getting a new order of things has often proved more problematic, slow or costly than anticipated at the outset. Over the past 30 years, much attention has been paid to the study of innovation: 'No other field of behaviour science research represents more effort by more scholars in more disciplines in more nations' (Rogers, 1995: i).

In 1962 there were 405 publications on innovation; by 1995, there were about 4,000 (Rogers, 1995) and more has been written since then, particularly in relation to new technologies. Education accounts for about 10 per cent of the innovation literature. Alongside this runs the study of educational change (reviewed in Fullan, 1992). Together they have increased our understanding of how we think or act in relation to change and cautioned against the search for easily applied algorithms or simple recipes. Productive educational change appears to proceed on an unsteady course, veering between over-control and chaos (Pascale, 1990). Fullan (1993) describes it as 'fraught with unknowns' and emphasizes problem solving as an integral part of the change process. Though research has produced deeper understanding of the processes, innovation is still a chancy business. Innovation in ODL may face even higher levels of risk because of its uncertain status and unfamiliarity in some contexts. An innovation is an idea, practice, approach, process, system or object which is perceived as new by an individual, group or organization. What is familiar in one context can appear as an innovation in another, as the literature on ODL shows.

What kinds of problems face innovators when introducing ODL into organizations? What lessons from experience and research are relevant? Which in particular are important for introducing new learning technologies? This chapter examines these three questions, starting with the experience of innovation in ODL before turning to research on the nature of innovation, to see what light this can shed.

The experience of innovation

Many organizations are beginning to use ODL for the first time, either as a small-scale departmental initiative or as a large-scale organizational strategy. What kinds of difficulties are encountered? Is there any commonality in the experience of those involved?

An attempt to explore these questions was made in a small study I carried out in the course of staff development workshops on ODL between 1996 and 1999. The summary here reflects the experience of 426 individuals who were involved in introducing and implementing a wide variety of new ODL courses in universities, development aid projects, businesses, industry and public services (such as police forces, social welfare and health services and the military). These initiatives were at varying stages of planning and implementation. The individuals came from 17 countries, developing and industrialized; 42.5 per cent (181) came from the UK and 57.5 per cent (245) from 16 other countries in Europe and Asia. Among other things, they were asked to identify the three main difficulties they encountered in introducing ODL; further e-mail discussion about the issues raised took place with 102 of the 426 individuals. From analysis of this information, four main areas of concern emerged, in order of priority: resource availability, organizational issues, human resource capacity, and use of the technology.

Problems in innovating ODL

The problems reported showed considerable consistency, despite wide variation in contexts, cultures and kinds of ODL application.

1. Resource availability
   - ODL initiatives were under-resourced in financial and human terms (for 63 per cent of informants) and senior decision-makers often required implementation within unrealistic time-scales. Both preparation costs and staff time for ODL were underestimated. This was reported as jeopardizing quality and creating pressure on personnel.
   - The cost structure and funding needs of ODL were 'not well understood' by senior decision-makers, so as well as under-funding, the flow of funds was sometimes inappropriate. ODL was usually expected to be a cheaper alternative though often no cost analysis or projections underpinned this expectation.
   - The scale of projects was sometimes too small to be viable financially. Expectations of future lucrative markets were often based on little more than optimism (no market surveys, scoping or environmental scans were done in nearly half of the projects). The most promising projects were based on clearly identified needs with few competing options for meeting them.
2. Organizational aspects
   - Staff involved in new ODL ventures (sometimes initiated by a policy directive) received inadequate 'buy-out' time and few rewards or incentives. Significant additions to existing workloads were common while at the same time ODL work had lower status than other kinds.
   - Administrative practices within organizations did not always fit with the operational requirements of ODL. Staff were sometimes too inexperienced in ODL or project management to anticipate the changes needed and lacked sufficient status to institute them. While *ad hoc* solutions worked for a few or small ODL initiatives within an organization, system-wide change, including more formalization of procedures, was necessary with expansion. This step appeared difficult to achieve.
   - Internal coordination and policy for ODL or information technology (IT) initiatives were weak. In some organizations, particularly universities, it was common to find a number of separate small ODL initiatives existing, unaware of each other's activities and with no mechanisms for coordinating them. Each project negotiated separately with administrators, duplicating effort. In some cases, different groups made separate contracts with external suppliers of products and services, leading to problems of compatibility and IT support within the organization.
   - Many ODL centres were under-staffed, of low status and with little representation on decision-making committees. They sometimes lacked a clear position within the organizational structure. Much uncertainty

was expressed about the best position and functional roles for ODL centres (a variety of arrangements existed). Nearly half the centres lacked a clear or earmarked budget allocation and funding for two-thirds of them was reported as more *ad hoc* than for other centres or departments.

- Teamwork within and across departments was difficult to achieve. About a third of ODL coordinators saw themselves as lacking the necessary skills for managing teams effectively, especially when members came from other departments and were equal or senior in status to the ODL coordinator who might also be on a short-term contract. The tendency for staff from different departments to work as individuals, rarely meeting as a group, resulted in weak communication about policy and practice, very limited knowledge about their organization's overall use of ODL and a failure to mobilize themselves as a pressure group when necessary.
- Making the shift from small individual initiatives to mainstream inclusion was a problem since ODL was often perceived as a marginal activity. When the shift to mainstream happened because a project was successful, it could result in a loss of the project (and the funds it generated) for the initiator or department, as more formal structures and senior managers took it over.
- Where innovation involved collaboration, the workload and difficulties of working with partners, especially overseas, were underestimated. Problems stemmed from lack of clear agreements or contracts and weak definition of roles, responsibilities and time-schedules.

3. Human resource capacity
   - Many staff lacked adequate knowledge of ODL and self-help seemed the main means of getting it. Staff development was sometimes too little and too late for critical phases, with inadequate budgets.
   - The level of planning for ODL projects tended to be too general. While adequate for face-to-face courses, it was not sufficiently detailed, specific or articulated for the smooth implementation of ODL courses. One consequence was the emergence of avoidable problems.
   - Many courses were the result of individual initiatives, tied to the enthusiasm and skills of their creators. An obstacle in extending capacity more widely among others was negative attitudes towards ODL, often because of the additional workload entailed.

4. Use of technology
   - In ODL projects using technologies, problems centred on insufficient expertise and technical support, given little attention in project planning.
   - The choice of a technology was often prompted by three main factors: an individual staff member's interest in it, its availability, or funding opportunities for obtaining it (not because it was the most appropriate choice for the learning purpose or target group. Other options would sometimes have been better (more accessible to students, lower cost to use, less demanding on the specialist skills and technical support needed, more appropriate for the intended learning goals).

● Not much evaluation was being done, owing to lack of time and expertise. Because of this, evidence on the effectiveness of a technology for teaching and learning was scarce. Some organizations had gathered feedback as part of quality assurance procedures but very few had evaluated the learning gains resulting from use of the technology.

Organizational change

Organizational issues figured prominently in the experience reported. New operational requirements needed the modification of existing systems and procedures or the design of new ones. Two-thirds of informants found their organizations slow or reluctant to make the changes. Strategies used by ODL innovators for coping with these realities included working around intransigent procedures, making informal arrangements with selected administrators on a personal goodwill basis and incorporating more of the administrative work within their own department or workload. Introducing ODL involved changes in:

● organizational practices (systems, procedures, record-keeping systems, access to learner records);
● new kinds of work groups and relationships across specialisms and administrative boundaries;
● the use of technology and additional media for teaching courses formerly provided face-to-face;
● the creation of new curricula and methods of assessment;
● adoption of new pedagogical approaches, to maximize the potential of new technology or media, or to fit new kinds of learners;
● forms and styles of communication and interaction with learners;
● new value and belief systems;
● the skills and expertise of individuals, roles, job descriptions and the creation of new specialisms;
● resource allocation and financial decision-making.

The introduction of ODL involved multi-level changes and getting to grips with these was a key part of the innovation process.

Innovating with learning technologies

Some similar findings come from a more substantial study by Alexander and McKenzie (1998) of 104 Australian projects introducing information technologies for student learning. They found that outcomes were affected by a range of factors whose weighting and combination were shaped by particular contexts of use. These factors related to organizational issues, resources, project planning and management, software development and production, availability of expertise and technical support, and issues of copyright. The most important factor in determining successful project outcomes was the design of the students' learning experience.

Features contributing to success in these projects were:

- the design of the students' learning experience ('success' depended on addressing a specific need, enhancing learning in ways not previously possible, using a soundly based design strategy integrated with learner support, and appropriately designed assessment);
- sufficient funding;
- adequate research, design and testing of software before beginning development;
- sufficient technical support and software development expertise;
- the inclusion of formative evaluation during the development phase;
- resolution of copyright issues before beginning development;
- ensuring student access to the hardware and software;
- realistic goals (in relation to time and budget);
- skilled project management;
- support and commitment of senior managers;
- shared goals in project teams and capacity to overcome differences between members;
- strong commitment by project members and adequate time for the work;
- conduct of ongoing evaluation activities;
- adequate support for all involved (staff and learners);
- support from senior managers and public acknowledgement of the project as a worthwhile activity;
- recognition and reward for the efforts of staff involved.

Most of these features apply to any ODL initiative. Alexander and McKenzie's (1998) overall conclusion was that the use of a particular information technology did not, of itself, result in more or better learning. While they report that some of the innovations were adopted by others, research in general concludes that many projects or pilots in the use of learning technologies have not subsequently been adopted more widely, even within institutions which invested in the infrastructure and equipment for IT. Instead, they tend to be limited to use by the initial developer. As Salomon (1991: 44) says: 'While computer technology *affords* a number of important possibilities, none of them can be assumed to become automatically realized only because of the technology's presence.'

Research on innovation

How does the above experience fit with findings from innovation research? What does the research lead us to expect? Does it offer any helpful insights for ODL projects? What kinds of models of innovation are there?

Models

The spread or diffusion of an innovation is defined by Rogers (1995) as the process by which an innovation is communicated through certain channels over time among the members of a social system. Two broad models of innovation can be found in the literature: the linear and the convergence. The linear reflects rational planning and a one-way view (usually top-down) of communication. It has been criticized for ignoring the social and political realities of project implementation. Bureaucratic societies and institutions tend to favour the linear approach. In contrast, the convergence model views planning as a participatory activity, with shared decision-making. In practice, it can appear messier and more *ad hoc* than the linear model and runs the risk of losing direction though generating wider ownership of the change.

These two broad models are paralleled by a distinction Fullan (1993) makes about approaches to educational change. On the one hand there is the rational planning ideal: mandated change, a mission stated at the outset with objectives set from above, a blueprint to follow, a plan of linear and sequential activities, linking cause and effect, controllable and predictable to a large extent. This approach has not been wholly successful and does not reflect the complexities of change within a given context or match what actually happens (Fullan, 1992, 1993). On the other, there is what Fullan describes as a new paradigm of dynamic change: an 'overlapping series of dynamic complex phenomenon', unpredictable, using both top-down and bottom-up strategies, focusing on process, evolutionary in character, a journey rather than a blueprint, allowing its mission to emerge over time from what is enacted. The second approach appears to have more potential for being responsive to a changing environment than the first.

Innovators in ODL may find it helpful to reflect on these models in relation to their own projects. Which is your project closest to? What forces shaped your choice? If your project is more similar to the second approach, how does this fit with the prevailing culture and practices of your organization?

Adoption patterns

Does the adoption of innovations follow a predictable pattern? A typical pattern found in a large number of studies in different fields is an S-shaped curve (Figure 2.1), showing that some individuals or units adopt an innovation earlier than others. The rate needs to reach between 10 and 20 per cent of the total (a 'critical mass') before the innovation takes on a momentum of its own, at which point interpersonal and informal networks of communication among peers are influential in spreading information and value judgements. One can also speculate that the achievement of critical mass is important for changing organizational practices at the systems level. For ODL planners, knowing about typical adoption patterns can help guide expectations and inform strategy.

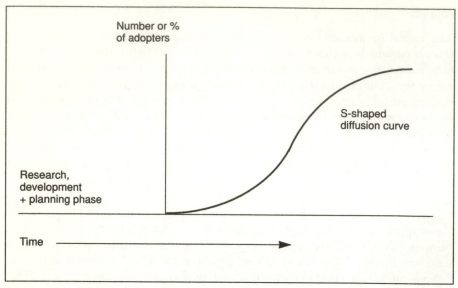

Figure 2.1 *The S-shaped innovation adoption curve (Rogers, 1995: 110)*

Within the S-shaped curve, different categories of adopters can be identified. One of the best known typologies (Rogers, 1995) is based on time taken to adopt:

- *innovators* (2.5 per cent): 'venturesome', able to cope with uncertainty, facilitating the flow of new ideas into a system;
- *early adopters* (13.5 per cent): confident users of new ideas, well integrated into local social systems, opinion-leaders;
- *early majority* (34.0 per cent): seldom opinion leaders but adopting new ideas before the average member, important in consolidating an innovation so a significant target group for change agents;
- *late majority* (34.0 per cent): sceptical and cautious about risking their scarce resources, adopting only under pressure;
- *laggards* (16.0 per cent): conservative and cautious, the past as their point of reference.

Though these are ideal types, based on abstractions from empirical investigations, they may provide some clues for planners, help set realistic expectations and shape strategy. However, this classification has little to say about those who choose (perhaps for good reasons) not to adopt an innovation. Its predictive capacity may be limited too.

Critical mass and rates of adoption

One preoccupation in the literature is the time taken to establish an innovation. In education, innovation has tended to involve relatively long time–scales (Fullan, 1992). These have varied widely – from more than 30 years to two or three. It is likely that the current use of information technologies and global interaction are generating shorter time-spans for the spread of knowledge about particular innovations, though perhaps increasing the hazards of technology-led innovations.

The concept of 'critical mass' helps explain adoption patterns. It comes from physics, referring to the amount of radioactive material necessary for a nuclear reaction. It has been used to describe any process that becomes self-sustaining after some threshold point is reached. The S-shaped curve for innovation is explained by the concept of 'critical mass' in terms of the relationship between the behaviour of individuals and the larger systems of which they are a part (Schelling, 1978). Critical mass occurs at the point when enough people have adopted an innovation to make the further rate of adoption assured or self-sustaining. Rogers (1995: 319) describes this as 'a kind of tipping point or social threshold in the diffusion process'.

The adoption rate for interactive communication technologies has its own characteristic variation on the S-shaped curve (Figure 2.2). Achieving critical mass in these tends to be slower than for other innovations, but once achieved, accelerates faster, even exponentially. An illustration is the development of the Internet. One reason for this difference is that other users are needed in order for

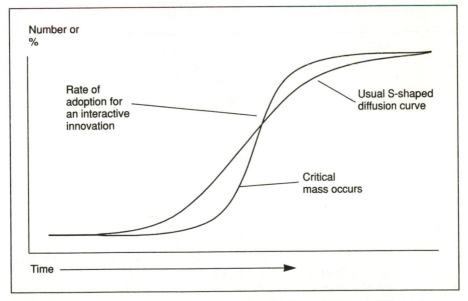

Figure 2.2   *The adoption curve for interactive technologies (Rogers, 1995: 314)*

the innovation to function. Another is the multi-directional information exchanges that interactive communication generates. In other kinds of innovations, earlier adopters have an effect on later adopters in a sequential chain, but with interactive communication technologies, earlier and later adopters influence each other, in what Markus (1990) describes as a process of 'reciprocal interdependence'.

Several strategies for accelerating the attainment of critical mass in the use of interactive technologies have been found useful:

- targeting senior managers and opinion leaders for support;
- shaping individual perceptions through providing information and evidence of its value;
- encouraging whole groups (or departments) of users to adopt the innovation rather than individuals alone;
- providing incentives for early adopters until critical mass has been reached (even providing a service free, as the French government did with the introduction of the Minitel videotext system);
- making its use for a 'real' work purpose and as the sole means of carrying out the work;
- finding significant champions who will themselves use the innovation in a highly visible way.

These strategies can apply to any ODL innovation.

Influences on the rate of adoption

Some innovations are adopted more quickly than others. According to research (Rogers, 1995), five main features affect the rate of adoption. You may find this a useful framework for reviewing the experience of innovation in your own context or for planning it. It may also help you to make a realistic appraisal of the proposed innovation's chances and highlight areas where effort needs to be concentrated:

- *Relative advantage:* the degree of perceived benefits and cost-benefit. The greater the perceived relative advantage of an innovation, the more rapid its rate of adoption.
- *Compatibility:* the degree to which an innovation is consistent with existing values, beliefs, experiences and norms. If a new value system is required the rate of adoption will be slower.
- *Complexity:* the degree to which an innovation is perceived as difficult to understand and use. Innovations requiring new skills and understanding (involving steep learning curves) are slower to be adopted.
- *Trialability:* the degree to which an innovation can be experimented with on a limited basis. Innovations that can be introduced by instalments will

generally be adopted more quickly than those that are not divisible since incremental implementation allows uncertainty to be reduced through learning by doing.

● *Observability:* the degree to which the results of an innovation are visible to others and demonstrably beneficial.

The organizational dimension

Any innovation disturbs existing systems. An innovation is essentially a process of social change and therefore complex, multi-level, culturally situated, occasionally irrational and unpredictable. An innovation in one part of an organization can have considerable consequences for the functioning of other departments, procedures and work cycles in direct and indirect ways. It is likely to have an impact on budgets and resource allocation beyond those of the project. Some of these consequences may be predictable, others not. Changes in teaching and learning methods, or the adoption of new learning technologies, are not simply technical changes, confined to a single department, but involve changes in other departments and the wider culture too. It is not possible to introduce a change and at the same time keep other things as they were:

> No innovation comes without strings attached. The more technologically advanced an innovation is, the more likely its introduction is to produce many consequences – some of them anticipated, but others unintended and hidden. A system is like a bowl of marbles. Move any one of its elements and the positions of all the others are inevitably changed also. (Rogers, 1995: 419)

Research shows that larger organizations are generally more innovative than smaller ones, though size is probably a surrogate measure of several things (total resource availability, the amount of 'slack' or uncommitted resource, the range of technical expertise across employees). Other features of an organization which influence its take-up of innovation are the degrees of centralization (power concentrated in a few strong leaders), formalization (rule-following), and system openness (the extent to which information is exchanged with the external environment – what Granovetter (1973) calls the strength of 'weak ties' to others outside the system, with strong internal effects). Centralization has sometimes been negatively associated with innovation, though particular organizational characteristics may suit different parts of the innovation process. For example, while the initiation of innovations is more frequent in a decentralized organization, a centralized organization can strongly direct and sustain a chosen innovation. Successful innovation is not likely to be a product of either central directive or local initiative alone. As Pascale (1990) says, change flourishes in a 'sandwich': where there is consensus above and pressure below, things happen.

Conclusions

The research and experience outlined above offer some lessons and identify common barriers to innovation in ODL. Finally, three broad conclusions seem worth bearing in mind.

The organizational dimension and quality of planning need more attention by innovators introducing ODL. This echoes Brown's (1997: 193) conclusion after reviewing 14 case studies of ODL: 'there are inescapable issues concerned with culture, roles and values that significantly affect the outcome of innovations depending on how they are addressed. Of course, if the key players in the situation are unaware of these issues they are unlikely to handle them very well.'

Problem-solving is an integral component of the process since innovation is never problem-free. However, if little evaluation is done as part of the innovation, evidence to guide solutions or improvements or to substantiate claims of effectiveness is lacking. Evaluation activities need to be planned into ODL projects from the start and their findings used; adequate resources (finance and time) need to be allocated for them.

Innovation in education and ODL is not a simple exercise so we should not expect it to be: 'Substantial change involves complex processes. The latter is inherently problem rich. A spirit of openness and inquiry is essential to solving problem. Change is learning' (Fullan, 1993: 27).

References

Alexander, S and McKenzie, J with Geissinger, H (1998) *An Evaluation of Information Technology Projects for University Learning*, Commonwealth of Australia, Canberra

Brown, S (ed) (1997) *Open and Distance Learning: Case Studies from Industry and Education*, Kogan Page, London

Fullan, M (1992) *Successful School Improvement*, Open University Press, Buckingham

Fullan, M (1993) *Change Forces: Probing the Depths of Educational Reform*, The Falmer Press, London

Granovetter, M (1973) The strength of weak ties, *American Journal of Sociology*, **78**, pp 1360–80

Markus, M L (1990) Towards a 'critical mass' theory of interactive media, in *Organizations and Communication Technology*, ed J Fulk and C Steinfield, pp 154–218, Sage, Newbury Park, CA

Pascale, P (1990) *Managing on the Edge*, Touchstone, New York

Rogers, E D (1995) *Diffusion of Innovations*, 4th edn, The Free Press, New York

Salomon, G (1991) Learning: new conceptions, new opportunities, *Educational Technology*, June, pp 41–44

Schelling, T C (1978) *Micromotives and Macrobehaviour*, Norton, New York

Chapter 3

The influence of teacher beliefs on flexible learning innovation in traditional university settings

Edward Peter Errington

Introduction

As an academic developer, I observe continually how the creation or adoption of flexible learning approaches within 'traditional', campus-based-only institutions remains a contentious issue – not at the level of physical resources, but at the more fundamental level of university teachers' beliefs.

It has long been recognized that teachers' beliefs can have a significant impact on the relative success of innovation in traditional settings. Teacher dispositions: constitute a 'personal set of guidelines for professional practice' (Combs, 1982); provide the substance of teachers' 'personal practical theories of teaching' (Marland, 1997); and inform 'personal practical knowledge' (Haigh, 1998).

What follows is an exploration of the nature of university teachers' beliefs and their likely impact on innovation within more traditional institutions perhaps contemplating flexible forms of learning delivery for the first time. Given the influence of teacher beliefs, I discuss the kinds of challenges facing academic developers, institutional managers, and other change agents wishing to engage teachers in more flexible forms of learning delivery within traditional settings. I have drawn out a number of explicit assumptions which academic developers might consider when formulating strategies to address the challenges to innovation posed by traditionally oriented teacher beliefs.

I do not underestimate the complex nature of institutions – the ways they encompass many different kinds of teachers, pockets of innovation and resistance, and diverse political groups – all exist at one and the same time. However, for present purposes, I pursue the discussion, assumptions and strategies 'as if' institutions possess a mono outlook – in so far as this enables a focus on the impact of teacher beliefs on the adoption, or otherwise, of flexible learning delivery.

Teacher beliefs are important

The beliefs of university teachers can profitably be viewed as part of 'belief systems' (Rokeach, 1970; Combs, 1982; Errington, 1985). Personal belief systems fulfil two important functions simultaneously: 'the need to know and understand, and the need to ward off threatening aspects of reality' (Rokeach, 1960: 70). It is the tensions between the two that can make or break flexible learning initiatives.

Within belief systems, the more central dispositions are seen to dominate other beliefs in the system, and are the most difficult to change. Central to a university teacher's belief system are likely to be dispositions regarding role. Although the relationship between teacher beliefs and practice has never been a clear one, it is reasonable to assume that those who see their role in one way are likely to differ in their practices from colleagues who view their role in some other way.

Linked to central beliefs about roles of teachers and learners are other dispositions about what constitutes 'worthwhile' knowledge; student learning; the organization of learning; assessment; and teacher-learner relationships (Errington, 1985; Schoenfeld, 1999). Toohey (1999) notes that these kinds of dispositions transcend individual teacher choices and enter the broader professional discourse used to define educational goals, delivery of subject content, and assessment practices.

For various reasons teachers may be open or closed towards innovation in their beliefs. Teacher beliefs heavily influence what is possible or appropriate within particular circumstances. Some teachers may believe that flexible learning is not a real option in the context of other held beliefs about student competence, degree of institutional support, or adequacy of institutional infrastructures.

Some challenges facing agents of change

Given the above, what are the challenges facing academic developers and institution managers wishing to employ more flexible forms of learning delivery in traditional settings?

Creating a teaching and learning infrastructure

One important consideration is the quality of institutional infrastructure in place to advance a particular innovation. The infrastructure consists of more than its physical, resource-bearing framework. Rather, the greater part is its human infrastructure – which operates at the level of beliefs, values and attitudes.

Teacher perceptions of support

Decisions about what teachers feel they can, or will, support by way of flexible learning initiatives are influenced by the degree of perceived support available at all levels of the institution. The quality of support for new initiatives is embedded within the institution's own culture. It determines the degree to which change will be facilitated by teachers. As Brown (2000) points out in Chapter 11, the challenges for universities wishing to adopt more flexible initiatives extend far beyond technical considerations to include a change of culture – signalled and led from the top. This culture consists of the belief climate prevalent at any one time. What kinds of teaching and learning climate does the institution promote? Is change welcomed? Or do teachers get the message that teaching is an inferior activity compared to the institution's more important 'research-led' aspirations?

Individual teachers working within traditional institutions are also influenced by the extent to which they believe colleagues support flexible learning initiatives. It is not unusual for a department to operate a variety of courses which demand a variety of delivery methods to meet the needs of a diverse student population. Nor is it unusual for departmental members to embrace a variety of beliefs about how learning should be delivered. Contestations about what constitutes 'real teaching' and 'real learning' still abound. Common departmental goals are needed if teachers are to achieve their educational ends – preferably linked to the university's mission. Students too play a part in influencing the adoption of flexible learning initiatives: for example, teacher views about lack of student access to computers may limit the kinds of flexible learning strategies they feel able to adopt.

Teachers particularly need to know that they are supported from the top, that there is a collective institutional vision with clear leadership, and that the institution is committed to flexible learning. Forster and Hewson (1998) observe the need for universities to develop a 'collective aspiration' if they are to achieve desired results. Lack of perceived support from any quarter can act as major constraints on practices teachers feel are possible within these circumstances.

Assumption:
Teachers need opportunities to identify and critically appraise resources and constraints at both a physical and a dispositional level. These may be allied to agendas of possibility in the light of held beliefs.

Managing innovation and change

To show teachers they are/will be supported, management need to send the correct messages via appropriate policies and strategies which are clearly designed to facilitate flexible learning options (Forster and Hewson, 1998). Institutional policies and strategies are likely to make explicit the targeted student population, intended modes of learning and teaching delivery, attendant resources including student and academic development requirements, and infrastructure needs (Marland, 1997).

Institutions need to be unequivocal about the kinds and degrees of flexible learning support they are willing to resource. Toohey (1999) points out that pressure generates the need for change, but it is support that facilitates such changes. The worst approaches to institutional innovation can occur when the institution is 'foggy' about its mission, and teachers are expected to use the existing infrastructure to deliver some very different kinds of courses. The best can occur when institutions have a clear message of intent, matched by a coherent strategy, fully resourced and underpinned by an explicit commitment to flexible learning at all levels – preferably formulated in consultation with middle managers, teachers, and student representatives. This message of intent needs to give a clear rationale why particular flexible learning initiatives are needed. Stephen Brown (2000) in Chapter 11 notes that the impetus for enhancing the quality of traditional provision at de Montfort University via mixed mode delivery was driven by the need for more flexible access to courses by students. Similarly, McLachlan-Smith and Gunn (2000) in Chapter 4 note the need to meet the flexible learning requirements of students unable to attend on-campus classes at Auckland University.

Experience shows that the most traditional of universities have a tendency to subsume open, distance and flexible learning activities within the resources of the broader campus-based remit. Where the characteristics of flexible learning are closest to the university's main campus-based mission, then support will be forth-coming (eg resources given for campus-based operations of summer schools). However, where the needs of flexible learning delivery differ from its traditional counterpart (eg costs of 'extra' audio-visual production support), then money may not be so readily available. 'Flexible learning delivery' at its most innovative may be too much of a radical departure for management. As Stephen Brown (2000) points out in Chapter 11, one way forward is to take existing institutional resources and 're-engineer' these to fit changing circumstances.

The place of academic development

When we examine the impact of teacher beliefs on the variable success of flexible learning initiatives, we do so in the knowledge that individual and shared teacher efforts have little chance of success without appropriately supported academic development from the top. Stephen Brown's (2000) experience related in Chapter 11 suggests that innovation can fail when it has no related academic development strategy.

In using academic development to introduce teachers to flexible delivery via the Internet, Toohey (1999) observes that a technology skills approach fails when it does not take into account the teachers' concept of teaching and learning.

Assumption:
Academic development is most likely to succeed when the teacher's own beliefs about teaching and learning provide the starting point. Articulation can lead to a critical examination of held beliefs and a reassessment of available options.

It is common for educational technologists to adopt a technical skills-only approach to training – leaving teachers to make their own connections between teaching, learning and the Internet (Murphy and Vermeer, 1998: 204). Questions of use, and subsequent criteria for discerning choice, are likely to be based on technological rather than pedagogical considerations. Some contemporary workshops involve teachers sitting in front of a computer screen in lab-like conditions – far removed from their real work setting.

Assumption:
Technical training needs to occur within the context of held teacher beliefs and values, not apart from them.

Teachers' beliefs about 'flexible' learning

What teachers believe about 'flexible' learning, how they interpret its (many) meanings, and put these into practice within their own traditional settings is also influenced by beliefs about teaching and learning (Mar and Mak, 1998). Teachers are only likely to view delivery options favourably in so far as they facilitate educational purposes.

Assumption:
The more academic developers know about teacher beliefs regarding flexible learning, the more likely they are to create appropriate development opportunities.

We more easily align ourselves with values similar to our own: a cursory glance at the literature on open, distance and flexible learning soon reveals a set of explicit teaching and learning values. Protagonists are seen to value a learning management approach (as opposed to an 'academic-as-expert' model); greater equity in teacher-student power relationships; diversity of student populations; equity of learning access; independent learning; negotiated learning tasks; variety of learning media delivery; and opportunities for reflective learning (Marland, 1997: 75). What is the degree of fit between traditional teachers' own beliefs and those espoused by proponents of flexible learning? If, fundamentally, teacher beliefs about 'flexibility' do not match those advanced by the institution or flexible learning exponents, what are the real choices facing teachers within the human infrastructure?

Assumption:
The more teachers' own beliefs are consonant with the professional values underpinning flexible learning approaches, the more likely they are to put these beliefs into practice.

When it comes to helping teachers choose appropriate forms of learning delivery, academic developers can facilitate decision-making by helping participants base their judgement on informed criteria.

One hurdle to confront academic developers is: How relevant is flexible learning delivery for the participant teachers? How will academic developers engage teachers in a judicious examination without making value judgements or undermining teacher confidence?

Without clear links between the flexible delivery option and held beliefs about teaching and learning, the relevance is likely to be lost. What is important for one teacher may not be so for another. To what extent will the innovative flexible delivery meet the teacher's learning objectives?

Assumption:
Flexible learning technologies which are perceived to facilitate learning objectives are the ones likely to be adapted and adopted most readily.

One measure of flexible delivery's relevance to teachers is its perceived application to 'real work' situations. According to Robinson (1998), academic development in open and flexible learning can fail when teachers are unable to connect the training content with their own 'real-work' needs or 'organizational realities'.

Assumption:
Knowledge gained about flexible learning alternatives needs to be embedded within the teacher's workplace – preferably on an ongoing basis.

Williams (1999) points out that changes may occur in traditional teachers' beliefs about technology *per se* – but the 'change' might simply involve a return to a central, traditional view of the teacher's role as 'expert' and student as 'knowledge receptacle'. That is, unless teachers have an opportunity to examine critically their pedagogical assumptions.

Assumption:
Teachers need opportunities to identify their held beliefs. They are then in a better position to examine them critically with a view to modifying beliefs and envisioning alternative practices.

Given teachers' often firm views about teaching and learning, there is a natural tendency to reproduce the same kinds of pedagogical approaches – regardless of the very different kinds of media employed (Forster and Hewson, 1998). Traditional teachers may use what Marland (1997: 86) labels a 'monologic model'. Here distance education study materials are prepared and packaged by the instructor and sent out to the many students, on a 'knowledge-as-given' basis. Students are not encouraged to engage in dialogue with the instructor, materials or peers. Rather, they are invited simply to 'digest' the package contents and regurgitate its contents later for examination purposes. Without alternative visions, teachers will apply their didactic beliefs to whatever constitutes a teaching event.

Traditional teaching at its driest follows the easier path of the known. 'We are happy with what we know best.' Familiarity with the path can lead to less innovative practices, and less interaction between teachers and students, and students with texts (Toohey, 1999: 91).

Recognizing the need for change

Teachers need to be aware of the need that change can be worthwhile, and have confidence in their ability to bring about the necessary innovations with appropriate support. As Forster and Hewson observe, teachers need incentives to modify their practices. What incentives does the institution have in place to reward those who accept the challenges it offers? Those working in the more traditional, 'research-led' universities may regard their efforts in the teaching domain as marginal if the institution gives a disproportionate amount of its rewards (eg career promotion) to those working in the research area – paying attention to university teaching and learning in so far as activities meet the standards set by the Quality Assurance Agency.

Helping teachers confront negative beliefs (fears)

A further challenge for academic developers is to find ways of helping teachers address and modify negative beliefs (fears) about the intended innovation in a non-judgemental manner. Those contemplating moves into more flexible forms of learning delivery express fears about: the potential loss of ownership of their learning materials when placed on the World Wide Web (WWW); learning assessment; students paying alumni to sit their examinations for them; and the lack of 'real' contact with students.

Assumption:
Teachers require opportunities to acknowledge and address their negative beliefs in a non-threatening environment.

The overall challenge for academic developers is to help teachers identify and critically examine beliefs about teaching and learning – and use these as informed contexts in which to site prospective learning innovations. I have found this approach to be most productive in promoting and achieving institutional goals. The assumptions extricated here form the basis of the strategies that follow.

Addressing challenges via academic development

Abdullah (1998) notes that teacher resistance to change is something that needs to be anticipated when planning for innovation. I believe that acknowledging and addressing the impact of teacher beliefs on any innovation provides one way of lowering resistance. The following strategies have proved useful:

Surveying teacher beliefs

- A brief audit of teachers' beliefs prior to meeting them. Academic developers can use this to gain a sense of where teachers are 'at' in understanding relationships between teaching, learning and flexible delivery (FLD) options. I also ask teachers what they hope to gain from attending the development event.

Teaching and learning as a rationale for practice

- We explore current personal visions of teaching and learning (their 'personal practical knowledge', Haigh, 1998). I ask them to describe recent teaching incidents of their own where an element of innovation was involved, and to reflect on their attitudes towards it.
- We explore *previous* experiences (if any) of flexible learning delivery (FLD). I enquire about the most/least useful aspects they have encountered, and to what extent they incorporate these useful aspects within current practice. The intention is to explore the practical dimensions of beliefs about FLD in relation to broader understandings of teaching and learning.
- We envision the kinds of *future* FLD courses they wish to construct in the light of held beliefs about what is (resource) or not (constraints) possible. I help focus on how to maximize resources and minimize constraints.

Focusing on 'flexible learning' practices

- In collaboration with colleagues, there are opportunities for staff to engage in hands-on training with selected forms of flexible delivery (audio, video, print, Internet) – consonant with the kinds of learning objectives they hope to achieve.
- Teachers are encouraged to link 'new' knowledge with earlier understandings in order to reconceptualize and redesign present, campus-based offerings. This can provide an opportunity for teachers to articulate what they have gleaned via explaining/presenting newly acquired understandings of FLD, and how these may fit into their 'real' workplaces.

Dispelling negative beliefs (fears)

- There are many reasons why teachers might be afraid to move towards more flexible forms of learning delivery, particularly the uses of the Internet. Teachers express concern about how they might:

– make students more visible?
– personalize tutor and student involvement?
– engage students in interactive learning?
– diversify and pace activities/tasks?
– develop strategies for learning reinforcement, review and reflection?

They come to realize that 'solutions' to these concerns (challenges?) are often embedded within the particular mode of delivery. For instance, teachers can be helped to understand that most traditional teaching and learning tasks have their equivalent forms of delivery via the Internet:

– students handouts = electronic publishing;
– group discussions = electronic conferencing; and
– person-to-person communication = e-mail.

Using the above examples helps teachers build bridges between the known (traditional delivery) and the less known (flexible learning delivery). They are urged to reassess their negative beliefs in the light of new information. The 'electronic solutions' above are seen as relevant to basic learning delivery tasks. We know teachers will more readily adopt those practices similar to their own.

Matching teacher beliefs with contemporary FL practices

● Notions of 'sameness–difference' are explored to help teachers compare their beliefs with those espoused by protagonists of FLD. Approaches closest to the teachers' own are most likely to be adopted. Those which radically depart from the teacher's own are the most difficult to promote.

● Notions of 'centrality' are also explored between teachers' held beliefs and those surrounding the selected learning delivery. If beliefs about FLD (the educational purposes it can facilitate) are viewed as peripheral to the teacher's main purposes (eg meeting specific learning objectives), the FLD approach is more likely to be abandoned. Teachers become aware of the 'goodness of fit' between held beliefs and FLD options.

Critically appraising media options

● Teachers are invited to investigate the best and worst that flexible learning can offer. Best practice might involve a significant review of the whole curriculum and a more carefully considered choice of content and teaching methods. Worst practice might simply engage teachers in delivering packages of materials, or down loading all lecture notes on the WWW (Toohey, 1999).

● Discussions are held about the appropriateness of media for particular purposes. Choices are set within the parameters of other (beliefs) constraints impinging on practice. The focus is on issues of teaching and learning and how technology can serve educational purposes. Teacher concerns are extended beyond 'technical fixes' towards a critical understanding of the principles involved.

Investigating teacher beliefs about resources and constraints

- Teachers are encouraged to explore perceptions of support provided by the current infrastructure. Are these perceptions realistic? Do teachers need further information that might modify their views of support?
- Teachers are helped to define the degree to which they enjoy colleague support. Where does the common ground lie with colleagues? Where are the differences? Do these have implications for resources?

Embedding FLD principles into current practice

- Teachers are encouraged to create action plans which firmly embed FLD principles. These may target current or planned courses and will outline the necessary strategies and steps needed to optimize chances of success. Teachers will require help to put principles into practice, via guidance, monitoring and evaluation.

Conclusions

The 'infrastructure' for flexible learning innovation exists as much at the level of dispositions (what is believed possible) as it does on any physically resourced plane. Those who believe that the introduction of more flexible learning practices is simply a matter of applying economic resources to targeted areas, or that academic development events should focus on short-term 'technical fixes', underestimate the impact of teacher beliefs on any proposed changes. Teachers' 'commitment' to an innovation might usefully be viewed as a set of beliefs they hold which they use to judge an innovation's 'relevance', 'connected-ness', and 'centrality' in relation to their more fundamental beliefs about teaching and learning. Academic developers are in an excellent position to help teachers embed flexible learning initiatives within these powerful dispositions.

References

Abdullah, S (1998) Helping faculty make the paradigm shift from on-campus teaching to distance education at the Institut Teknologi Mara, Malaysia, in *Staff Development in Open and Flexible Learning*, ed C Latchem and F Lockwood, Routledge, London

Brown, S (2000) Campus re-engineering, in *Innovation in Open and Distance Learning*, ed F Lockwood and A Gooley, Kogan Page, London

Combs, A W (1982) *A Personal Approach to Teaching: Beliefs that make a difference*, Allyn and Bacon, Boston

Errington, E (1985) Teacher belief systems, attitudes towards drama and educational outcomes, unpublished PhD thesis, University of Wollongong, New South Wales, Australia

Forster, A and Hewson, L (1998) Universities learning: the lure of the net, in *Staff Development in Open and Flexible Learning*, ed C Latchem and F Lockwood, Routledge, London

Haigh, N (1998) Staff development: an enabling role, in *Staff Development in Open and Flexible Learning*, ed C Latchem and F Lockwood, Routledge, London

Mar, H and Mak, D (2000) Staff development in open learning at the Hong Kong Polytechnic University, in *Innovation in Open and Distance Learning*, ed F Lockwood and A Gooley, Kogan Page, London

Marland, P (1997) *Towards More Effective Open & Distance Teaching*, Kogan Page, London

McLachlan-Smith, C and Gunn, C (2000) Promoting innovation and change in a 'traditional' university setting, in *Innovation in Open and Distance Learning*, ed F Lockwood and A Gooley, Kogan Page, London

Murphy, D and Vermeer, R (1998) The catalytic staff development effects of a CD ROM project, in *Staff Development in Open and Flexible Learning*, ed C Latchem and F Lockwood, Routledge, London

Robinson, B (1998) A strategic perspective on staff development for open and distance learning, in *Staff Development in Open and Flexible Learning*, ed C Latchem and F Lockwood, Routledge, London

Rokeach, M (1960) *The Open and Closed Mind*, Basic Books Inc, New York

Rokeach, M (1970) *Beliefs, Attitudes and Values*, Jossey-Bass, San Francisco

Schoenfeld, A. (1999) *Toward a Theory of Teaching-in-Context*, University of California, Berkeley. Located electronically at: http://www.gse.berkeley.edu/faculty/aschoenfeld/TeachInContext/tic.html

Toohey, S (1999) *Designing Courses for Higher Education*, The Society for Research into Higher Education & Open University Press, Buckingham

Williams, D J (1999) *Teaching with Technology or the Technology of Teaching: Reconstructing authority in the classroom*, Abilene Christian University, Abilene. Located electronically at: http://www.morehead-st.edu/people/r.royar/williams.h

Chapter 4

Promoting innovation and change in a 'traditional' university setting

Claire McLachlan–Smith and Cathy Gunn

Introduction

The University of Auckland is the largest 'traditional' university in New Zealand with approximately 26,000 on-campus students. It has specialized in face-to-face, large lecture or small group teaching across disciplines and professional fields since 1883, and takes pride in attracting the country's largest pool of research funding. The university recently joined 'Universitas 21', an international consortium of research-led institutions, and is looking to national and international markets for new teaching and research opportunities. While these global ambitions are clear, the current infrastructure does not support large-scale open, distance or flexible learning opportunities. Other New Zealand universities currently lead the field in this area.

Brown (1997) in Chapter 11 states that there are no validated blueprints for change for institutions that wish to move into flexible delivery, and that there is considerable competition to contend with from the mega-universities with global aspirations (Daniel, 1998) and the rapid emergence of online, virtual universities. Given that the costs of initiating flexible delivery are considerable, Brown states that tight parameters for development of flexible courses are needed. These parameters at the group and institutional level might include:

- policy development, central funding and resourcing for flexible learning from the highest levels of the institution;
- 'learning development managers' in faculties who oversee project management, instructional design of courses, and ensure adequate staff development occurs;
- a choice of development strategies for instructional design (in house, embedding of other courseware, or collaboration with other institutions), with local and centralized production and monitoring of learning materials;
- provision of appropriate support for learners (Laurillard, 1993);
- promotion of the flexible approach within the institution;
- embedding flexible learning into the institution through staff development, rewards, infrastructure and strategic development.

At the individual level, Errington (2000) in Chapter 3 contends that teachers have a set of beliefs about their role, which influences their practice as a teacher. These beliefs include sets of assumptions about teaching, learning and the teaching:learning relationship. Teachers' personal beliefs about themselves as teachers in a flexible delivery context will be influenced by some of the following factors:

- perceptions of institutional support (where change to flexible learning is signalled and led from the top);
- institutional development of policies and strategies that identify student populations, modes of delivery, resourcing and infrastructure;
- the congruence between their own beliefs and the proponents of a flexible, 'learning management' approach;
- challenges to existing beliefs will occur most readily when the flexible innovation is seen to facilitate learning opportunities and when alternatives are embedded in the workplace.

Errington argues that infrastructure also exists at the level of individual disposition (at what is believed to be possible), as it does on any physically resourced plane, if the innovation is going to be successful. However, as he cautions, 'The worst approaches to institutional innovation occur when the institution is "foggy" about its mission, and teachers are expected to use existing infrastructure to deliver very different kinds of courses' (2000, Chapter 3).

Developments in flexible learning at the University of Auckland have primarily been driven at the individual, department or faculty level by 'early adopters', where individuals and groups have worked on flexible learning projects, using diverse learning methodologies. There has been parallel development of policy for flexible learning at the institutional level, but the two processes have not necessarily influenced one another. This paper discusses the rationale, planning and evaluation of two demand-driven developments in flexible learning that succeeded in the current climate. Evaluation of staff and student experiences and the implications for institutional strategy are examined.

Example one: distance education diplomas for general practitioners

Introduction

The Goodfellow Unit in the Auckland School of Medicine was established in 1978 as a centre for continuing medical education specializing in postgraduate study for primary health care professionals. Students on the Goodfellow Unit diplomas in Emergency, Sports and Geriatric medicine are practising general practitioners who enrol to gain further knowledge and clinical skills. The diplomas were first offered by distance in 1995, following demand from students who were travelling in excess of two hours a week to attend two-hour seminars for the course. Students need the flexibility of time and place to be able to fit study into their working lives.

Project description

Although formal needs analyses were undertaken before the diplomas were designed and offered to internal students in 1993, further analysis was not undertaken before offering them to distance students in 1996. Although little is known about how New Zealand doctors prefer to update their medical knowledge and skills, some studies have indicated that they prefer enrolment in a postgraduate course to attending seminars or personal reading (Tracey, Arroll and Richmond, 1998). However, the model of attending seminars run by experts has been very influential in both undergraduate and continuing medical education. The challenges for the diploma coordinators were to overcome the obstacles of isolation for rural doctors, provide intellectual stimulus, disseminate information, and provide appropriate feedback.

A consultant recommended a combination of studio-produced videos of 'expert' seminars and written materials as the most effective media for teaching doctors at a distance. Limited resources meant that video or audio-taping live lecture sessions was a more practical option, and feedback from students indicated that they preferred a tape of the live seminar with student questions. By 1998 the majority of students were enrolling as distance learners, and the target audience had changed to include 25 per cent overseas graduates for whom English is a second language.

Students attend an introductory weekend workshop, where they receive a ring binder to hold written materials, including an overview of course modules and objectives, core knowledge and skills to be learnt, and contact information. Typically each module contains a topic overview, written notes from the lecturer and relevant journal articles. Once per month students are sent a package containing written materials and videos. They receive 15–20 videotapes in total, depending on the length of the course. Access to a journal review service is provided, and regular phone or e-mail contact is maintained. Assessment includes a demonstration of competence in practical skills to a clinical mentor and a multi-choice examination. To complete the diploma, students must do 200 hours of supervised practical and clinical experience, produce a practical skills diary and write up 20 case studies.

The evaluation methodology

In 1998 an evaluation form designed by the first author and Dr Jocelyn Tracey, a former Director of the Goodfellow Unit, was sent to all enrolled students (73). It was checked for content and ambiguity by the course coordinators and the administrators. The survey was based on Massey University's extramural evaluation form, and previous forms used in the Unit.

Data included:

- where students had trained;
- years since graduation;
- reasons for studying;
- effectiveness of course content and delivery;
- appropriateness of assessment;
- preferred learning formats;
- typical methods of studying.

Many of the questions asked students to respond to positive statements on a five point scale from 1 = 'strongly agree' to 5 = 'strongly disagree'. One targeted follow-up letter and a reminder were included in the diploma newsletter sent to students. Responses were entered into an EXCEL database and descriptive statistics obtained. Open-ended questions were coded separately by the principal investigators and the results compared and discussed. Of the 73 forms sent to students, 46 (63 per cent) replies were received.

In addition to student data, ongoing discussion with the diploma coordinator provided additional detail from a teaching and institutional perspective.

Summary of evaluation findings

Student profiles

Primary reasons for enrolling were updating knowledge and skills, personal interest or satisfaction, and the possibility of being able to study in their own time. Five to ten years was the most common period since graduation for these students. A third of all students had trained in overseas medical schools.

Course structure and delivery

In terms of format, content and quality of the courses, students all agreed that the overall quality was high and that the courses had clear learning objectives. The format of videos and folders was considered easy to use, and videos and handouts were seen as relevant and useful to the course.

Students cited a few problems associated with using videos and written materials, including:

- technical problems such as the quality of video recordings;
- understanding the relationship between the video lecture and the supplied readings;
- learning difficulties such as applying techniques without practice opportunities;
- lack of opportunity to interact with other students.

The usual method of studying was watching the videos and taking notes or reading the written materials and annotating them. Students studied an average of seven hours per week, on an average of 10.8 occasions per month, with a range from 2–30 occasions. Two-thirds of students studied at irregular intervals, while the remainder studied at regular times to fit in around their work schedule.

Preferred delivery formats

The first weekend workshop was identified as a valuable part of the course by both students and the course lecturers. Videotaped lecture sessions were rated as 'most preferred format' for learning, followed by CD ROM plus study guides, audio–tapes plus study guides and then study guides only. Teleconferences plus study guides, e-mail discussion lists plus study guides and then Internet-only courses were the least preferred learning formats. It is important to note that students are unlikely to have actually experienced these learning formats. According to the diploma coordinator, only 25 per cent of students currently use e-mail.

Comments were also invited on the potential usefulness of common features of other flexible learning formats. All students said that a greater amount of activity in the materials (such as self-review tasks) and interactivity with other students via e-mail or chat rooms would help them to learn.

Despite the familiarity of the expert 'talking heads' on the videotapes, two-thirds of students said they had to use a different method of study as a distance student than they had used during their medical training. Reasons included finding time to study around work and family, and the need for greater motivation and self-direction to succeed, although being able to review tapes was a bonus. Others missed the human interaction and found it a harder method of studying.

Course assessment

Only half of students agreed that the amount and type of assessment was appropriate.

One area for concern was assessment methods, particularly the examination. Although students liked the practical assessments, they queried the relevance of having a multi-choice examination to assess knowledge, understanding and ability to apply core content to their work situations.

Conclusions and recommendations

Most students liked the package format of videotapes and relevant readings and considered the assessment methods fair and appropriate. Students study at irregular times to fit in with their personal and professional lives and have had to develop different methods of study to cope with isolation from other learners and the complexity of a busier life. Although they are unlikely to have experienced other flexible learning methodologies, they are open to the possibilities. The most important finding was that distance learning is a viable method of gaining further knowledge and clinical skills for general practitioners, as long as it can be self-paced, practical and relevant to the work situation.

Instructional design could be strengthened by using models such as Rowntree's (1990) 'reflective action guide' which could be effective for students who do the bulk of their learning activity away from their materials in clinical work. Drawing on constructivist models that encourage a learning apprenticeship between the student, their clinical supervisor and the course coordinator would also be useful. A stronger pedagogical structure is indicated, to ensure that required reading, thinking and activity are signposted for the needs of the target audience.

Personal contact between teachers and students is established at the workshop in the first weekend of the course and students receive written materials, personal direction, meet other students and assess their own clinical skills. The workshop is crucial in terms of keeping postage costs of materials to a minimum. Further use of flexible learning technologies such as e-mail discussion lists, chat rooms, and CD ROM or online resources is indicated in order to disseminate information, reduce isolation and ultimately reduce production costs, although doctors will need compelling reasons for learning to use the technology.

All these improvements have time and workload implications that the current employment of lecturers in part-time positions does not cater for. Securing resources for designing, writing and producing courses is an ongoing concern in a university that is not used to the 'front end' resource implications of flexible learning. Other obstacles to development include the perceived need to upgrade audio-visual production facilities in the School of Medicine, versus an institutional move towards centralization of resources.

Example two: the Diploma in Business as a flexible learning option

Introduction

Students on the Diploma in Business are full-time working professionals who want to gain further qualifications to enhance their career prospects and business performance. The Auckland Business School qualifications enjoy a reputation for high-quality, practically oriented courses. It is impractical for most students to suspend their careers to undertake full-time study, so the course has relied on evening and weekend attendance for some years. Even this does not suit some students as their work involves travel and irregular time commitment. Recent trends towards internationalization provoked concern that overseas institutions might penetrate the local market. Although there was no overarching policy to support it at the time, the proposed solution was a flexible delivery option, which is now in the third year of operation. A number of valuable lessons have been learnt, though some delivery and course management issues remain unsolved. This initiative has set an example for other departments in an institution that aspires to moving with the times but finds it difficult to do so for structural and political reasons.

Project description

The flexible learning option was offered on a self-selection basis for the first time in 1997. The course structure was not clearly defined at the outset because there was little experience of how the crucial elements of effective communication and teamwork could be maintained in off-campus mode. An evaluation study was designed to assess how the strengths of the existing course translated into flexible mode, and to explore ways that multimedia and communications technology might be used to support future courses.

The initial venture into off-campus learning involved a very small number of students ($n = 5$ yr1, $n = 12$ yr2), but still produced important indicators of how flexible options might be fine-tuned and how the potential of technology might be further exploited. It also identified institutional and administrative issues related to flexible learning, a mode then offered for very few, specialized courses.

The flexible learning option ran in parallel with a long-established, lecture-based course, the major differences with the flexible option being:

- greater forward planning so 'packaged' course materials could be given at enrolment;
- less (perceived) scope to encompass 'breaking issues';
- the lack of regular, face-to-face contact between students, their peers and staff.

The flexible option made intensive use of packaged readings, written commentaries and videos. To address the lack of classroom contact, an electronic discussion list and direct e-mail contact between students and staff were established. The use of these channels was actively promoted from the outset, as experience suggests there must be compelling reasons for students to make the transition to new and unfamiliar study methods (Draper, Brown *et al*, 1996; Gunn, 1996) before they can be expected to use them efficiently.

It was considered essential to stay with the established assessment structure to ensure the quality and comparability of the two study options. This required off-campus students to proceed at a similar pace so assignment and exam deadlines could be met.

The evaluation methodology

Despite the small numbers involved, it is proposed that the evaluation findings provide useful pointers to issues for consideration in future initiatives.

The qualitative study was conducted in three stages:

1. Discussions with staff to identify the aims and objectives of the evaluation and to define the context, course structure and difference from the lecture-based option. Preliminary questionnaire data collected from students provided points of reference at later stages, on:

    ● individual levels of computing confidence and experience;
    ● education and previous experience of distance learning;
    ● reasons for choosing the flexible learning option;
    ● motivation for choosing and completing the course;
    ● expectations of the flexible learning option.

2. Communications on the mailing list were monitored (with permission from the students). Questions were posted occasionally by the evaluator and students were invited to submit any comments directly.
3. Debriefing sessions were held separately with the course coordinator and the students on completion of the course. The students presented opinions on topics related to course organization, presentation, assessment and structure. A second questionnaire was completed at the end of the meeting.

Summary of evaluation findings

Flexibility

Perhaps the most significant, positive outcome of the evaluation was that the flexibility allowed busy professionals to engage in further study without having to take a career break. On a less positive note, students felt the course simply mirrored the established classroom version and that this structure did not work well in some crucial aspects. This implies a potentially high level of demand for flexible learning options in business and professional education if courses were properly reconceptualized for distance education.

This would require the pace of study to be less dependent on the lecture-based course. From a general perspective, this requires introduction of more flexible time and assessment formats. The institutional implications of this are significant and no decision has so far been reached.

Contact and support provision

The high level of personal support and guidance was rated as a strength of the programme. This was only possible because of a high staff–student ratio. Despite this advantage, a time delay involved in e-mail responses sometimes hindered progress and a system for fielding student queries to specific lecturers broke down when no responses were received.

Proposed remedies include establishment of a mentor system with eg graduate students assigned to one or two students, and publication on the WWW of relevant information and a dynamic list of frequently asked questions (FAQs).

Relevance and quality of material

The currency and relevance of course material to professional life was considered a positive factor and learning was immediately reinforced through application to real situations. Project work related to the students' own companies added further relevance and was a strong motivational influence. The implication is for more work-related assignments to be included as course assessments. However, the separation of responsibility for lecture-based and flexible learning options was identified as problematic.

Course structure and delivery

Initially the course appeared to the students to be 'a rather crude adaptation' of the on-campus version and the readings sometimes seemed out of keeping with the stated objectives. This improved as the semester proceeded with the inclusion of commentaries on lecture topics sent out by e-mail.

The common problem arose of an excessive volume of material for the time available, so in-depth coverage was excluded. The presentation of material was criticized as poor and uninteresting since most content was photocopied readings. This reflects an initial, limited view of the potential of technology to enhance delivery and media to enhance presentations. Circulation of student-generated paper synopses was a useful way to clarify the main ideas and introduce different perspectives. However, the main technology used in the course (e-mail) was basic and involves only one sensory channel, so there is much scope for improvement.

Project work was logistically difficult in flexible mode and e-mail communication between students was slow and disjointed. This begs the question of whether the projects should involve work-place colleagues and mentors rather than fellow students. A course more specifically geared to off-campus delivery could make more use of electronic communications such as chat rooms with specific times for synchronous discussion. Reconsideration of project work requirements and materials update and delivery is also implied.

Course assessment

The requirement that all students sit a final exam proved unrealistic because the content was geared to work done in class, some of which differed from the flex-ible learning course. No computers were available for the exam, although this was the predominant method of writing and communicating during the course. To some extent though, the assessment accommodated individual needs and professional interests, and building on this perceived strength is recommended.

Conclusions and recommendations

The experience of the teaching staff and findings of the evaluation provide a 'snapshot' of a trial setting. Three significant findings were that:

- increased flexibility of time and place offered a major advantage to the target group for courses of this nature;
- high levels of personal communication would be unsustainable at current staffing levels with large student numbers, although technology could make a significant difference;
- the WWW could be used to deliver continuously updated course materials instead of requiring all materials to be packaged at the start of the course.

Although technology offers much potential, both staff and students need addi-tional training and support to fully realize this. Reconceptualization of course structures, assessment and the role of technology is required to shift away from the less successful conversion of an on-campus course to development of an effective, flexible learning experience. Establishment of standard hardware and software platforms and a student guide to independent study would eliminate many minor problems.

Sourcing of multimedia resources could add to the richness of the largely text- and video-based course. If the department intends to move into the distance education market, these issues would be well placed high on the planning agenda. Perhaps the most significant findings from an institutional perspective are the different administrative and assessment procedures required for campus learners and the need for a review of policies and practice updates to reflect these differences.

Discussion and conclusions

If we return to Brown's and Errington's suggestions for how to shift to flexible delivery at the personal, group and institutional level in a traditional university setting, some of the following issues begin to emerge.

- *Policy development, central funding and resourcing for flexible learning from the highest levels of the institution*
  The primary issue affecting development of both courses is that development

has occurred at local level, without a central locus of control on policy, strategy, funding or monitoring of quality. Using Errington's (2000) description, the institution is 'foggy' about its involvement with flexible learning, so these teachers have essentially mounted flexible courses within the traditional infrastructure, and against all odds. Their relative success is a testimony to the dedication of staff and students involved.

There is actually great opportunity for innovation in an institution which does not need to overcome the prepared package mentality of distance education, but equally there is tremendous scope for empire building, resource grabbing, and really sub-standard courses to be offered. The institution needs to bring the policy makers and innovators together in a planned process of resource allocation and standard setting to prevent worst-case scenarios from occurring, while best practice is established.

The crucial factor for success of these initiatives was ownership of the innovation by someone for whom it was a passion. Without this, it was unlikely to succeed. These people are typically 'early adopters' with a passion for trying something new, but they also need to have experience, credibility and a voice in the institution. The reality is that they are often part-time contract employees. As most staff in departments will have little knowledge or interest in flexible learning, this person has to be an advocate for resources, and a key contact for students who are enrolled in the flexible option. The lack of infrastructure means they will be the first port of call for any difficulties that arise. The paper coordinator has a greater rather than lesser role in promoting learning in a flexible course.

- *'Learning development managers'*
Although both authors play a role in providing staff development for academic staff on flexible learning and delivery, the role of 'learning development manager' does not exist at the university at institutional or faculty level. We can provide advice and support in terms of instructional design and use of educational technology, but we are unable to play a full role in project management. There is no coordinated strategy for preparing teachers for flexible learning.

- *A choice of development strategies for instructional design, with local and centralized production and monitoring of learning materials*
Both examples used an adaptation of existing course-ware for the flexible option, with local production of learning materials, and in-house coordination of quality assurance. Neither course was completely reconceptualized for flexible learning. This resulted in some difficulties with the courses. For instance, the choice to videotape the lecture format for the diplomas in medicine can be seen at best as a conservative choice of media, and at worst an inappropriate choice. In both examples, the assessment used for the flexible option was identical to the internal class, but not necessarily appropriate to students' learning needs. In the first example, students completed a factual multi-choice examination at the completion of a practical and applied course

of study. In the second example, students had to sit examinations in a controlled university environment. In both cases, alternative strategies would have increased the flexibility and the applicability of the assessment. The institution has to learn to think flexibly about achieving learning outcomes in comparable but different ways.

In terms of production, lack of a centralized production facility in the School of Medicine meant that students were sent current information with each posting, although this clearly involved a costly and naïve delivery schedule and could have potentially resulted in low-quality presentation of materials (Lockwood, 1998). For the Diploma in Business, technology offers the opportunity of maintaining currency through students receiving late-breaking news via e-mail commentary, although this route has the potential of simply transferring costs to learners. However, one of the major advantages of using technology is that the latest information can be sent to students as it arrives. With traditional distance study, materials preparation occurs months in advance of its dispatch to students, so it can be significantly out of date by the time it arrives. Greater use of the Internet for delivering information can only improve flexibility, and there is huge potential for fast delivery of course materials. As the institution develops infrastructure for flexible learning, it will be important to ensure that opportunities for flexibility of delivery are maintained, while costs to students are monitored.

● *Provision of appropriate support for learners*
As the institution is not equipped for flexible learning, students have little to no support beyond that which lecturers are able to provide. This lack of infrastructure resulted in the sorts of delay in e-mail response to queries experienced by students in the second example, and for the need for paper coordinators to check personally on students' progress in Example one, as there was no 'help desk' available to students.

● *Promotion and embedding of flexible learning into the institution*
Although the institution has developed a policy for flexible learning, it looks unlikely in the current climate of cost cutting that the institution will do anything meaningful in terms of resourcing and supporting flexible learning. In fact, recent indications suggest that the institution will actively encourage flexible learning at the level of individual innovation rather than institutional strategy. However, as Peters (1998) and Daniel (1998) argue, institutions that wish to compete in national and international markets have to dedicate resources and policy to making it happen. The university at present can be seen to be strong on rhetoric and gestures, but weak on implementation through revision of infrastructure, resources, training, support and quality assurance of materials.

● *Teachers' beliefs about flexible learning*
It is perhaps at the personal level that these courses have had their strongest support. Although staff have not had perceptions of institutional support, in fact they have had to battle for it, and nor have they had institutional policies,

strategies and resourcing, they have had a very strong set of personal teachers' beliefs in the importance of providing flexible learning options for students. The coordinators of these programmes see flexible learning as one of the most effective ways of students meeting learning objectives, and therefore they have wholeheartedly thrown their energies into course development.

In conclusion, these flexible courses have been successful essentially against the odds: due in part because they met the needs of their niche market and in part to the time and dedication of the 'early adopters' who coordinated them. The danger of such an approach is obvious, however, as so much of the work of developing these courses is hidden. The institution could look upon the success of these courses as an indication that further resourcing and support is unnecessary, where in fact they have only worked as well as they have because of the efforts of the 'early adopters' involved. Without the personal beliefs and championship of the paper coordinators for these flexible courses, we could be discussing a very different outcome for learners, teachers and the institution.

References

Brown, S (ed) (1997) *Open and distance learning: Case studies from industry and education*, Kogan Page, London

Brown, S (2000) Campus re-engineering, in *Innovation in Open and Distance Learning*, ed F Lockwood and A Gooley, Kogan Page, London

Daniel, J S (1998) *Mega Universities and the Knowledge media: Technology Strategies for Higher Education*, Kogan Page, London

Draper, S W, Brown, M I *et al* (1996) Integrative evaluation: an emerging role for classroom studies of CAL, *Computers and Education*, **26** (1–3), pp 17–32

Errington, E P (2000) The influence of teacher beliefs on flexible learning innovation in traditional university settings, in *Innovation in Open and Distance Learning*, ed F Lockwood and A Gooley, Kogan Page, London

Gunn, C (1996) CAL evaluation: what questions are being answered?, *Computers and Education*, **27** (4), pp. 57–60

Laurillard, D (1993) *Rethinking University Teaching: A framework for the effective use of educational technology*, Routledge, London

Lockwood, F (1998) *Design and Production of Self-instructional Materials*, Kogan Page, London

Peters, O (1998) *Learning and Teaching in Distance Education: Analyses and Interpretations from an International Perspective*, Kogan Page, London

Rowntree, D (1990) *Teaching through Self-instruction*, Kogan Page, London

Tracey, J M, Arroll, B and Richmond, D E (1998) Changes in CME uptake caused by reaccreditation, *New Zealand Medical Journal*, 10 April, pp. 118–20

Chapter 5

Making a virtue of necessity – a low-cost, comprehensive online teaching and learning environment

Bruce King

Introduction

There is a growing literature on the problems faced by universities at the present time that reflects a striking unanimity on the issues involved, whether the institution be in the developed or developing nations, has a long and proud history or is a relative newcomer to the tertiary scene, and teaches principally on-campus or at a distance. [See, for example, Margolis (1998), Noble (1998) and Turoff (1997)].

A common thread in these analyses is the impact of the new communications and computer-based technologies on teaching and learning. Further, there are agreed infrastructural, technical support and professional development commitments that universities need to make to accommodate these changes which are generally seen as inevitable, although there is debate about the scale of their ultimate impact.

As universities seek to address these issues, it rapidly becomes apparent that they are closely interconnected with a range of other matters within the institution. These include how teaching and learning are regarded, the nexus between changes in course delivery and a range of administrative issues, the potential of the new technologies to alter power relationships in the teacher–learner interaction, and even tensions between traditional views of the role and function of a university and an emerging organizational culture that accommodates more specific notions of social accountability, customer service, and accommodation of student diversity.

The way universities choose to respond to these pressures depends very much on how they see their competitive advantage relative to other institutions (Daniel, 1996; Yetton *et al*, 1997). Such perspectives are frequently tinged with a greater degree of pragmatism than many in universities may wish to acknowledge.

This chapter considers how a new, financially constrained Australian university approached the development of a technologically mediated teaching and learning environment.

The thinking behind the innovation[1]

In 1993, all Australian universities were invited to participate in a three-year cycle of quality audits undertaken by the Commonwealth Government. There would be an initial focus on teaching and learning and as the audit outcomes involved a significant ranking and reward component, all 37 publicly funded institutions committed themselves to the process. The audit considered both outcomes and embedded policies and structures for fostering quality practice.

The University of South Australia is located in a small city with two other, older universities, both with higher status and strong research traditions. The new institution recognized that its strongest chance for a positive ranking in the Quality Audit rested on the policy and planning framework it had put in place to improve the quality of its teaching and programme delivery. Senior management also exploited the situation to consolidate long-term commitments to a radically different approach to teaching. Documentation prepared for the Quality Audit Committee contrasted the current situation (in 1993) with the characteristics that would prevail in 2003 under a proposed Future Learning Environment. A critical outcome of the identified changes was to be a student-centred learning environment that was significantly technologically mediated.

The University had developed the broad policy framework for this initiative through a series of needs analyses and carefully formulated plans in 1992 and 1993 and the necessary technical and capital infrastructure was identified in the

---

[1] This section draws on King (1998). The papers referred to are all internal documents of the University of South Australia.

Corporate Plans (1993 and 1994). The changes to the teaching and learning environment were outlined in three further reports prepared in the year from July 1993.

These were summarized in the University's (1994) first *Report to the Committee for Quality Assurance in Higher Education* in July 1994. Here the University described its changing learning environment and predicted a staged process to a future learning environment from 1993 to 2003. The University intended to create a teaching context which derived its legitimacy from the learning needs of its students, that is, a flexible and student-centred environment. Further, the application of technology to teaching was to be strategic, directed to increasing student choice, and underpinned by a strategy to develop information literacy in students. Finally, the necessary changes to the teaching environment would be adequately resourced and supported by appropriate professional development of staff.

The movement towards a student-centred learning environment *per se* is not the subject of this chapter. It is sufficient to report there has been substantial progress at the level of curriculum development, changed teaching and learning strategies, and proposals for new assessment strategies that are both more student-centred and reflective of the concerns of the professions into which students would wish to proceed upon graduation.

In 1996, the Electronic Access to Teaching and Learning (EATL) Report set out recommendations for the next stage of development in the Future Learning Environment. This was accepted by the Senior Management Group as a framework for the future. It constituted the most significant discussion of the issues faced by the University and outlined a series of strategies for action.

The purpose of the plan was to:

- develop and maintain a distinctive and cost-effective capability in the electronic delivery of courses on campus, throughout Australia, and internationally;
- improve the quality, flexibility, efficiency and effectiveness of teaching and learning;
- provide an effective infrastructure to support the achievement of the University's graduate qualities;
- create opportunities for course delivery, new markets and diverse student groups;
- build the University's competitive advantage in existing areas and create major new opportunities.

A major sub-theme was acknowledged as the need to move the University from *ad hoc* to planned processes and arrangements in the area of electronic access to teaching and learning. The ultimate goal was that all students and staff would progressively integrate information technologies into their learning in appropriate ways.

There were three critical assumptions in the EATL Report:

● the capacity of information technologies (IT) to enhance the teaching and learning process and do so cost effectively;
● systematic integration of IT as essential to the University's future and not a matter of choice; and
● the need to make choices of direction and position IT commitments strategically.

There had been substantial developments in the University since the EATL report was produced. Most important was the commitment to Microsoft Exchange as the universal e-mail environment for all staff and students. This was facilitated by awarding a joint tender to a local firm to provide ISP services to students of the three universities in South Australia. In addition, there has been significant resource redeployment to IT at the University through an internal budget reprofiling strategy and specific resource commitments in the *Corporate Plan 1997*.

What is clear, however, is that for a combination of circumstances, the thrust of the EATL report towards the establishment of an online teaching and learning environment within the University was not comprehensively implemented.

In summary, at the beginning of 1998, halfway along the nominated timeframe, there was discernible progress towards achieving institution-wide commitments to student-centredness in teaching and learning arrangements. However, despite various attempts to use the collegial decision-making structures of the University to advance the technological dimension of the Future Learning Environment, little had been achieved beyond a strengthening of the network infrastructure across the six campuses of the University and an institution-wide common e-mail and messaging system. The Vice Chancellor demanded a 'breakthrough' intervention in relation to the application of technology to teaching and learning.

Within four months a conceptual outline of the online educational environment had been prepared, together with a project timeline for its development and implementation. This was presented to the University community in May 1998. The first stage of the project was completed by March 1999 at which point UniSAnet was officially launched and operational.

The University of South Australia has developed an online environment for teaching and learning, UniSAnet, that is low cost, scaleable to all staff, students and courses, requires very little technical skill to implement, and presents a common interface to students of the University regardless of the programme in which they enrol.

The current situation

The development of UniSAnet was shaped very much by the three assumptions of the EATL report identified above, which can be summarized as (1) IT applied to learning had to add value and be cost effective, (2) was central to the University's mission rather than an option, and (3) had to be applied strategically.

In developing the conceptual framework, I wrote:

> UniSAnet will be a coordinated teaching and learning facility which stands as an additional dimension to the University's existing teaching and learning program. Its purpose is to add value through increasing the quality and flexibility of course offerings by extending choices both to academic staff and to students. It should also secure efficiencies in program delivery and extend the capacity of the University to make its programs available to a greater number of students, nationally and internationally. The teaching programs and support services of the University should be presented to current and potential students in an accessible and integrated fashion. Finally, it should assume the widest possible range of student and staff expertise in relation to using information technologies. (King, 1998: 4)

The resource situation of the University was extremely constrained. The UniSAnet proposal had to acknowledge that to have any chance of success. Further, to make something substantial with limited resources, there would be no room for mistakes. So, for a mix of strategic and pragmatic reasons it was proposed that:

- the technological developments should be as simple as possible;
- emphasis should be on adding value to existing offerings, particularly distance teaching materials;
- initially the focus should be on transforming those existing resources to make them more accessible and interactive, using the capacities of online delivery;
- to avoid user-end technological commitments, both staff and students should be able to operate UniSAnet using a standard browser without further specialist software, particularly plug-ins; and
- this basic platform would be the standard, from which more comprehensive developments would build.

The proposal had to accommodate those existing initiatives of academic staff, sometimes specially funded, where subjects or courses had already been put online. This was a potentially disruptive issue, for such developments were very much the product of individual expertise and enthusiasm. In a number of instances, they were on a platform different from that proposed for UniSAnet. What mattered was that such developments should thenceforth be planned for compatibility. Conversely, it would be incumbent on UniSAnet to provide links from the common University system to these individual offerings and to ensure that the system would be robust enough to accommodate other developments.

Secondly, it was acknowledged that the University could determine to target key course areas for faster development than proposed for UniSAnet for strategic and commercial purposes. Such initiatives may well require more sophisticated elements than provided for in the common basic package, yet they would have to be compatible.

It was held that the University had a responsibility to its students about provision of a consistent interface for online study programmes. The modular nature of courses within the institution, the significant contribution of service programmes, commitments to broadening undergraduate education by including non-specialist components in every programme, and the capacity to exercise significant levels of choice in some fields, all made it crucial that decisions about authoring software and the adoption of a standard authoring platform be made on a University-wide basis.

This was important for staff as well as students. Given the limited capacity to provide technical or professional development support, it was argued that academic staff would require a consistent method by which they design materials, moderate online discussions, and administer the delivery of their subjects.

Of course, an institution's capacity to provide necessary technical and professional development support to staff is diminished significantly when expertise has to address a range of software products. Experience in other Australian universities suggested that as courses increasingly have online components, the support needs of students proliferate in ways that create significant resource demands, eg through necessary maintenance of a help-desk. The matter is complicated further as other services, such as enrolment and fee collection, are also offered online.

In conclusion, it was clear that the University was at a critical point and must take action to bring a degree of rationalization to a range of exciting but uncoordinated activities. It took the decisive step of agreeing that:

- its online teaching and learning services would have a common front-end, ie UniSAnet;
- there would be a consistent use of authoring and communication tools within and between courses;
- increased attention would be given to supporting staff so they could readily place materials online;
- technical support would be constrained to nominated authoring and communication tools;
- students would be supported by a teaching and learning help-desk, initially maintained through corporate resources; and
- where possible, existing online courses and subjects would be brought within UniSAnet during its first year of operation, typically by electronic linkage.

The UniSAnet model

The approach taken was that UniSAnet would be a common, universal system for the university community, capable of mass customization. That is, it would be available to every staff member, all students, and represent as many courses and subjects as were required without further technical development. It involves the linking of both existing corporate databases and custom-built data stores to Web pages, operated upon through standard Web interfaces using Web forms and wizards. These are prepared by the UniSAnet project team and allow academic staff to create content and shape the teaching and learning arrangements of online subjects without requiring specialist expertise or other necessary support.

Thus UniSAnet can be accessed by staff and students alike through a standard Web browser without user need for specialist software, especially plug-ins. The decision has been taken to present essentially text-based material, appropriately ordered and linked, online discussions, interactive quizzes and a range of assessment activities so that any subject can have an online dimension that extends students' learning options or removes administrative or time and place restrictions on study.

Course content can be structured for Web-based learning in one of two ways. Either an academic can create directly online, using the tools developed within UniSAnet, or existing distance teaching resources can be converted by Flexible Learning Centre staff to attractive and acceptably formatted online materials without additional academic input. Starting this year, Centre staff automatically create online administrative materials for every subject taught off-campus in time for the semester of offer and approximately 450 subjects have been so prepared in the two months since the March launch.

It was argued that UniSAnet should be implemented strategically, with very clear targets in mind. These include the following:

- Establish immediate success at basic levels for the whole university community by creating Web pages for all staff, courses and subjects offered by the institution. Students should be able to gain access to simple and straightforward teaching and learning resources using any standard Web browser, without requiring academic staff to develop any new skills. The authoring environment must be flexible and afford a reasonable level of interactivity for students.

- Use the experience of this minimalist online presence to encourage academic staff to author materials using Web forms and wizards, thus releasing them to concentrate on academic content and educational issues rather than mastery of technical detail.

- Generate enthusiasm and interest in creating more sophisticated learning resources and interactive teaching strategies within specific courses, using the success of early innovators as exemplars of good practice and models for the involvement of a wider group of academic staff and courses. Such developments can be funded in part through the internal Grants for Innovation in Teaching and Learning. The recommended authoring software is MS Front Page because of its integration with other desktop software provided to staff.

● Integrate over time (1) online forms of student support (eg access to a range of library services) and (2) online administrative functions (enrolment and fees payment) with teaching and learning resources available through UniSAnet to provide students with comprehensive electronic access to the University and its courses.

It needs to be stressed that UniSAnet is a University-wide initiative. As such, standards will prevail that are consonant with the University's mission and reputation. While it is intended to provide opportunities for staff and courses to be represented online, this will be within the context of University ownership of the online presence, both in terms of its presentational standards and existing delegations which control information relating to the institution and its programmes. It success will be subject to annual review and, in the first instance, by an external consultant.

Reflection on the development of UniSAnet

The development of UniSAnet is part of an Australian-wide movement to more flexible forms of educational delivery in higher education. In terms of the Teaching and Learning Strategy of the University of South Australia, flexible delivery is the enabling concept that underpins our commitments to an environment shaped by student-centred learning and an agreed set of learning outcomes, the Qualities of a Graduate of the University of South Australia. By flexible delivery I mean:

the provision of learning resources and the application of technologies to create, store and distribute course content, enrich communication, and provide support and services to enable more effective management of learning by the learner. In particular, the concept involves a view of learning in which a teacher does not predominantly mediate the student's experience. (King, 1999: 271)

The decisions taken by the University of South Australia need to be seen as part of a national (and probably international) trend. They have their origins in three disparate developments: (1) distance education, (2) open learning and (3) technological change. I will briefly discuss each of these as it contributes to the more general concept of flexibility in education.

Distance education in Australia has predominantly been offered from dual-mode institutions in which the conventions of on-campus teaching have been very influential components of the organizational culture (King, 1999). However, the growth and acceptability of distance education demonstrated that there were approaches to resource-based education that could be as successful as more conventional approaches to university teaching in terms of student learning outcomes as indicated by retention and graduation rates.

Open learning has had increasing acceptance, too, in this country. That is, there has been a growing acknowledgement of the legitimacy of removing constraints in the educational choices students make. At its most developed, this constitutes a political transfer of control over the learning experience from lecturer to student. More pragmatically, it manifests itself in such relatively mundane matters as the number of teaching periods per year, more relaxed approaches to prerequisites for study, opportunities for assignments to be undertaken in contexts that value practical experience and perhaps the students' employment aspirations, greater recognition of prior learning, the capacity for students to create acceptable degree study patterns from a diverse range of specialisms, etc. What is key to our understanding of open learning, however, is the acknowledgement that it is not a distinctive form of educational delivery but the assertion of certain value positions in relation to education that are primarily student centred in their orientation.

The availability of technologies with the potential to improve both communication and access to information in education settings has increased enormously in the last decade and has had probably the greatest single impact on the way academics practice their teaching role. It is, however, the other two elements discussed above that have afforded this application of the new technologies a particular legitimacy in the Australian university scene. This is discernible in the approach taken to the development of UniSAnet which, in a number of ways, emphasizes access to learning opportunities rather than the creation of teaching situations. Consequently, it embodies a greater range of opportunities for students to exercise control over their own learning rather than reinforce the power of the academic to determine the manner in which educational transactions occur.

The national trend described above has been analysed by researchers from the Fujitsu Centre of the Australian Graduate School of Management at the University of New South Wales (Yetton and associates, 1997). By analysing the circumstances surrounding the introduction of information technologies into the activities of 20 Australian universities, Yetton and his colleagues (1997: xii–xiii) deduced that institutions use different strategies to gain strategic advantage over competitor universities in the application of technologies to teaching and learning, and created three generic categories to accommodate these strategies:

- value adding – wherein traditional universities seek to provide high-quality experiences for students as new members of a high-service, high-variety and high-reputation educational community;
- mass customization – typically where large devolved universities seek to employ it through a low-cost central infrastructure to empower innovation and a focus on student use of technology in strong and relatively autonomous academic units (eg faculties);
- standardized delivery – typically where new universities use a separate, centrally resourced unit to build competencies across the institution such that

IT–enabled learning can be used to deliver quality, standardized programmes to a large number of students.

In the Fujitsu analysis, the University of South Australia was identified as a strong example of the third approach. This was before the development of the UniSAnet concept and we would argue that it constitutes a fourth model, or possibly some combination of the second and third of the generic approaches.[2]

UniSAnet involves a set of common tools and interface designs, but allows the individual academic considerable capacity to customize their course in the manner of their own choosing. The Learning Guide Wizard, for example, prompts standard components of good learning materials (Figure 5.1).

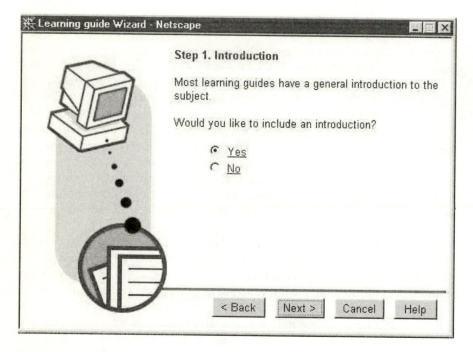

Figure 5.1 *The Learning Guide Wizard*

It does not prescribe or predispose a particular outcome for any learning product and a central planned characteristic is the capacity for individual developments to be built from its robust foundation. By establishing templates and frameworks in-house, there is protection for the intellectual property generated within the institution in that this is not committed to an externally provided authoring and communications package and retrieved under licensing arrangements. However,

---

[2] In this, I am modifying a position argued by my colleague, Ian Reid (1999).

the same templates and authoring tools allow academics the capacity to structure learning experiences without having to focus on technological issues and that are constrained only by the educational expertise and imagination of the lecturer concerned.

UniSAnet is a limited, but positive achievement. It has enabled a university with constrained resources to establish an online presence for all its staff, courses and subjects. To date, some 450 subjects (ie the constituent elements of a degree programme such as History 1, History 2) have significant resources available for learner support. These are part of the success story. The University also committed itself to annual evaluation of the initiative and the first of these was undertaken by an independent expert from another university. His conclusion included:

> The project team needs to be congratulated for the current development. Starting from scratch, they have had the vision, technical and management expertise to develop a comprehensive, valuable and useful educational Web information system. Their foresight has included the integration with the university's information systems, which has only recently been recognized by other online Web developers in its importance. The current implementation is already functional and will be both beneficial and a major factor in the movement to Web based online teaching and learning at the University of South Australia. (Hansen, 1999: 12)

At the present time, UniSAnet serves only to add options for students to their existing programs. Progressively, however, we anticipate student usage will see online services become the study medium of preference.

References

Daniel, J S (1996) *Mega Universities and Knowledge Media*, Kogan Page, London

Hansen, S (1999) *Report on the University of South Australia UniSAnet Project*, Centre for the Enhancement of Learning and Teaching, University of Western Sydney. Photocopy

King, B (1998) *Establishing UniSAnet: The online environment of the University of South Australia*, paper presented to the Information Technology Advisory Committee, University of South Australia

King, B (1999) Distance education in Australia, in *Higher Education Through Open and Distance Learning, World Review of Distance Education and Open Learning: Volume 1*, ed K Harry, p 271, Routledge, London/Commonwealth of Learning, Vancouver

Margolis, M (1998) Brave new universities, *First Monday*, **3**, 5. http://www.firstmonday.dk/issues/issue3 5/margolis/index.html

Noble, D F (1998) Digital diploma mills: the automation of higher education, *First Monday*, **3**, 1. http://www.firstmonday.dk/issues/issue3 1/noble/index.html

Turoff, M (1997) *Alternative Futures for Distance Learning: The force and the darkside*, Keynote presentation at the UNESCO/Open University International Colloquium, April. http://eies.njit.edu/Papers/darkaln.html

Reid, I (1999) Beyond models: developing a university strategy for online instruction, *Journal for Asynchronous Learning*, **3**, 1, May. http://www.aln.org/alnWeb/journal/Vol3_issue1/reid

University of South Australia (1994) *Report to the Committee for Quality Assurance in Higher Education*

Yetton, P and associates (1997) *Managing the Introduction of Technology in the Delivery and Administration of Higher Education*, Evaluations and Investigations Programme, Higher Education Division, Department of Employment, Education Training and Youth Affairs, AGPS, Canberra

Chapter 6

Experimenting in Lotus LearningSpace

Sheila Tyler, Mike Green and Claire Simpson

Three years ago, Glas[1], a multinational corporate, took a bold move to develop management capabilities among staff across Europe, the Middle East and Africa. Its decision was strategic: the aim was to accelerate culture change, create new leadership and build a learning organization capable of sustaining adaptability and flexibility among managers. For this, it wanted to form a partnership with a major business school capable of delivering an MBA programme by distance learning to a large number of managers.

Small cohorts of Glas managers had already been following The Open University Business School's Certificate, Diploma and MBA programme for several years. But in 1996, 500 young people of high potentials were selected by Glas and signed up in two successive cohorts; they were joined by a further 200 in 1997. Students progress through the four-year programme, taking a fixed menu of courses (Strategy, International Enterprise, Creativity and Managing Knowledge) at MBA level. This chapter describes a project by The Open University Business School (OUBS), UK, to use Lotus LearningSpace for the delivery of courses to Glas's students at the company's request. Glas was keen to enhance teamwork and action learning among managers and OUBS cast this as an opportunity to move beyond a simple conferencing model of student communication and support.

---

[1] The name of the corporate has been changed.

The OUBS teaching and learning methodology

The Open University Business School delivers part-time supported distance education across the UK, Europe and beyond. The core elements of this education are course materials (text, audio-visual), and learning support components (learning facilitation by tutor, tutorials (UK only), Day Schools, Residential Schools, assignments and examinations). Courses draw on the concept of the reflective practitioner in professional learning (Schon, 1983, 1987). They require students to apply course concepts and techniques to their own work contexts and to demonstrate this in assignments. Tutors (part-time associate lecturer staff who work largely remotely from the OUBS) play a key role as learning facilitators. They have responsibility for groups of up to 16 students, and mediate and support the core 'dialogue' between course components and individual students, and between students who are encouraged to share perspectives, experiences and practices. Computer-mediated communication facilitates these dialogues and supplements the face-to-face opportunities provided. In addition to marking assignments and holding face-to-face sessions with students, tutors are trained to moderate and host online discussions using FirstClass (Salmon, 1998). The Open University Business School was an early adopter of electronic networking and conferencing although computer access as a requirement on Certificate and Diploma courses post-dated the start of Glas's initiative.

Lotus Notes and Lotus LearningSpace

Lotus Notes is an electronic groupware system that combines messaging, groupware, and Internet access. Its integrated messaging and groupware combines 'push/pull' methods of information sharing (users can upload information to the server and retrieve information from it). Notes is the platform for the LearningSpace application.

Lotus LearningSpace can be thought of as a pre-structured, pre-labelled set of filing cabinet drawers (databases), to be filled with anything that can be put in digital form. The standard version of Lotus LearningSpace has a number of databases: schedule, resources, courseroom (discussion database), assessment and profiles (details of users). Advantages of using Lotus Notes/LearningSpace, compared with Web-based methods of delivery, are that both Notes and LearningSpace can be used offline (saving connection charges) and that the functionality of the Notes platform in particular reduced technical design time while allowing experimentation appropriate to OUBS's own Web-based system, currently under development.

On the basis of student feedback, course by course, we have made a number of changes to the standard version of Lotus LearningSpace (LLS), including the recent introduction of a navigation tool to replace the 'drawer-opening' system and allow seamless access to resources (including other students) outside LLS. We also introduced more work and debating spaces for student groups of different sizes (from small team rooms to course-wide conferences) for collaboration: the primary innovation.

The desire to move beyond conferencing was consistent with our understanding that changing organizational realities 'increasingly require employees to work in teams, to have good interpersonal skills… and to value individual differences' (Baldwin et al, 1997). Furthermore, the adoption of an action model (Resnick, 1987) involving a learning community embracing teachers, management experts and Glas personnel in addition to students held the possibility of blurring the boundaries between formal learning and the workplace (Mumford, 1997).

The specific objectives of teamwork and action learning accorded with the pedagogical approach of OUBS, which is constructivist and uses instructional strategies designed to maximize flexible application of knowledge. Teamwork and action learning offered additional opportunities for students to relate knowledge to action, to examine subject matter from multiple points of view to construct more flexible knowledge (Prenzel and Mandl, 1993) and to examine a wider variety of contexts in which knowledge could be applied. Simply stated, teamwork and action learning offered richer opportunities for development which could be systematically embedded in the learning programme, rather than left to the more serendipitous possibilities of electronic conferencing. And by making explicit the features of successful team/group learning (Stevens and Campion, 1994), it was hoped to provide students with strategies for continuous learning outside formal educational programmes.

Critical success factors in online working, revealed by a wide body of literature (eg Mason and Kay, 1989; Kaye, 1991; O'Malley, 1998), were identified as follows:

● competence among group members;
● shared understanding of the goal;
● mutual respect and trust;
● creation and manipulation of shared spaces;
● clear lines of responsibility;
● selective use of outsiders;
● the realization that collaboration ends when the goal is achieved.

These critical success factors both shaped the approach to teamwork and activities, and distinguished teamwork from large-scale electronic conferencing. Team formation was regarded as an activity in itself; team autonomy was considered vital (Simons, 1993) and it was clear that activities needed to be structured with clear, overtly useful goals and with careful attention to process. The small team, working in a focused way on a structured activity, contrasted with the 'big and boundary-free' electronic conferences (these were seen as functionally distinct and complementary).

The autonomy of teams extended to student decisions about their composition and regulation (Baldwin *et al*, 1997). Students' technological self-efficacy (Compeau and Higgins, 1995) was thought to be high given the nature of Glas's business.

The project team was aware that teamwork needed to be embedded in course design, content and presentation and that the existing text-based courses designed for more individual use offline were less than ideal. A resource-based course model with a loose assemblage of materials through which students would be guided via group activities was necessary but was known to be unachievable. This was not merely because of the time-frame, but because of the enduring success of the OUBS course model and its position as the largest provider of MBAs in Europe and the UK. Instead, a compromise was attempted: a time trade-off between participation in team activities and individual study.

Apart from this, accommodating team-based action learning was considered possible. The following were seen as essential:

● clear and specific learning objectives such that teamwork added value to the learning experience and had practical outcomes for students;
● the (re)design of assignments and other activities so that students could work on issues and material relevant to Glas and which (critically) required constructive sharing of information, experiences and interpretations;
● a compelling purpose for collaboration, albeit the production of an assignment or preparation for an examination.

The result – 'Action Centred Learning Activities' – was an alternative means to the production of an assignment but with potentially larger and different gains for students. Progression planning accommodated the authority students were expected to exercise over the size and constitution of teams, and problems such as under- or over- participation by members. Activities were simpler with fewer consequences earlier in a course, and more complex with higher stakes at the end (eg working on a seen case study for the final examination). An additional tutor role was helping students with time trade-offs and facilitating teamwork. Attempts to involve Glas senior management were not wholly successful for a variety of reasons, but for one course Glas linked a final assignment (a critique of strategy) to a student 'challenge'. This involved an online debate with two senior executives as part of the preparation and an opportunity to present the final assignment to Glas executives: a means of quickly liberating innovative thinking into the organization via an influential audience.

The first course versioned for Glas was piloted with four tutorial groups using Lotus Notes which Glas was then introducing throughout the organization; Lotus LearningSpace was used thereafter with all Glas's students. Action Centred Learning Activities (ACLAs) were structured and detailed, involving three phases: individual study, teamwork involving a Glas issue/focus, and individual reflection on the teamwork results. The time-frame for each phase was sufficiently generous to allow for individual differences in study pace and asynchronous working. For the pilot, each activity required a tangible output in the form of a text one week before the due-date for an assignment to enable students to make use of it. Students and tutors were provided with information and advice on online teamwork (Einon, 1998) and tutors were involved in developing the ACLAs (a continuing practice). Towards the end of the course, three students from each of the four tutorial groups were interviewed. The main points are set out below.

Technical

- Despite Glas's assurance that all students were Notes users, many were very new users and a number experienced technical set-up problems.
- Glas's firewall meant students needed a separate ID to access OUBS databases.
- Replication of databases (information exchange between Glas's server and students' machines) was not always successful or fast.

Content and learning issues

- Students' views on collaboration in an educational context were very mixed: they ranged from 'cheating' to a sophisticated view of the gain from being exposed to different perspectives and approaches. The majority regarded collaboration as information exchange.
- Students saw the Action Centred Learning Activities as additional to the core course requirements.
- Students who did follow the activities saw the benefit of them but found them over-structured and more time-consuming than individual study; they disliked the idea of a joint output.
- Participating students who worked in teams found that online teamwork was harder to manage than they anticipated; they had not expected to need 'rules and regulations' to deal with team members who did not pull their weight so had spent insufficient time establishing a framework initially, to the cost of the team.
- Despite knowing one another and studying together for 18 months, participating students felt the need for initial trust-building before working together.
- Some non-participating students would have participated but could not find like-minded people to work with in their tutorial group; some had collaborated on the activities offline.

As a result, activities for the courses that followed were 'loosened up': greater variety, less structure and no requirement for any output independent of the assignment. Instead, some assignments could be submitted jointly but with an individual conclusion. Facilities for more discussion databases – team, tutorial group and course-wide – were also introduced at this point. Induction days, covering an introduction to the technology, the activities and team formation, were planned for both students and tutors for the follow-on courses and the first formal activity was timed to begin after the first Day School one month into courses. Before that, more informal conferences would be facilitated by tutors for trust-building and developing a 'critical mass' of students. More emphasis was placed on team autonomy: students were to be actively encouraged to create virtual team-rooms and establish procedures to deal with unethical behaviours. A move to allow students to work across traditional tutorial group boundaries, by allowing them to form teams via a course-wide conference, was blocked by tutors on the basis that, potentially, such teams would be tutored by two or more people who might give conflicting input. However, the project team's interpretation was that much about the new collaborative style of working among students threatened to undermine the tutor role and shift the power/authority balance in favour of the student. Given OUBS's student-centred approach, this was something of a surprise, but prepared us for resistance that can be interpreted as 'cultural' from students, tutors, course teams and other academics.

Obstacles and barriers

Not all our intentions and planned changes to Action Centred Learning Activities or facilitation of student collaborations were acceptable to successive Course Teams as the project rolled forward. In particular the 'time trade-off' between individual and group activities met with resistance. Obstacles and problems were encountered at many levels, for example: the need for centralized decision-making conflicted with the historical autonomy of Course Teams; changes that were felt to require re-validations of courses could not be implemented; there was concern about the non-comparability of the student learning experience on different versions of courses ('if it ain't broke, don't fix it'; resistance to external demands); there was sometimes lack of belief in teamwork as an effective means of learning; there were time constraints.

Recent evaluation

During presentation of the two most recently completed courses (run simultaneously with different cohorts of students), student feedback was sought in three phases: telephone and face-to-face interviews with subgroups of students, and an end-of-course questionnaire completed by all students. The response rate for the questionnaires was 76 per cent. Issues generated in each phase of feedback were used to form the questions to be posed in the next phase ('progressive focusing'). For brevity, feedback from one course (Strategy) is presented.

The benefits of discussion and collaboration (including the Action Centred Learning Activities) were recognized by almost all the students interviewed and they remarked that this was the way they worked in Glas. However, disappointingly few students participated. The feedback from students places their lack of participation in a wider context which has implications both for the education provider and the corporate sponsor.

General use of LLS

Student use of LLS was greatest for accessing materials (79.5 per cent of students used it for accessing presentation-specific materials and 62.1 per cent for accessing course units); 32.6 per cent used it for general collaborative work, 24.2 per cent for tutor contact and 10.6 per cent for keeping in touch with other students; 8.5 per cent used it for participating in the ACLAs online (19.4 per cent participated in ACLAs off line). The breakdown is shown in Figure 6.1. Some students acknowledged the difficulty of abandoning old study practices.

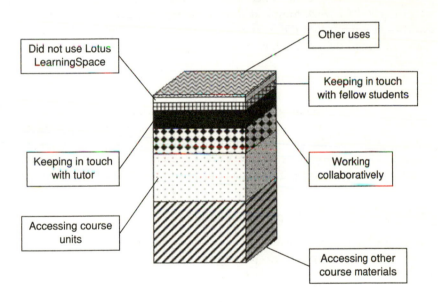

Figure 6.1   *What did you use Lotus LearningSpace for?*

Technical problems

Technical problems were widespread: only 36.6 per cent did not have difficulties with set-up or ongoing connectivity such as slow server connections. Use of LLS appeared to be determined by initial experience and technical problems (lost messages/contributions; loss of format when manipulating digitized materials): 'If you know there are people in your group who are not connected, there's no point in sending out general notes.' The firewall problem, requiring students to switch IDs, inhibited frequent use.

Time and study habits

Factors that deterred collaboration and team activity were:

- lack of time, both for participation and reading other people's contributions ('When you don't have time to read thoroughly, you don't have time to discuss things online');
- lack of response to their own contributions (a 'critical mass' problem);
- a preference for face-to-face or synchronous (telephone) contact.

Many students made reference to the demands Glas made on them in their day-to-day work. Glas was described as a 'pressure company' in which personnel were required to work long and unsocial hours. Students also mentioned that studying in English (not the mother tongue of the majority) slowed their rate of study, adding to their difficulties. Students reported study times from eight hours a week to 'minimum of 20' with increases when assignments were due. Typically, students spent one or more weekends on each of the three assignments.

Almost all students belonged to self-help groups which met face to face, sometimes with great regularity (eg three times a week over coffee) and most worked collaboratively in these groups, providing little incentive to work online. Virtually all students spoke of the value of such groups and their part in a 'survival' strategy for getting through courses.

Students' views on ACLAs and teamworking

The majority of students felt positively about teamworking and team activities; the 'Glas Challenge' was seen as particularly exciting and relevant but few took it up because of insufficient time, lack of response within Glas (some students could not get information essential to the assignment from their management), and problems with the business strategies Glas had chosen. Thus, the ACLAs and Challenge were largely eschewed by students: 'Our aim is to reduce the material we have to read; anything on top of that is disregarded.'

Some 29.5 per cent of students thought the ACLAs were an 'add-on' to the course, an equal proportion thought they were not, but a worrying 40.9 per cent were not aware of any activities (despite the claim by 76 per cent that it had been easy to find their way around LearningSpace). Of teamworking students, 75 per cent thought the ACLAs were useful for working towards assignments, 37.5 per cent thought they enhanced their learning and 37.5 per cent thought they saved time. Reasons for not participating in the ACLAs are shown in Figure 6.2. The

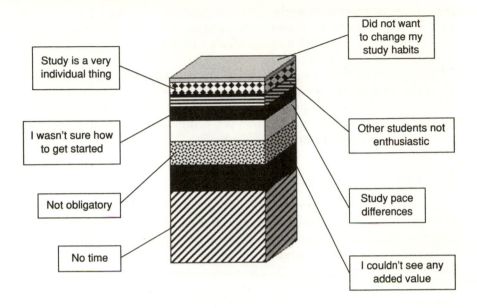

Figure 6.2 *Reasons for non-participation*

predominant reason was 'no time' (69.8 per cent). Other reasons were not being able to see any value in the ACLAs (23.3 per cent); not obligatory (22.1 per cent) and differences in study pace (19.8 per cent). The large majority of those who had not participated in the ACLAs studied collaboratively in their own self-help groups (79.6 per cent).

Glas strategy and support

Issues of Glas strategy and support were very dominant. Most students felt that if the four-year management development programme was central to Glas human resource strategy, Glas should provide time and opportunity for students to apply their learning. This would require support at local (line) management level brought about by 'top-down' initiative. Many students alluded to the lost opportunities for Glas. Suggestions for appropriate line-manager support included discussing assignment topics with line managers and working with them so that assignment preparation and writing could become part of work – a view wholly consistent with Action Learning.

Reading time and other issues

A question about workload was framed in terms of a comment frequently made by students: 'There's so much reading to do for the course, I don't have enough time to think about it properly.' A large majority of students (78.6 per cent) agreed with the statement; almost the same proportion (76.7 per cent) said that to get through the course they do only what's necessary, although many (61.2 per cent) were unhappy about this way of studying.

Students' main concerns, based on a checklist taken from emergent issues, were the demands of work and lack of time (equal at 82.6 per cent), followed by the overall length of the programme (61.4 per cent), lack of support for the programme by Glas's executive (37.9 per cent), and lack of support by local management (30.3 per cent).

Discussion and actions taken

The emerging pattern with the Glas group is one of increased activity online over time both within single courses and from course to course, and successful 'pockets' of activity, eg single tutorial groups and geographical locations.

However, the overall picture is one of overburdened students often unable and seemingly unwilling to change study habits that have helped them to 'survive' a programme of study which, though wholly sponsored by Glas, appeared not to be supported in a way that tangibly acknowledged students' efforts, or made studying or applying learning easier by providing appropriate opportunities. Students, though, were not the individualists that the pilot groups had suggested: students not only saw the benefits of collaboration but worked with other students regardless.

Acting on the feedback to ensure more appropriate use of LearningSpace for follow-on courses, we made the following changes:

- a shift in strategy to use LearningSpace more for student support than for collaboration;
- retention of collaborative activities, but devised to be more discursive and amenable to a conferencing model of online work;
- a greater emphasis on tutor support and additional tutor training (technical and facilitation);
- the introduction of a navigation tool;
- information for students (help line; Web-based information for students to show line managers);
- abandonment of plans for non-geographical tutorial groups (implementation would have disturbed students' long-standing self-help groups).

Regarding the introduction of a navigation tool, it was becoming increasingly clear that the standard Lotus LearningSpace style of navigation was not conducive to guiding students through a process. Many students missed seeing the ACLAs, or were confused. Additional tutor training will ensure that all tutors are free of technical problems before students arrive online, and are better equipped to deal with initially sub-critical masses of online students. Part of the training will take place online and cover their role as role models and champions (Middleton, 1999).

Our own learning

The project has been of significant value to the OUBS as it progresses towards online delivery of courses. Within the OUBS, the project has provided a focus for the development of new methods of teaching and learning. Content and delivery are no longer contemplated as separate systems. In pioneering new methods of producing teaching and learning materials for use online, we have engaged with the need for multidisciplinary teams, new systems and processes of generic value.

These successful outcomes are balanced by (a) the traditional study habits and survival strategies of students in a 'pressure company', (b) Glas's implementation and support of the education programme (including teamwork and the attempt to take the MBA 'into the workplace'), and (c) OUBS's traditionally successful systems which will bend only so far to the impact of new technologies. Approaches to technology include addition and/or replacement of processes and content (features of incremental/gradualist change), and restructuring/re-engineering for which processes must be revisited ('big bang' change). The fundamental issues for OUBS as it moves to fully online courses are that gradualist change leads to 'additionality' – a consequence of addition – and that the learning objectives for its traditionally delivered courses are not necessarily compatible with new objectives that technology makes possible. It became clear from the Lotus project that an adequate course model would need to be an eminently flexible one to accommodate different paths through a more 'raw' set of resources (Figure 6.3) and all that that entails (Macdonald, 1999).

A consequence of our learning is the introduction of a communication plan within OUBS to address the culture and process changes that course *requirement* for distributed collaborative working and learning are likely to pose. Working online (compared with online communication) requires the time and motivation to acquire new skills and techniques. These will need to be part of an explicit curriculum for use with next-generation digital technology which will include 3D learning environments and smarter intelligent agents, taking us far beyond electronic messaging for both work and learning. The future is not merely a matter of revisiting the social learning and resource-based course models of the past (Cresswell, 1998). It offers the possibilities of new methods of working consistent with the re-engineering of processes (e-commerce), distributed industry and sustainable development. The future is exciting, but how do we proceed? The Lotus project shows that the gradualist approach (addition and adaptation) is unlikely to work: it is necessary to break out of text-heavy courses geared to individualist approaches to learning. The required flexibility and its consequences produce the same dilemma currently faced by the commercial

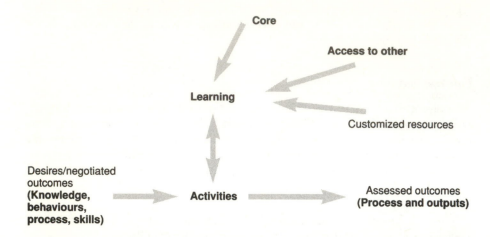

In the process model 'activities' embrace a wide variety of learning tasks; learning resources are flexible outside a core assembly, and assessment is based on the desired and negotiated outcomes (processes, behaviours, skills and knowledge). Courses can be customized, with strategic guides through a programme of activities which draw on the resources. The model is capable of embracing a continuum of teaching/learning methods from offline individual study through networked learning to online teamwork.

Figure 6.3 *Process model*

world (Angehrn, 1999): that preparation for change may mean abandoning successful practices. But how? The Apollo moon landings were achieved on the back of the Gemini programme which tested critical processes. The analogy looks useful.

References

Angehrn, A (1999) *Visions of the Future*, Keynote address at the efmd Annual Conference, Edinburgh

Baldwin, T, Bedell, M D and Johnson, J L (1997) The social fabric of a team-based MBA program: network effects on student satisfaction and performance, *Academy of Management Journal*, **40**, pp 1369–97

Compeau, D R and Higgins, C (1995) Computer self-efficacy: Development of a measure and initial test, *MIS Quarterly*, **19**, pp 189–211

Cresswell, J E (1998) Back to the future: team-centred, resource-based learning as the antecedent of computer-based learning, *ALT-J*, **6** (1), pp 64–69

Einon, G (1998) *Issues in Computer Supported Collaboration*, T293, Block 5, Chapter 6, The Open University, Buckingham

Kaye, A R (ed) (1991) *Collaborative Learning Through Computer Conferencing: The Najaden Papers*, Springer-Verlag

Macdonald, J (1999) Appropriate assessment for resource-based learning, Unpublished PhD thesis, The Open University, Buckingham

Mason, R D and Kay, A R (eds) (1989) *Mindweave: Communication, computers and distance education*, Pergamon Press, Oxford

Middleton, C A (1999) *Asynchronous Computer Conferencing in the MBA Classroom*, Proceedings of the 32nd Hawaii International Conference on System Sciences

Mumford, A (ed) (1997) *Action Learning at Work*, Gower, Aldershot

O'Malley, C (ed) (1998) *Computer Supported Collaborative Learning*, Springer-Verlag

Prenzel, M. and Mandl, H (1993) Transfer of learning from a constructivist perspective, in *Designing Environments for Constructive Learning*, ed T M Duffy, J Lowyck and D J Jonassen, Springer-Verlag in cooperation with NATO Scientific Affairs Division

Resnick, L B (1987) *Relationship between learning at school and what we do in the rest of our lives*, Presidential address at the Annual Meeting of the American Educational Research Association, Washington

Salmon, G. (1998) Developing learning though effective online moderation, *Active Learning*, December, pp 3–8

Schon, D (1983) *The Reflective Practitioner*, Basic Books, New York

Schon, D (1987) *Educating the Reflective Practitioner*, Jossey-Bass, San Francisco

Simons, P R-J (1993) Constructive learning: the rôle of the learner, in *Designing Environments for Constructive Learning*, ed T M Duffy, J Lowyck and D J Jonassen, Springer-Verlag in cooperation with NATO Scientific Affairs Division

Stevens, M J and Campion, M A (1994) The knowledge, skill and ability requirements of teamwork: implications for human resource management, *Journal of Management*, **20** (2), pp 503–29

Chapter 7

Generic structures for online teaching and learning

Lindsay Hewson and Chris Hughes

Synopsis

While the WWW has proved an effective medium for the dissemination of flexible learning materials, it has so far lacked the capacity to support the complex human interactions and richness of the classroom learning experience. At best, Web-based learning environments have used e-mail or proprietary bulletin boards to enable messaging between teachers and learners and relied on the pedagogical design and expertise of the teacher to build these into a meaningful instructional process. What is missing in many cases is an instructional design that goes beyond the incorporation of activities within the materials to implement a planned process of teaching and learning over time and among a group. The knowledge base and skills built over a century of classroom teaching are seldom transferred and applied to the new medium. In addition, some teachers have argued that the new medium demands new methods and in doing so, have perhaps discouraged the wider diffusion of the WWW as a teaching tool.

The authors have developed a Web-based learning environment called WebTeach that attempts to recognize the existing experience and skills of teachers by offering online correlates that build on the strengths of established classroom practice. It represents an attempt to model a range of sound pedagogical approaches and to ease the transition to the online learning environment for both teachers and students. It is believed that, by providing generic structures that facilitate familiar classroom interactions, both teachers and learners will more easily adapt to online teaching and learning. The current version of WebTeach provides scaffolding for discussion, brainstorming, class quizzes, task setting, both formal and informal debate, case studies and questioning.

To date, the authors and colleagues have used WebTeach within a Masters of Higher Education programme, and successfully used a number of the structures to support innovative online group processes in postgraduate Philosophy, Medicine and French at their university. The WebTeach system and the teaching strategies it provides find application in both distance delivery and the flexible delivery of on-campus subjects.

Introduction

During 1995 we faced a dilemma at the University of New South Wales not uncommon throughout the higher education sector – financial constraints and increased global competition demanded the restructuring of our existing post-graduate Masters in Higher Education programme for flexible delivery. While this process had begun by developing traditional text, video and audio–taped modules, there was a reluctance by colleagues to move to entirely off-campus delivery for fear of losing the valuable personal interactions that had been a successful feature of the programme to date. In fact, we had felt, since its inception some years earlier, that the teaching and learning in our Higher Education programme should model and reflect the fundamental principles of reflective practice (Schön, 1987) and deep learning (Marton and Saljö, 1984; Ramsden, 1992) that we espoused throughout the course. While some staff resisted the move towards online teaching as a poor imitation of sound classroom practice, one particular subject (Information Technology for Teaching and Learning – ITTL), which had previously been outsourced, suggested potential for the development and trial of new techniques and technologies that might diffuse throughout the programme.

The focus of ITTL challenged us to use the Internet as much as possible as the delivery medium, both for resource reasons and to provide our students with the experience of learning with and through the new media, as they learned about them. The subject involved a range of assessable projects and tasks, from library work and evaluation exercises to the prototyping of mediated teaching resources. To ensure some satisfaction for ourselves and our students and in order to be able to realistically address some of the discursive outcomes we had set, we needed communication tools which were as robust and as rich as possible. The geographical spread of our students (they work in universities all over Australia, and some participate while on leave overseas) meant we could not make great use of synchronous tools, so the standard asynchronous tools available at the time, e–mail and news group/bulletin boards, were our first choice. An examination of the currently available online tools for teaching and learning revealed a selection of sophisticated messaging systems with abilities to form groups, attach documents and hyperlink content.

However, it soon became apparent that these tools could support only a limited range of teaching strategies and processes when compared with classroom interaction. Few, if any, had a pedagogical basis for their design or functionality. Some had emerged from management information systems to seek new markets in education, but in doing so, brought with them the hierarchical access and control structures of corporate management or the military. Others, such as newsgroups, had their origins in the Internet, and were premised on a sort of anarchic egalitarianism. We considered that the appropriate infrastructure to support the constructivist, collaborative relationships of teachers and learners would lie somewhere in between the two extremes. Since our innovation, several other agencies within the Higher Education sector have identified and addressed this same issue which has led to more considered responses. For example, the Frontier system in use at the Open University, UK within the Masters of Distance Education course models and facilitates appropriate teacher/learner interactions through the provision of platform–independent, multi–user groupware. Others such as the ANTA Multimedia Toolbox (see Chapter 9) and University of South Australia's UniSAnet (see Chapter 5) provide authoring environments for the production of online learning that are consistent for teachers and students across the institution.

As teachers moving into an online environment, we brought with us a well-developed and highly refined knowledge base for teaching, together with skills in facilitating a range of methods for classroom teaching. We also derived some satisfaction from our classroom efforts and looked forward to similar rewards in the new environment. We soon realized that few online teaching systems allow much of this knowledge and skill to be fully utilized in the new environment. Ideally an online infrastructure should build on the teaching and learning processes familiar to both teachers and learners, facilitate dialogue and offer some intrinsic rewards to both parties. If we could gain access to tools and processes that were equal to or better than those we used in the classroom, we could transfer our methods to the online environment and also develop new approaches in response to the new medium. The Internet clearly does offer new possibilities but linking these to our existing knowledge and skill base was a problem. The infrastructure we sought would need to support the types of learning activities and strategies commonly encountered throughout our teaching, yet remain sufficiently flexible to permit the switching of strategies and changing of methods during use. It had to achieve this asynchronously and without penalty to the remote learners who were also participating in other subjects both on and off campus.

We decided to try to do better for ourselves and for our students by developing a prototype for use within our subject.

Description of innovation

The innovation we eventually developed in response to our situation and concerns is now called WebTeach. WebTeach is a Web-based package designed initially to support our own teaching, but since extended to support teacher–student and student–student interaction for teaching on the Web in a variety of contexts. Unlike most other Web teaching packages, it does not focus on supporting the development and uploading of Web pages, nor on student administration. The major commercial packages such as Top Class and Lotus LearningSpace already perform these functions well. There was therefore no need for us to reinvent the wheel by building an application that addressed these functions. Rather WebTeach is designed to facilitate discussion and the use of familiar classroom teaching strategies within a virtual classroom. Our system also attempts to provide a richer communication environment by employing structural and graphic devices to indicate the educational and communicative expectations and intent of the contributions. In this way we hope to draw on teacher and student's familiarity with classroom processes and teaching strategies to support their transition to online learning. We judge WebTeach to be successful partly because it becomes transparent in use, by which we mean that it does not seem to be a barrier for teachers or students to the implementation of the communicative aspects of what Rothkopf (1970) has termed mathemagenic activities – 'activities that give birth to learning' (p 325).

We identified and addressed three levels of communicative interaction in sound classroom practice. These are reflected in the three virtual locations that WebTeach supports:

A Class Notice Board

- The Notice Board is for official class communication and hence only a group's teachers can post notices to the Notice Board. Notices are just Web pages containing text and hence are a one-way form of communication. In practice teachers use notices to advise of changes to the class schedule, of arrangements for assessments and other activities and for any other purpose that calls for official notification of information to students.

A Seminar Room

- Unlike the Notice Board, the Seminar Room is the place where the teaching of the class occurs. Items posted to the Seminar Room are called activities and are intended to be the equivalent of a teaching session, perhaps an hour or two's worth of teaching in a live class. Activities are interactive in that the students and teachers must contribute to them for them to work, just as in a real class. Only teachers can *initiate* activities in the Seminar Room, but anyone can join in. Activities can employ a range of teaching strategies, including discussion, brainstorming, questioning, debating etc. These will be described more fully below. By default, teachers have control over the teaching strategies in each activity, but they may nominate students as discussion leaders (allowing for student-led seminars). A student who is nominated as a discussion leader for an activity can draw on the full range of strategies available in order to facilitate the activity. It is also possible to nominate everyone as discussion leaders, but this can lead to chaos.

A Coffee Shop

● The Coffee Shop is just like the Seminar Room, except that anyone can initiate or join a conversation in the Coffee Shop. The Coffee Shop is thus a free-for-all discussion within the class group. Unlike most Web teaching tools, all the teaching strategies that are available in Seminar Room activities are also available in Coffee Shop conversations. Anyone initiating a conversation in the Coffee Shop may nominate others as discussion leaders, just as they can in the Seminar Room. Those initiating conversations in the Coffee Shop may choose to remain anonymous if they wish.

The software automatically distinguishes between teachers and students and it allocates some access and control privileges accordingly.

A significant feature of WebTeach that was introduced after our first experience of using the software is its integration with e-mail. The software notifies by e-mail either the teachers of the group or the whole group (depending on the nature of the contribution) whenever contributions are received (see Figure 7.1).

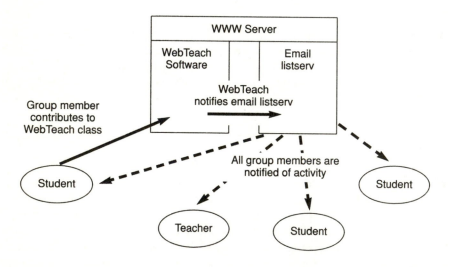

Figure 7.1 *WebTeach and integration with e-mail*

Our experience with WebTeach before this function was added was that both teachers and students quickly lose the habit of checking the Web pages if there is little activity in the group for a week or so. There is nothing more frustrating than posting your comment only to be ignored for a week or two. With the e-mail notifications, everyone is made aware of each submission, and of the topic of the activity or notice that triggered the e-mail. Relevant URLs are included in the e-mail notifications as live links to facilitate quick access to the Web pages. This has been found to improve participation in real classes and it also leads to flurries of activity from time to time.

The teaching strategies supported by WebTeach

The original version of WebTeach supported only discussion within Seminar Room activities, and it did so in a manner similar to most newsgroups, with the main difference being that the Web page that represents the activity takes the form of a transcript of the entire session to date. Many other bulletin boards and threaded discussions display messages as individual items that are flipped through using 'next' and 'previous' buttons. WebTeach has evolved in response to the experience and needs of its users and now supports a number of asynchronous teaching strategies aimed at promoting a deep approach to learning in students in a range of contexts. These teaching strategies provide some support for teachers seeking to implement the discursive, adaptive and reflective exchanges nominated by Laurillard (1993) as characteristic of an acceptable teaching strategy, within a virtual classroom.

The teaching strategies available in any Seminar Room activity (and Coffee Shop conversation) are:

- *Discussion:* the ability to start a discussion and solicit comments. Teachers may have their comments in the discussion highlighted if they wish. Contributors can choose to comment anonymously. Comments are displayed as bullet points in a list, preceded by the contributor's name or pseudonym and a verb indicating the intended speech act, eg 'Chris says:'.
- *Meta-comments:* the ability to make a comment on the process in use, or on other meta-issues, at any time, no matter what strategy is in use. Meta-comments appear as double indented bullet point blue text, preceded by the contributor's name or pseudonym, and a verb indicating the intended speech act, eg 'Mary meta-comments:'.
- *Brainstorming:* the ability to pose a question and receive only short anonymous responses. Responses are displayed in rows in a table as they are received (see Figure 7.2).
- *Questioning:* the ability to pose a question and gather responses while instituting a 'wait time'. Responses received are only revealed to students when the teacher decides that it is appropriate to do so. When revealed, the

- **Charles** says: There are a couple of proprietary systems in use at Sydney. Mechanical Engineering is using WebCT to set some online multiple choice revision questions, and Medicine is using TopClass to discuss case studies. Other than that, some individuals are using a standard Newsgroup threaded discussion to maintain virtual chat rooms for postgraduates who seldom meet on campus.
  (submitted by Charles via c.smith at IP: 120.34.27.190. on 24/5/99 at 12:51 PM)

- **Maria** says: University of Technology has decided to use TopClass as the enterprise standard, so all online classes must be developed in this system. Some faculties are doing a good job (e.g. http://www.chemeng.uts.edu.au/class.html) while others are resisting the imposition of standards. They say they cannot afford the staff development time.
  (submitted by Maria via maria poulos at IP: 129.45.67.18 on 24/5/99 at 12:54 PM)

- **Claus** says: Newcastle is still in the past, and hasn't yet developed any 'house standard' for online teaching. A few colleagues have experimented with WebCT and LearningSpace but cannot afford to pay for the license.
  (submitted by Claus via c.vonneuman at IP: 120.88.120.156 on 24/5/99 at 12:55 PM)

Lindsay H starts a brainstorm by saying…
OK, that is fairly typical of most institutions. Some centralised policy, but mostly early adopters having a little experiment in their own time. Let's see if we can build a list of possible tools from which to choose.
(submitted on 24/5/99 at 12:58 PM)

TopClass
Lotus LearningSpace
WebCT
Some combination of TopClass and WebTeach??
I believe there is another system called BlackBoard that's specifically for teaching

Lindsay H resumes the discussion by saying…
These are most of the main players although there is a much more comprehensive list at Murdoch Uni (http://cleo.murdoch.edu.au/teach/guide/res/examples/course-servers.html) with comparative data.
(submitted on 24/5/99 at 3:55 PM)

Lindsay H seeks arguments on the following proposition(s)…
As a more formal exercise, I would like each of you to help build a case FOR and AGAINST the use of a proprietary system (say LearningSpace) in an undergraduate university setting. Let's start with the case FOR the standardisation of LearningSpace.
(submitted on 24/5/99 at 3:58 PM)

- **Frank** (a pseudonym) **argues FOR the proposition(s)** by contending…
  It would save money by enabling a site license to be negotiated, and it would reduce the maintenance costs for the university.
  (submitted on 24/5/99 at 3:58 PM)

- **Cynthia argues FOR the proposition(s)** by contending…
  The students would get to use a single interface across several subjects/courses.
  (submitted by Cynthia via cynthia pitt at IP: myhome.usyd.edu.au on 24/5/99 at 3:59 PM)

- **Charles argues AGAINST the proposition(s)** by contending…
  I don't think it would work because you can't get academics to agree on anything!
  (submitted by Charles via c.smith at IP: 120.34.27.190 on 24/5/99 at 4:01 PM)

  o **Lindsay meta-comments:** Sorry Charles, you could be right, but let's wait to hear the arguments FOR LearningSpace, before we begin to look at the negatives.
    (submitted by Lindsay via lindsay hewson at IP: thepit.pdc.unsw.edu.au on 24/5/99 at 4:06 PM)

- **Karina argues FOR the proposition(s)** by contending…
  A standard system would allow the teachers to build up a library of practical activities over time and share their development work.
  (submitted by Karina via k.samuel at IP: 128.45.67.108 on 24/5/99 at 4:07 PM)

Figure 7.2   *Responses to brainstorming*

responses are displayed in a table format, each preceded by the contributor's name or pseudonym, and a verb indicating the intended speech act, eg 'Lindsay answers:'.

- *Setting a task:* the ability to set a task for individual or group attention, and to hold further interaction until a number of students indicate with a comment that they have completed their work on the task. Indications are displayed in a table format, preceded by the contributor's name or pseudonym, and a phrase indicating the intended speech act, eg 'Sue indicates readiness to proceed with the comment:'.
- *Case studies:* the ability to describe a case and ask for comments on it. Information can be added to the case at any time. Comments on the case are displayed in the same way as discussion comments. However, additions to the case are placed in a box to separate them from the ongoing discussion and are prefaced by a statement in green indicating that the named teacher has added the following information to the case.
- *Informal debate:* the ability to state a proposition and to request that students submit arguments for or against it. The software requires students to indicate if they are for or against the proposition when they are submitting their arguments. Arguments submitted are displayed as for discussion comments, but are preceded by the contributor's name or pseudonym, and a phrase indicating the intended speech act, eg 'Mary argues for the proposition(s) by saying:'.
- *Formal debate:* the ability to conduct a formal debate on a topic. The software stages the debate by sequentially requesting cases for and against the proposition, then a summary statement. Submitted cases are displayed in boxes and identified by the contributor and a statement in green text indicating the stage of the debate, eg 'Cathy presents the initial case for the affirmative:'.
- *Closing a discussion:* the ability to close off a discussion with a concluding comment. The closing comment is displayed in the same way as a discussion comment, but the final contribution form is removed and a button allowing the teacher to reopen the discussion is substituted.

A further facility can be made available in the Seminar Room:

- *Quiz items:* the ability to pose a question with a suggested response (or criteria for an acceptable response), but to withhold the suggested response until the student has responded to the question. Students are not able to view the suggested and other submitted responses until they themselves have submitted a response. The software accepts only one response from each student. Other submitted responses submitted are available to students anonymously, once they have submitted. However, the contributors are identified when the responses are viewed by teachers, so that quiz items can be used for assessment purposes as well as for providing formative feedback. Both teachers and students can pose quiz questions, but they appear in separate sections of the Quiz page.

All submissions to a WebTeach group may also include URLs, graphics and e-mail addresses. The software attempts to convert these to appropriate live links. It detects URL references to image files and automatically converts these to image references so that the image becomes part of the activity page. This facility allows students and teachers to refer to Web sites and other Web elements without having to master the intricacies of HTML. Of course, raw html codes can also be included in a submission and will be rendered faithfully.

WebTeach requires students to have a standard Web browser and e-mail program only; no special client software is required. Online registration is supported, so teachers can register usernames, passwords and e-mail addresses for students via their Web browser, or they can allow students to register these themselves, depending on the situation.

Evaluation and impact

WebTeach, in various stages of development, has been in use for over five years. The first version supported the three virtual locations, but only offered a simple discussion strategy within activities. It was used successfully for our own teaching in the subject 'Information Technology for Teaching and Learning'. This initial version was developed in an attempt to make the transition to online teaching as easy as possible for both teachers and their students. Hence the use of familiar descriptions and functions for the virtual locations, and a simple chronological transcript format for the activities. It represented to us an improvement on the 'newsgroup' style of communication tools that were employed by the commercial products of the time to support educational communication.

Our experiences in using the software to teach this subject led us to begin expanding the range of teaching strategies supported. At first we drew on our experiences, on good classroom practice and on relevant pedagogic theories to expand the range of strategies supported from discussion to questioning, task setting, brainstorming, and the quiz function. From our experiences and from comments in the reflective journals submitted by our students, we also added the possibility of beginning anonymous Coffee Shop conversations and of being anonymous when contributing to an activity, and the e-mail notifications of submissions.

This second version, augmented with these additional strategies and functions, was used for a further two years by ourselves and by a range of other teachers from within our discipline of higher education and from several other disciplines. Among the other groups using the system at this stage were architects, French linguists and high school teachers. Notable among the other discipline groups were a group of philosophers using the system to teach a Graduate Diploma in Professional Ethics at a distance, and a research group in anxiety disorders teaching a Master's Degree in Psychological Medicine to general practitioners all over Australia. Each major group, the educators, the philosophers and the doctors, used the system extensively, but in different ways. An analysis of the different patterns of use led to a further development of the system into its current form.

The educators tended to use all three virtual locations, but relied mainly on the discussion strategy to support their teaching. However, within this broad trend there were still differences. Some teachers ran seminar discussions for a defined period, say two or three weeks, then closed the discussion before opening another one, others started several activities at the beginning of a course and left them open for comment throughout. Some groups 'took off' in the sense of engaging in extensive discussion, some produced desultory engagement, perhaps submitting a single comment to an activity, with little ongoing engagement. The authors are still exploring the factors involved in these disparate outcomes. Some groups made heavy use of the Coffee Shop for informal contact, others rarely used it. Some teachers experimented with the brainstorming function and others with the quiz facility, but the dominant strategy was discussion. Uses of the anonymity facility were rare.

The philosophers, not unexpectedly, took to the discussion strategy easily, and produced lengthy activity transcripts debating points arising from their textbook and regular reading assignments. These groups, or at least the local members of them, also met regularly in live classes. Thus for some students in this course, the WebTeach activities supplemented face-to-face teaching. Seminar activities were started almost weekly, focusing on the topics featured in the syllabus, but activities were kept open once started, and many instances of students returning to an earlier discussion to add a comment arising from a later topic occurred. Many of the discussions took the form of arguments around an original contention, often for or against it. Other discussions took the form of more general discussion over the validity or defensibility of positions. The philosophy groups also used the Coffee Shop extensively.

The doctors were probably the most extensive users of the system, and they adapted it to suit their most familiar teaching strategy: the case study. They employed the seminar activities, primarily as discussions, to focus on a case, starting the discussion with a description of the initial presentation of a patient, inviting comments, then periodically adding information to the initial description to complicate or refine the information available, before inviting further comments. This process of adding to the case and then resuming discussion often went through several cycles within an activity. At times up to 40 messages would be added overnight, a process facilitated by the e-mail notifications.

Further development of the system was undertaken in an attempt to support the patterns of use emerging from these groups more effectively. Towards the end of 1998 the teaching strategies supported were again expanded to include case studies, informal arguments, and formal debates. In addition, the ability to submit meta-comments within almost any strategy was added. Thus meta-comments seeking clarification of the topic could be submitted while a brainstorm is in progress, or a teacher may meta-comment on the tenor of a discussion without actually joining in.

To lighten the administrative load the ability to register students for a group online was added, along with some other administrative functions allowing the suspension of e-mail notifications and the blocking of all further contributions. This version of WebTeach is now in use by some 25 class groups at UNSW in a range of disciplines now expanded to include immunology, food science, and drug and alcohol studies.

We have monitored the use of WebTeach from its inception by a range of devices. Apart from our own reflections on its use in our teaching, we draw on the experiences of our colleagues and on student journals and evaluations.

In our own subject (ITTL), students are required to keep a regular journal of their experiences in the subject, including their reflections on the experience of online learning which is submitted online, for peers to see, as part of their assessment. For some this is the first such experience. Significantly, these journals reveal little frustration with the system (the bulk of student frustration is reserved for their attempts to master FTP and HTML). Moreover, many students indicate that they would like to use something similar to WebTeach to supplement their own prototype teaching resources. As indicated above, journal comments reflecting on the barriers to participation led us to include the possibility of requesting anonymity for contributions.

Similarly, feedback from colleagues in the full range of disciplines so far mentioned has indicated that teachers take to the system quite easily and find it able to support their teaching practices well. Most teachers begin teaching on the system with no instruction at all, apart from access to the standard help file for all students, and the online demonstration.

However, despite all these evaluations, it is still a legitimate question as to whether the communication supported by the system can be genuinely mathemagenic, such as can be achieved in the best of classroom practice. A colleague of ours, Olga Dysthe, who is a linguist from the University of Bergen in Norway, has analysed the transcript of one activity from the philosophy group to try to track the communicative chains displayed (Dysthe, 1998). Her intent was to try to discern evidence of true dialogic interaction in which contributors respond not just to the original topic or teacher contribution, but to the contributions and ideas of others. Drawing on work by Bakhtin (1981) she argues that mere turn-taking does not qualify as dialogue, but rather that it is reciprocity and active engagement with the ideas and thoughts of others that make an interaction dialogic. Olga further argues that genuine dialogue, as its defined characteristics, can be used as an indicator of truly mathemagenic activity. In her words, 'multi-voicedness creates learning potential'. She found evidence in the transcript she analysed of genuine dialogue as indicated by a number of criteria, and she argues that this can be used to indicate the ability of this medium to support effective learning.

Finally, in our own work with teachers at UNSW facing a move to online delivery and contemplating their options for supporting communication, many describe their ideal product in terms similar to WebTeach. Some of our colleagues are integrating WebTeach with commercial packages, using the former for handling the communication in the class, the latter to facilitate the distribution of information and assessment activities. We also find that after having worked with it for some time, many colleagues are unable to articulate significant changes they would like to see in it. This does not at all mean that we can see no aspects that could be improved, far from it, but it does indicate that the software and the approach has had some success in easing the transition for teachers and students. Making full use of the repertoire of skills they have developed for classroom participation in this new world appears, from the data we have gathered, to play no small part in this success.

References

Bakhtin, M M (1981) *The Dialogic Imagination: Four essays by M. M. Bakhtin*, ed M Holquist, trans C Emerson and M Holquist, University of Texas Press, Austin

Dysthe, O (1998) *The Multivoiced University Classroom: The educational relevance of Bakhtin, Rommetveit and Lotman's dialogue theories*, Paper presented to the Literacy and Numeracy Conference, 10 November

Laurillard, D (1993) *Rethinking University Teaching: A framework for the effective use of educational technology*, Routledge, London

Marton, F and Saljö, R (1984) Approaches to learning, in *The Experience of Learning*, ed F Marton, D Hounsell and N Entwistle, Scottish Academic Press, Edinburgh

Ramsden, P (1992) *Learning to Teach in Higher Education*, Routledge, London

Rothkopf, E (1970) The concept of mathemagenic activities, *Review of Educational Research*, **40** (3), pp 325–35

Schön, D A (1987) *Educating the Reflective Practitioner*, Jossey-Bass, San Francisco, CA

A demonstration of the WebTeach software is available at http://www. online.unsw.edu.au/Webteachdemo/welcome.html

Chapter 8

Selecting an integrated electronic learning environment

Alistair Inglis

Introduction

The major shift that is now under way in the delivery of distance and open learning programmes via interactive multimedia and the World Wide Web, or what are being termed the 'knowledge media' (Daniel, 1996), is presenting challenges for educational managers responsible for leading the shift as much as it is for teachers who are being asked to teach such programmes. Many of those who are coming to this area for the first time are tending to conceive of this mode of delivery either in terms of the development of Web-based course materials or in terms of the creation of virtual classroom environments (Freeman *et al*, 1999). However, as experienced distance educators know, the delivery of programmes at a distance involves much more than simply providing educationally effective learning opportunities. It also involves the provision of a range of academic and administrative support services such as tutorial, counselling and library services (Simpson, 2000) and may involve provision of weekend and residential schools. All of these support services rely in turn on a complex series of support systems. If the intention is to make the transition from face-to-face delivery or more traditional modes of distance education delivery to delivery via the knowledge media, then one of the tasks involved in making that transition is putting in place the appropriate delivery infrastructure.

In the case of traditional distance education programmes, the architecture of the infrastructure required to support learners assumes that communication with them will be maintained largely through the post and telephone. However, when courses are delivered online, the delivery systems require quite a different architecture – especially if the cost savings that are generally hoped for from the automation of functions are to be achieved. Any Web server package is capable of delivering courseware over the Internet. However, to provide a complete range of support services, more specialized software is required.

The rapid intensification of interest in online delivery has led to the development of a growing array of software systems that combine the functions of delivering Web-based courseware with support for other functions needed for the delivery of courses online.

As might be expected, a field of rapid innovation and education and training providers wanting to move into online delivery are keen to know which system would best serve them. However, providing specific advice on this question is not at all easy – especially as the information on which any advice is based is soon out of date. For most education and training providers, what will be of greater value than being given advice on which system currently represents the 'best buy' will be to be provided with a framework for making their own selection decision. This chapter will therefore look at how this task might be approached. It will in addition provide a number of entry points into the available information in the field.

Terminology

There is as yet no generally accepted term for referring to this type of software. One term that was used in the past and is still sometimes used is 'learning management system'. However, the term 'learning management system' came into use as a way of referring to systems for computer managed learning (CML). Such systems directed the pathway that learners followed based on their performance on computer administered tests (Inglis, 1995). Many systems of the type being referred to here do not support learning management in the sense in which that term was originally used. Moreover, even those that do, now support a wider range of functions than the original CML systems. It would therefore seem appropriate to restrict use of the term 'learning management system' to those components of delivery systems that are specifically concerned with the management of learning.

A term used by McGreal (1998) in comparing eight such systems was 'integrated distributed learning environments' (IDLEs). The term 'distributed learning' is being used in the North American context to distinguish this mode of delivery from distance education. In the North American context the term 'distance education' generally refers to remote classroom mode of delivery mediated by audio or video conferencing. However, the term distance education is not used with this meaning elsewhere in the world and consequently in countries other than the United States and Canada there is no necessity for this distinction to be made. The term 'distributed learning' also tends to imply that the systems themselves are distributed. This may or may not be the case. Many such systems are designed to operate off central servers even though learners may be directed to resources that exist elsewhere on the Web.

Maurer (1997) used the term 'integrated network based learning environment' in identifying what he considered to be 10 critical requirements of such systems, while Inglis *et al* (1999) have used the less specific term 'integrated electronic learning environments'. Both of the terms 'electronic learning' and 'electronic learning environment' have some currency (see, for example, Walker and Lambert, 1995) and offer the advantage of subsuming laboratory contexts. This is the term that will be used here.

Some readers may take the view that what is being spoken about here is a 'system' and an environment is the learning context that the system provides. However, the term 'system' tends to downplay the multifaceted nature of these products. In a very genuine sense, the software and the context they provide cannot be separated.

Types of integrated electronic learning environments

Integrated electronic learning environments differ considerably in terms of the range of features they provide and the way they have originated.

Inglis *et al* (1999) subdivided integrated electronic learning environments into three broad types:

- custom design – systems which have been designed specifically to meet the needs of a particular organization;
- building block – systems that have been assembled from a range of pre-existing components;
- off-the-shelf – systems that have been designed to provide a total support environment.

Development of a custom-designed system is an option for education and training providers that do not experience serious resource constraints. This approach offers the advantage that the system can be tailored closely to the needs of the organization. However, the cost of securing this advantage is high and there is also a high ongoing software maintenance cost. For most education and training providers the only practicable options are therefore either the 'off-the-shelf' or 'building block' approaches.

Elsewhere in this book, Bruce King explains the rationale for the University of South Australia's choice of using a building block approach in developing UniSAnet, while Stephen Brown indicates that De Montfort University has chosen to use the off-the-shelf product WebCT in Electronic Campus trials that are currently under way there.

Adoption of either of these approaches involves the acquisition of existing products, and consequently acquisition of an integrated electronic learning environment will involve undertaking some form of evaluation and going through a selection process.

Is there merit in standardizing on one system?

Before considering how one ought to go about selecting a system to implement, it is worthwhile taking a closer look at the question of whether it is worthwhile standardizing on one particular system. If you are looking for a system for your own individual needs then this question does not arise. However, if you are looking for a system which will be used by a number of courses and staff in a department or institution then whether or not at the same time you are trying to achieve standardization becomes a key issue.

Standardization is often held out as the ideal to be aimed for in information technology. It is true that standardization can yield significant savings, particularly in the areas of staff development and equipment and software maintenance. The types of advantages that can come from standardization are discussed in relation to the ANTA Multimedia Toolbox initiated by Ron Oliver and his colleagues and described elsewhere in this book. However, savings are often achieved at the cost of opportunities for innovation. If the aim in implementing an integrated electronic learning environment is to gain experience in online delivery then an argument can be made for spreading that experience across two or more systems. This reduces the possibility of making an inappropriate decision and provides experience with alternative implementations of the basic functions.

The decision taken in relation to standardization needs to give consideration to the circumstances that apply in the individual situations. If you are planning to mount a series of small-scale trials, it might be appropriate to use this as an opportunity to gain first-hand experience with a number of systems. On the other hand, if you are about to implement a programme that will extend across an institution, the advantages of standardization will need to be considered.

Side-by-side product comparisons

The classic method of comparing computer software is by means of a product comparison chart. Product comparison charts are commonly used by computer magazines in reviewing software in specific application categories; for example, desktop publishing software. This is an area in which computer magazines have acquired considerable experience. Numerous examples of this type of comparison may be found in publications such as *PCWeek* and *PCWorld*.

Examples of side-by-side comparison charts for integrated electronic learning environments are already to be found on the Web (see Table 8.1). The most detailed comparison is the Online Educational Delivery Applications developed by Bruce Langdon. This is periodically updated and is available in different formats on two different sites: http://www.olin.nf.ca/langdonline/index.html and http://www.ctt.bc.ca/langdonline. The original version of the comparison listed integrated electronic learning environments separately. However, the current version also includes site development tools and hosting services. McGreal's (1998) is a useful comparison available in print.

Table 8.1 *Comparisons of integrated electronic learning environments published on the Web*

Source	URL
Comparison of online course Delivery software products (Centre for Instructional Technology, Marshall University)	http://multimedia.marshall.edu/cit/webct/compare/
Online educational delivery applications: a web tool for comparitive analysis	http://www.ctt.bc.ca/landonline http://www.olin.nf.ca/landonline/index.html
PCWeek Online	http://www/zdnet.com/pcweek/stories/jumps/0,4270,2393036,00.htm http://www8.zdnet.com/pcweek/reviews/0818/18chart.htlml

Because of the rapid developments in the field, published comparisons are likely to be out of date. When it comes to comparing products with a view to making a selection decision it will generally be necessary to compile one's own information. However, published comparisons can provide a starting point for that process. This may be augmented by information in the specifications provided by suppliers. Table 8.2 provides a list of some of the more widely used systems together with the names and Web addresses of their suppliers.

In preparing a comparison chart it is important to identify what information is going to be useful. It will be useful to distil the information down to that which will be most pertinent to making a selection decision. The type of information that will be most valuable is that which enables one product to be distinguished from another. Features that are common to all products belonging to the category may be disregarded. Similarly, features subsumed under or implied by other features may also be removed from consideration. For example, it would not be necessary to specify cross-platform operability if the system is only going to be accessed via a standard Web browser, because the Web browser will take care of

Table 8.2 *Some integrated electronic learning environments*

Product	Source	Web site
Courseinfo	Blackboard Inc.	http://company/blackboard.com/Courseinfo/index.html
Docent Enterprise	Docent Inc.	http://www.docent.com/solutions/products/index.htm
First Class Collaborative Classroom	MC2 Learning Systems Inc.	http://www.mc2learning.com/products/FCCC/index.html
LearningSpace	Lotus Development Corp.	http://www.lotus.com/home/nfs.learnspace/
Pathware	Lotus Development Corp.	http://www/macromedia.com/software/pathware/productinfo
Serf	University of Delaware	http://www.udel.edu/serf
The Learning Manager	The Learning Management Corp.	http://tlmcorp.com/
Toolbook II	Click2learn	http://www.awymetrix.com/products
TopClass	WBT Systems	http: www.wbtsystems.com/index.html
Virtual-U	Simon Fraser University	http://virtual-u.cs.sfu.ca/vuweb/Vuenglish/what/what.html
Web Course in a Box	MadDuck Technologies	http://www.madduck.com/
WebCT	WebCT Inc.	http://www.webct.com/global/webct/
WebMentor	Avilar Technologies Inc.	http://www.avilar.com/

this function. On the other hand, if one is also planning to use the system on a local area network in conjunction with the system's own client application, cross-platform operability would need to be specified. Generally speaking, it is advisable to start out by compiling as detailed a list of features as possible in order not to overlook important information.

Rating products

Preparation of a detailed comparison chart can be a good way of identifying the differences between different products but it can leave one floundering in a sea of information. What is also needed is a way of making sense of that information.

The computer magazines generally assist readers by giving 'Editor's Choice' awards for what they consider to be the best all-round product in each product category. These awards are based on such factors as the range and type of features offered, usability, and cost.

Selecting the 'best' product may be possible if products are reasonably similar or if there is one product that stands out from the remainder. However, software of the type being described here is not sufficiently mature for absolute comparisons to be meaningful. Integrated electronic learning environments have originated in a variety of ways. FirstClass <http://www.mc2learning.com/products/FCCC/index.html> started out as a computer conferencing system, LearningSpace <http://www.lotus.com/home.nfs/learnspace/> was built on top of Lotus Notes, The Learning Manager <http://www.lotus.com/home.nfs/learnspace/> has evolved from LMS, one of the earliest commercial CML systems. Products therefore tend to be stronger in some areas and weaker in others. It is quite likely that in an objective sense there is no best system.

Even considering the possibility that there might be one system that offers more features, or a better combination of features than the remainder, ignores the fact that with the rapid developments in the field products are tending to 'leapfrog' each other in terms of their capabilities. What may be regarded as the 'best' system today may well be rated only a 'solid performer' tomorrow, as another product moves to the front of the field.

Systems that have arisen more recently generally offer a more comprehensive range of functions. However, that does not necessarily make them better products. Companies that have less experience in serving users in the education and training market may be less familiar with the needs of the market.

The importance of analysing one's requirements

In a market where only small differences distinguish different products, it is possible to rely mainly on a side-by-side comparison of features in making a selection decision. However, given the considerable differences that exist between different products in the market for integrated electronic learning environments, selecting the appropriate product or combination of products depends on finding the optimum match between one's requirements and the features individual products offer.

Many education and training providers do not yet have a good understanding of their requirements as far as online delivery is concerned. They may not even have a strategy for analysing their requirements. This is particularly likely when there has been no previous history of involvement in the off-campus delivery of courses.

There are two broad approaches that may be taken by an educational institution or training organization in defining its requirements. The first is to identify the types of transactions that presently take place with students in on-campus courses. This list should encompass the full range of teaching situations, including:

- lectures;
- tutorials;
- seminars;
- small-group discussions;
- practical classes;
- projects;
- laboratory work.

However, the list should also include responding to students' enquiries of various types as well as administrative transactions such as processing enrolments and providing results. Each of these functions will need to be supported in some way in the online environment. Table 8.3 provides a list of the types of functions that will need to be supported.

Table 8.3   *Basic functions of integrated electronic learning environments*

Student administration, including
Enrolment/registration
Group mailing
Management of student progress details
Reporting of assessment result
Class management, including
Establishment of classes
Management of access to class resources
Delivery of courseware
Asynchronous conferencing
Synchronous conferencing
Exchange of documents
Provision of access to support services
Computer-marked testing

The second approach is to canvass the views of other education and training providers that have had substantial previous experience in off-campus delivery. These providers have already had to devise ways of communicating with and supporting students who seldom appear on campus and are therefore much more conscious of the variety of needs that must be provided for. Table 8.4 provides a list of the needs that distance education providers commonly provide for. Certain types of courses will give rise to other more specialized needs, such as the need to provide laboratory kits in science courses.

Table 8.4 *Types of needs identified with traditional off-campus provision*

Distribution of informational materials
Distribution of course materials
Distribution of readers
Responding to administrative problems (eg enrolment variation, missing material)
Provision of access to academic support
Provision of library borrowing service
Conduct of teleconferences
Facilitation of the establishment of local study groups
Despatch and receipt of assignments
Provision of opportunities for supplementary face-to-face meetings such as residential schools and tutor visits
Notification of examination timetable
Distribution of information on examination centres
Provision of re-enrolment information
Provision of a newsletter

An alternative to canvassing the views of other education and training providers is to turn to the extensive literature on open and distance education delivery which contains many case studies describing the methods of delivery used in different fields of study. The International Centre for Distance Learning database of literature on open and distance learning, which is maintained at the UK Open University and is accessible via the World Wide Web, offers one of the best points of access to this literature. The Web address for this database is <http://www-icdl.open.ac.uk/icdl/lit.htm>.

Some critical selection factors

All features are not equally important. The suitability of a product may be critically dependent on certain functions. Maurer (1997) has provided 10 guidelines for what his research group considers to be the necessary ingredients for an integrated electronic learning environment. However, these guidelines are pitched at a conceptual rather than an operational level. For example, the first two guidelines state respectively that insights obtained from traditional courseware design should not be ignored and that the production of high-quality should be made as easy as possible. While one would not want to argue with these principles, it is necessary to base selection of products on somewhat more concrete criteria.

What an individual provider regards as 'essential' will vary according to circumstance. However, the following are some features that are likely to be critical.

Cost

Cost is invariably a consideration in making this type of choice and it is more so in this case because the basis upon which the type of software is licensed is generally the number of students who will be taking courses concurrently. The cost may therefore be substantial and may increase with time.

The cost of the software licence is generally the cost upon which attention is focused. However, the total cost of implementing an integrated learning environment is not just the cost of the software licence. Table 8.5 lists other costs incurred in implementing a system of this type.

Table 8.5   *Some of the costs of implementation of an integrated electronic learning environment*

Software licence
Capital cost of server hardware
Capital cost of associated communications hardware
Maintenance costs of server and communications hardware
Consumables for server backup
Training of academic staff in use of system
Development of instructional material for students on use of system
Staffing of help desk to support use

Scalability

Scalability refers to the capacity of a system to accommodate expansion, for example its capacity to accommodate additional students or additional courses.

In some situations it is known from the beginning that a project will be scaled up if successful. In this type of situation, it is possible to anticipate the eventual need of the organization from the beginning, although even in this situation, new needs may arise unexpectedly. However, it is more common for the eventual needs of the organization to be indeterminate. Moreover, irrespective of whether expansion has been allowed for, there is a tendency for all successful projects to lead on to other projects. Scalability is an important factor because successful projects generally lead to the initiation of other projects. Use in one situation will suggest applications in other situations.

What is important is that the system should be capable of being scaled up to the level that might conceivably be required within a five- to seven-year timeframe and that the degree of disruption and cost involved in scaling up the system should be acceptable. As a general rule it is more desirable for a system to be infinitely scalable than for there to be limits on how much expansion can be accommodated. If there are limits, then it is important for the nature of those limits to be understood right from the beginning.

Compatibility with existing systems and processes

What distinguishes integrated electronic learning environments from single-function delivery systems such as Web servers and asynchronous conferencing servers is their capacity to integrate disparate functions. However, the value of this capability is negated to a considerable extent if the systems do not fit in with existing processes and systems. Acquiring new hardware to support a specialized suite of software can be more readily contemplated than replacing administrative systems that have been developed over several years or reorganizing procedures for student admission and progression.

Rating the importance of individual needs

While it is necessary to distinguish between functions you consider 'essential' and those you consider 'desirable', there may be value in going further and using a rating scale with more than two-point scale values to indicate the relative importance you place on different functions.

In considering the capabilities that an integrated electronic learning environment needs to offer in order to meet your needs, it is important to distinguish between the functional capabilities of the system and the way in which the system is used. For example, it is generally considered desirable to provide learners with direct e-mail access to their tutor as part of the online learning environment. However, whether or not this feature is provided in the case of an individual course depends on how the course's Web site has been set up, not necessarily on the capabilities of the software. E-mail support is generally provided through a dedicated e-mail system.

Ratings of the importance of different functions should also take into account the experience of others in the field. This is where consulting with other education and training providers can be particularly useful if you don't have previous experience in off-campus delivery of courses.

Making the selection decision

The process of making a selection decision will involve matching the set of requirements that have been identified against the capabilities of the products that are available. This is likely to be an iterative process. It may lead you to recognize the need to re-rate the importance of some requirements.

In comparing the capabilities of different products with your set of requirements you have defined, you ought to start with the capabilities you ranked 'essential' or 'most important', working down to those that you have ranked as 'least important'. For example, if you ranked synchronous conferencing support as an 'important' requirement then the products that provide such support should appear high on your list.

The end to which the process of evaluation is directed is making a selection decision. Once the selection decision is made, users will have to live with the consequences of that decision for some considerable time. Also, when the time comes to review the choice that has been made, there will be a cost involved in switching to a new system. Therefore, the price of making an inappropriate decision can be high.

When it comes to the stage of making the selection decision it is important to take into account whether a system as a whole makes a good match with one's requirements; in other words, whether the *combination* of features that a system offers is optimum. This is largely a matter of 'feel'. It is easy to lose sight of how different components of a system work together while making a feature-by-feature comparison of different products. When it comes to making the final choice, therefore, it is worthwhile taking time to stand back and ask 'Does this feel like the right choice?' If the choice doesn't feel right, you should go back to your list of requirements and compare this with what the product that you have selected offers in order to establish the source of your concern. Any lingering doubts you may have will have their origins in a mismatch between what you are being offered and what you require.

References

Daniel, J S (1996) *Mega Universities and Knowledge Media*, Kogan Page, London

Freeman, H, Ryan, S, Patel, D and Scott, B (1999) *Towards the Virtual University: Resource based learning and the Internet*, Kogan Page, London

Inglis, A (1995) Promises, promises..., *Journal of Law and Information Science*, **6** (1), pp 19–34

Inglis, A, Ling, P and Joosten, V (1999) *Delivering Digitally: Managing the transition to the knowledge media*, Kogan Page, London

Maurer, H (1997) *Necessary Ingredients of Integrated Network Based Learning Environments*, Proceedings of EdMedia'97, Charlottesville, VA, AACE

McGreal, R (1998) Integrated distributed learning environments (IDLEs) on the Internet: A survey, *Educational Technology Review*, **9**, pp 25–31

Reid, I C (1999) Beyond models: Developing a university strategy for online instruction, *Journal of Asynchronous Learning Networks*, **3** (1), pp 19–31

Simpson, O (2000) *Supporting Open and Distance Learners*, Kogan Page, London

Walker, R A and Lambert, P E (1995) *Designing Electronic Learning Environments to Support Communities of Learners: A tertiary application*, Proceedings of the Annual Conference of the Australian Association for Research in Education. http://www.swin.edu.au/aare/conf95/walkr95.220

Chapter 9

Flexible toolboxes: a solution for developing online resources?

Ron Oliver, Stephen Towers, Peter Skippington, Yvonne Brunetto, Rod Farr-Wharton and Anne Gooley

Introduction

Regardless of the motivation, the development of online learning materials has become an imperative for most education and training providers. Many providers who have experienced online development have found that their fore-most challenge is meeting the cost of development. Despite what some may believe, online development is not cheap, nor is online always the most effective way to learn. It is also unlikely to be inexpensive compared to other modes (face-to-face or print) until there is a considerable increase in efficiencies of production or in consumer demand. One of the challenging aspects is that design and delivery models are formative and changing rapidly as we learn about developing quality learning programs that take best advantage of the technology. It is also very simple to consume a lot of resources quickly in developing multimedia components for online learning materials that have dubious benefits for learners. Consequently, many providers are asking how they might be able to afford to develop online learning materials.

One approach is for providers to collaborate in the development of common resources. In this way expenditure is shared and organizational resources can be directed to differentiating products and services rather than duplicating them. While this sounds eminently sensible and obvious, as many can attest, it is difficult for teachers and lecturers within a school or faculty to agree on teaching approaches and resources, let alone involving other providers. However, there is an excellent example of just such collaboration and consolidation at a national level in the vocational education and training sector in Australia. It is called the 'ANTA Multimedia Toolbox Initiative'. The intention of this chapter is to describe this initiative and to discuss its implementation so that others seeking to carry out similar projects can be guided by the wealth of valuable information gained through this project.

Developing online resources

For many years, people have been critical of the development processes often used in building instructional and educational software systems. In many instances, the development has resembled that used in cottage industries where a small number of people take responsibility for all aspects of the process and where the product is destined for small-scale use in limited settings (eg Hanley, Schneebeck and Zweier, 1998). Bates (1999) uses the term 'lone ranger' to describe much of the development occurring in universities where many enthusiastic novices work independently on small-scale projects to support their own teaching and learning programmes.

The outcome of many of today's current practices in developing instructional software is a proliferation of discrete products often being used quite successfully in single classrooms. The Web promised to end this software proliferation by providing developers with a means of seamlessly integrating educational products from servers worldwide. In reality, the Web appears to have exacerbated the problem by creating and encouraging many more small developers into the fray.

Collis and Oliver (1999) in the preface to the Ed-Media 99 Proceedings describe a pattern, which appears to have emerged worldwide in the development of educational software, presented at this conference. The authors report large numbers of papers describing new ideas, their development and implementation but relatively few papers describing projects that have gone beyond the trial setting to mainstream applications. It appears that planning for sustained and external use is not part of the current thinking and planning among teachers and institutions developing educational software applications.

Planning and developing software for use beyond the immediate setting requires unique and particular design strategies. The development of products for widespread usage and application gives rise to many new considerations in the design and implementation process. The design must consider such attributes as scalability, 'the ability to undertake a large number of software projects in a systematic way that produces consistent and reliable results, and to distribute those products widely so as to gain large strategic benefits' (Hanley *et al*, 1998: 1).

Simultaneously the design must carry sustainability, 'the ability to maintain, revise or otherwise provide the technical and user support necessary so that software developed will continue to be available and of value to learners over time' (Hanley *et al*, 1998: 1).

There are many instances in this book which describe initiatives taken at the institutional or classroom level where sustainable and scalable use has been an important component of the process of designing online materials. Oliver and McLoughlin (2000) describe small teaching tools they have developed to provide scaffold and support for learners in online environments. A critical consideration in the design of these tools was use and application beyond the immediate setting. Other authors, for example King (2000), Brown (2000) and Hewson and Hughes (2000), describe initiatives at the institutional level designed to encourage and support teachers using online technologies and teaching strategies. In all these instances, key aspects of the system design included facilities and strategies associated with supporting large-scale use in sustainable ways. And in a more encompassing mode, Inglis (2000) describes strategies by which institutions can provide structured support for online and open learning through the appropriate choice and use of systems to support electronic learning.

Software toolboxes

The design and development of sustainable and scalable software for online learning requires planned and deliberate strategies. There are many factors to consider and currently there are a few structures to guide teachers and developers who seek this goal. One approach that appears to have merit is that of *software toolboxes*. The concept of a software toolbox carries the forms of flexibility and functionality required for scalable and sustainable software developments. A software toolbox is essentially a package that has been designed with flexible use in mind. The toolbox represents a product that can be used in a variety of ways to achieve essentially the same end. Toolboxes are usually created in open-ended and generic ways to enable users to customize and adapt the products to their own unique needs and purposes.

In the context of instructional software, toolboxes provide many opportunities to a variety of stakeholders, from training providers through teachers to the students. Toolboxes appear to have the prospect to break the short-term usage cycle characteristic of most educational software products. The deliberate design of a software system with flexibility for adaptation and change immediately creates new options for its use. In this chapter we describe a recent project in Australia, the ANTA Flexible Toolbox Initiative, which sought to support the development of toolboxes for national vocational education and training applications. We draw upon the outcomes from this project to suggest strategies that might guide others involved in the large-scale development of online learning materials for general use.

The ANTA initiative

ANTA, the Australian National Training Authority, is the national body in Australia representing the post-compulsory schooling sector in vocational education and training. It has a mission to 'ensure that the skills of the Australian labour force are sufficient to support internationally competitive commerce and industry and to provide individuals with opportunity to maximize their potential' (ANTA, 1998a, Preface). ANTA's agenda has been 'to deliver training more responsively and efficiently and to a wider catchment area' (ANTA, 1998b: 1). The Authority recognizes that technological advances have been the catalysts for new forms of educational and training communication systems and that the demand for, and supply of, vocational education and training is globalizing. Consequently it has enacted and sponsored strategies to encourage the Vocational Education and Training (VET) providers to provide more flexible, technological-based, delivery for domestic and international markets (Brunetto, 1999). The implications of technology advances and globalization for ANTA are that they require 'new ways of creating and customizing training material' (Eccles, 1998: 3). It was within this context that the pilot Toolbox initiative emerged.

ANTA believed that a Toolbox initiative was one of its best potential strategies to encourage development and delivery of online learning materials for the training market. In 1998–99 ANTA invested A\$ 3.8 million in 'toolboxes' with the aim of producing a 'smorgasbord of multimedia resources from which providers can pick and choose in designing online training programs' (Eccles, 1998: 3).

How was a national approach achieved?

The Flexible Delivery Multimedia Toolbox Development Initiative was a significant component of the ANTA Flexible Delivery National Project. The Toolbox Initiative was identified and canvassed in the 1998 Flexible Delivery Options Paper (1998c) and subsequent Action Plan. It built upon and complemented the outcomes of the previous year's projects, including Establishing Online Networks and National Online Learning Environment. It represented a national response to the need for quality products for online training delivery and has the potential to leverage a currently limited expertise in this area by allowing training organizations to customize online training programs through access to Toolboxes.

Outcomes

In the context of this project, a Toolbox was defined as 'a set of multimedia resources that provides a framework for the development of training programs for online delivery to meet the requirements of Training Packages' (ANTA, 1998d). The project set aside a substantial sum of money to support the development of Flexible Toolboxes for a range of Training Packages in the Australian Vocational Education and Training sector. At the time of the commencement of the project, many VET institutions were actively pursuing an online agenda and creating materials and resources for their own purposes. This development activity saw the proliferation and duplication of online materials for identical courses and programs. The Toolbox Initiative was a national strategy that could potentially reduce the duplication by providing one set of resources that all course providers in particular areas could draw upon.

A key aim of each Toolbox was to enable providers to customize the contents to meet the needs of learners and their enterprises. The toolbox was required to constitute two essential components: (1) a completed multimedia program designed to satisfy specific training competencies; and (2) a range of tools and functions which provide access to the program's components and resources. The building blocks that could come together to form the multimedia package were conceived to be available as separate resources. The toolboxes were expected to utilize various combinations of a wide range of the building blocks (refer Table 9.1).

While the Toolbox could include some authoring tools, the emphasis was on the generation of content specific to particular Training Packages. ANTA Toolboxes were purposefully content-oriented, aligned with specific Training Packages in order to provide a base set of online and multimedia learning materials that could be customized by training organizations for their learners. After an exhaustive selection process, 12 Toolboxes across eight organizations were chosen for development. The Toolboxes covered a cross-section of training areas and education levels. They were planned to be built using a range of authoring tools for delivery through CD ROM, LAN or Web services.

The Toolboxes were developed over a nine-month period and delivered to the Australian National Training Authority for storage and distribution. A comprehensive evaluation was undertaken during the development stages to assist with risk management and quality assurance and to create a learning environment for the project leaders and managers to guide future activities of a similar nature. ANTA was well aware that unforeseen considerations would emerge because of the scale and innovative nature of the pilot initiative. It was with this in mind that they commissioned the evaluation to identify and address issues proactively. Consequently, the findings from the evaluation provided some fascinating insights into the processes associated with the design and development of large-scale flexible software systems for learning environments. The evaluation studied the broad spectrum of strategies and approaches being used and provided some insights leading to a list of recommendations to guide future developments. In essence the evaluation provided formative and summative advice to both developers and ANTA and supported a *learning community* for online development during the project.

Table 9.1 *Potential components of Toolbox building blocks*

Packages of generic resources in a variety of media (including but not restricted to HTML material, video, audio, CD ROM, digital photographs, animated segments)

Developer's notes, guidelines, supporting documentation and technical guidance to facilitate online provision

Learning materials 'translated' from the Training Package and combined with authoring software to facilitate the development of further, customised materials

Assessment instruments which meet the assessment guidelines contained in the Training Package and combined with authoring software to facilitate the development of further, customised materials

Interactive tutorial packages on researching through the Internet, including directory services, and World Wide Web with simulated search examples, search tasks and tests

Generic case studies

Interactive simulation games

Guidelines for communication functions (eg e-mail, Web forums and chat) and student management systems

Tips, hints, ideas for student-friendly, student 'grabbing' instructional design

Web site with e-mail for comments, support and feedback on material developed as part of the toolbox

Listings of publicly accessible Web site relevant to the content of the targeted Training Package. Web sites might be reviewed with comments on the areas in which they could provide a useful learning resource

Project outcomes

On completion of the project, the eight development teams provided ANTA with multimedia resources for nine Training Packages. Each development team created, on average, toolbox resources for 10 to 15 units of competency, each representing approximately 40 hours of resources or independent study. Despite the broad range of subject areas involved and the range of industries represented, the evaluation team identified many patterns and consistencies between the learning materials. Some comparisons and descriptions of the various toolboxes in terms of teaching and learning processes, functionality, flexibility and utility are given below.

Teaching and learning processes

Content. Sourcing content for multimedia development is often a significant barrier and in many situations it is simpler for developers to produce it in-house to avoid intellectual property or copyright issues. The degree of difficulty for content development for this project was considerable because of the radical changes to concepts of curriculum, delivery approaches and the education and training markets. Consequently, obtaining and developing content in the required format was problematic for some development teams and influenced the potential models of contemporary instructional design that could be incorporated in the development of the learning strategies. In the development process, content writers were selected to provide the content to form the basis of the training packages. In some instances, 'experts' undertook content development with little or no experience of the emerging education and training environment or multimedia/online learning. Without strategic intervention, such content often resulted in a narrow collection of multimedia resources with an emphasis on text-based materials. Consequently, for these Toolboxes text formed the basis for online materials with accompanying media being a secondary consideration used to enhance or supplement the information presented as text. On the other hand, in instances where the content developers were guided in their tasks by expert instructional designers, the resulting materials reflected these interventions in positive ways. The following section describes this influence in more detail.

Instructional design strategies

Where text is the dominant source of content, instructional approaches tend to be didactic whereby learners are presented with screens of information followed by assessment activities to demonstrate recall and comprehension. Information is mainly presented using text on screen, often accompanied by a graphic (cartoon, diagram or photograph) with occasional audio and video sequences. Consequently, the general format is very much that expected in conventional paper-based learning materials.

While this outcome was echoed for some Toolboxes because of the type of content gathered, a number of the Toolbox teams had predicted this and implemented mitigating strategies. Effective processes were those that were integrated and inclusive. Effective processes included those where development team members participated in the development of quality systems based on relevant and proven approaches. Comprehensive handbooks and training sessions were useful for guiding content writers to consider the new and alternative forms of learning available within an electronic environment. Furthermore, there was a clear indication that resulting materials benefited from adding instructional design considerations within the content development process.

Interactivity. Interactivity is the Holy Grail of multimedia. Most Toolboxes included engaging interactions such as selecting and dragging elements to complete sequences, choosing from lists for elaborating comments, and manipulating graphics to test and simulate. Across the entire range of products there were many strong examples of engaging interactions for the learners. There appeared to be a tendency among some developers to restrict the forms of interactivity that could be applied. Interactivity for some development teams was constrained by the content provided, the view of the content experts and industry expectations in terms of how a learning package should appear. Where this occurred, interactivity was sometimes limited to special events rather than being provided as a matter of course or to 'point and click' to respond to questions or 'turn pages'.

Assessment tasks. Assessment is a learning process that can be used for many purposes. Some argue that assessment is the process that has the most significant impact on student motivation. Across the Toolbox projects, there were outstanding examples of effective and meaningful assessment tasks. Meaningful assessment proved challenging for development because of the potential scope for customizing the Toolboxes inherent in their design and the generic nature of the content provided. For example, the extent of relevant content could vary considerably depending upon the legislative province, sub-category of industry or size of enterprise. All of the Toolboxes sought to assess student competency, and the forms of competency being measured were clearly stated. But in some instances, the assessment tasks stopped short of measuring competencies and tended to rely on general questions that required further elaboration or support from training organizations using the Toolboxes. The challenge for future Toolbox development will be to engineer more creative assessment strategies and activities that enhance the learning experience as well as measure achievement. The existing Toolboxes provide some sound examples to guide future developments.

Flexibility. One of the main requirements of the Toolbox materials was a capacity to be adapted and changed to meet the needs of the various course providers who might choose to use them. The flexibility needed to achieve this included being able to add, delete or edit the text, the ability to change images and graphics and a general capacity to modify and customize the materials. The majority of developers used various strategies to cater for this customizability requirement. Some provided tools that could be used to manipulate the materials, some provided blank templates and others demonstrated the information structures for users to enable them to manipulate the HTML code directly. As previously mentioned, the degree of flexibility and customization increased design complexity and in some ways limited instructional models. The emphasis of flexibility and customization was for training organizations rather than for learners. Designing and balancing flexibility and customization for both training organizations and learners is a considerable challenge for developers, particularly considering that flexibility to this degree is a difficult capacity to achieve.

Authenticity. One of the major criticisms of education and schooling in the past is that it has been abstract and removed from reality. Multimedia and online learning provide ways to reduce the abstractness of education by providing learners with access to real-life settings, realistic environments and authentic information and cases. Several Toolbox development teams used the opportunity provided by this project to create information and content that reflected this real-world use. They used examples drawn from real life and presented cases rather than abstracted descriptions. These types of Toolboxes contrasted sharply with those that tended to present text descriptions instead of videos or pictures to portray real-life settings, content experts talking about processes in place of videos showing the processes, and studio re-enactments in place of real-life footage.

Portability and utility

A purposeful and highly successful strategy underlying the Toolbox initiative was to encourage innovation and diversity. This was seen to be important considering the formative nature of multimedia development for education and training and the range of development tools available (such as authoring languages and learning management systems). An anticipated consequence of diversity was the potential scope for the materials being developed to create impediments to the distribution and use of these materials by various training providers. It was recognized that the intended users, the training providers, would require a variety of systems and supports to make use of all the project Toolboxes.

Hardware. An alternative strategy would have been to create minimum hardware specifications to which all projects would adhere unless there were special circumstances. Setting the specification ahead of the development phase enables the challenges associated with subsequent organization and distribution to be considered in the appropriate place in the design process. For example, it is possible to create a specification that would enable materials to be served off all types of servers. While this would create efficiencies in terms of usage and application, such a generic specification could reduce the diversity and functionality of some aspects of the materials.

Software standards. A complementary activity to creating hardware specifications is to consider the same process in relation to software. These standards influence each other and should be determined in concert. In developing their Toolboxes, most developers chose to create the online materials in the form of a complete learning sequence via a courseware delivery system. In this project, the preferred delivery systems included proprietary products such as WebCT and Palace. As well as variations in the courseware delivery systems, the projects varied in small ways in their use of: HTML version; browser compatibility; use of plug-ins; and the use of Javascripts and interactive media elements. On completion of the project, Toolboxes were delivered as complete systems. Again, the variety of software systems tended to complicate distribution and usage among other training providers.

Examination of these issues raised the question of defining portability standards for the various projects. The specification of portability is necessary because it recognizes and deals with the needs of the learners and the tools used by the instructional designers to create the online learning environment. When portability is not considered, the finished products can have limited use in many settings and can defy the economies and efficiencies that have driven the development process. As well as considering software selection and application, portability also involves the establishment of protocols and standards describing internal components and aspects of the HTML files, media resources and database components. It is important for these to be developed and stored in a way that reflects the wide use to which they will be put to ensure minimum difficulty in their use for various training providers. Key specifications include: Metadata standards; HTML file size specifications; linking and navigation procedures (eg linear, hierarchical or flexible); windows (ie procedures for cascading and use of frames); file naming conventions (eg. names and suffixes and default files); and file and media organization (eg media files and use of CGI-bin folder). The more consideration that is given to specifying some standards for the very flexible elements in the design process, the more flexible and usable the final Toolboxes can be.

Setting some standards in terms of hardware and software would help in many ways to make the delivery more economical and efficient. Making these decisions to balance strengths and weaknesses of outcomes in an informed and deliberate fashion is an important component for projects of this nature.

Summary and conclusion

The use of toolboxes is a powerful strategy for creating scalable and sustainable learning resources for open and online learning. A national approach to multimedia development for education and training offers considerable scope for optimizing scarce resources and innovation, but it also brings many challenges and the need to balance competing factors. This chapter has described this strategy and provided information gained from a national project in Australia in which a variety of toolbox developments were supported and coordinated. The initial outcomes from the project indicate that there are a number of key factors that act to influence the quality of learning materials produced in this fashion. In the first instance, it is important to consider the expectations of the various industries and training agencies in terms of the form and format of online learning materials. It is apparent that the move to online technologies should be accompanied by a move in thinking and outlook on the nature of the training materials provided. The scope and opportunities offered by the new technologies to enhance and improve learning need to be recognized and actively pursued if the full potential and value of online learning is to be gained.

At another level, the development of scalable and sustainable software in the form of toolboxes needs to be based around a very firm framework describing the technical specifications of the resulting software systems. Apart from developing flexible systems, it is important to consider the hardware and software standards necessary to enable products created by a range of developers to integrate seamlessly into learning tools for the students. This project has demonstrated that it is possible to initiate and undertake large-scale projects that produce flexible online learning materials that can be used by a variety of training providers and integrated into their training programmes. It is important, however, to recognize the factors that limit the application of the software and to include detailed guidelines and specifications for developers to ensure that the products will find the forms of use and application intended.

References

ANTA (1998a) *A Bridge to the Future: Australia's national strategy for vocational education and training 1998–2003*

ANTA (1998b) *National Investment in Flexible Delivery Products: A preliminary options paper*

ANTA (1998c) *Eyes Wide Open – Vocation Education and Training in the Information Age: A Supporting Paper to Australia's National Strategy for Vocational Education and Training 1998–2003*

ANTA (1998c) *Action Plan: An options paper for national investment in flexible delivery*

ANTA (1998d) *Action Plan Project 1 – Online Product Development: Project brief toolbox development project*, Australian National Training Authority, unpublished, Brisbane

Bates, A (1999) *Thinking Digitally: Restructuring the teaching environment for technological change*, Keynote address presented at ED-MEDIA 1999, Seattle, USA, June

Brown, S (2000) Campus re-engineering, in *Innovation in Open and Distance Learning*, ed F Lockwood and A Gooley, Kogan Page, London

Brunetto, Y (1999) *Developing a consensus view of policy goals for toolboxes*, Queensland Open Learning Network, unpublished, Brisbane

Collis, B and Oliver, R (1999) Preface, in *Proceedings of the 11th World Conference on Educational Multimedia, Hypermedia and Telecommunications*, ed B Collis and R Oliver, Association for the Advancement of Computers in Education, Virginia

Eccles, C (1998) *A New Training Culture for Australia: The right stuff*, ANTA, Brisbane

Hanley, G, Schneebeck, C and Zweier, L (1998) *Implementing a Scalable and Sustainable Model for Instructional Software Development.* Available at http://www.cdl.edu/html/syllabus98.html

Hewson, L and Hughes, C (2000) Generic structures for online teaching and learning, in *Innovations in Open and Distance Learning*, ed F Lockwood and A Gooley, Kogan Page, London

Inglis, A (2000) Selecting an integrated electronic learning environment, in *Innovation in Open and Distance Learning*, ed F Lockwood and A Gooley, Kogan Page, London

King, B (2000) Making a virtue of necessity – a low-cost comprehensive online teaching and learning environment, in *Innovation in Open and Distance Learning*, ed F Lockwood and A Gooley, Kogan Page, London

Oliver, R and McLoughlin, C (2000) Using networking tools to support online learning, in *Innovation in Open and Distance Learning*, ed F Lockwood and A Gooley, Kogan Page, London

Chapter 10

Lifelong learning: generating new learning opportunities

Anne Gooley, Peter Skippington and Stephen Towers

Introduction

> A lifelong learner is an individual with the motivation and
> capability to continue learning throughout life in a range of social
> and work contexts so as to achieve personal fulfilment and
> maintain employability.
> Kearns *et al* (1999: 6)

Realizing the potential of lifelong learning in rural and remote communities poses specific challenges. The first major challenge is to ensure access to learning opportunities. Access to learning for people living and working in rural and remote locations and unable to attend campus-based institutions is greatly enhanced through information and telecommunications technologies. This fact has been widely recognized by both learning institutions and rural and remote communities for many years. Building and maintaining a technological infrastructure is a foundational task; it provides a platform for the services and products that assist rural and remote people to become motivated, self-directed learners. In many ways building and maintaining an equitable infrastructure is an easy task compared with the challenge of using the technology effectively to progress the objectives of lifelong learning. There are a number of barriers to the effective use of technology in rural and remote communities, including a deficiency of relevant programmes; limited opportunity to access technology and associated services; and the lack of experience and confidence of many potential learners. Services and programmes to overcome these barriers should be delivered within a context of supporting the educational, cultural and economic needs of communities so that learners can become active, independent, lifelong learners and communities can become learning communities using learning as a key strategy to promote social cohesion and economic development.

   This chapter examines the role of learning technologies in supporting learners in rural and remote locations; learners who, because of the location of where they choose to live and work, have limited access to the learning opportunities taken for granted by people living in metropolitan and regional areas. In particular, it reports on current initiatives that foster a lifelong learning capacity for rural and remote people so that they can fully participate in the opportunities presented by a knowledge-based information society.

Learning for rural and remote people – more than just access to technology

With 37 per cent of the Australian population living outside metropolitan areas, it is not surprising that Australia has been at the forefront of distance education for many decades. Correspondence education has a feature of some university and school provisions since early in the twentieth century. Australia's world-renowned School of the Air was established in 1951 using High Frequency (HF) radio signals to support remote school-aged learners. The rapid growth of information and communication technology, especially over the past 30 years, has provided continuing opportunities to build on these foundations to further improve access to education and training programmes and services.

   However, the emphasis on access has sometimes overlooked cultural and attitudinal factors which impact on an individual's capacity to learn. If rural and remote communities are to participate actively in the new socio-economic milieu that will characterize the 21st century, they will need to be 'able, motivated and actively encouraged to learn throughout life' (OECD, 1996 :15)Success depends on the adoption of a dual approach that, on one hand, builds and continuously enhances technological infrastructure, while, on the other hand, uses the infrastructure as a platform for the delivery of programmes and services which foster motivation and encourage the desire to learn. Strategies should build self-esteem and confidence and encourage participation in a knowledge-based, information society. This approach is presented diagrammatically in Figure 10.1.

Supporting lifelong learning in rural and remote communities

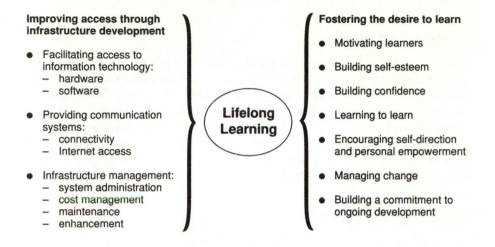

Improving access through infrastructure development

- Facilitating access to information technology:
  - hardware
  - software

- Providing communication systems:
  - connectivity
  - Internet access

- Infrastructure management:
  - system administration
  - cost management
  - maintenance
  - enhancement

Lifelong Learning

Fostering the desire to learn

- Motivating learners

- Building self-esteem

- Building confidence

- Learning to learn

- Encouraging self-direction and personal empowerment

- Managing change

- Building a commitment to ongoing development

Figure 10.1   *A dual approach for rural and remote learners*

This chapter reports on programmes and initiatives of the Queensland Open Learning Network (QOLN) to achieve this dual approach.

Lifelong learning in rural and remote communities – overcoming the barriers

There are many issues relating to the differences in participation rates between metropolitan and non-metropolitan people. Through its experience in offering learning services and programmes to rural and remote communities, QOLN has identified the key issues impacting on learning participation rates. These are (1) low self-confidence related to previous educational experience; (2) high costs associated with telecommunications, travel and distance; (3) the availability of relevant learning programmes and services for rural and remote client groups; and (4) limited access to information and communications technologies.

Previous education experience

Low self-confidence as a learner, related to previous negative experiences of schooling and low education levels, is prevalent in rural and remote areas and is a barrier to accessing education and training, particularly for older people already in the workforce. Furthermore, as young rural people are currently less likely to complete secondary school, future low levels of educational attainment are likely to continue to be a barrier to participation (Kilpatrick, 1997).

Travel costs and distance

The most visible access issue for rural and remote people is the travel required to access training delivery sites. Over 70 per cent of recent graduates who reside outside capital cities relocated to study because there was no local facility or their local facility did not offer the course they wanted to take (Kilpatrick and Bell, 1998). The cost of travel and the opportunity cost of the time spent travelling are barriers to participation. However, people will travel if the training is perceived to be of sufficient benefit (Kilpatrick, 1997). High costs of telecommunication services are also a barrier to participation.

Relevance of programmes

Recent studies (Butler and Lawrence, 1996; Kilpatrick, 1997; Sher and Rowe-Sher, 1994) have found that programmes that are perceived to be relevant to the needs of non-metropolitan communities will attract higher participation rates. Relevant programmes acknowledge local issues and the culture and skills of potential participants. Community and local employer participation in the design and formulation of learning programmes and services allows local needs and demographic characteristics to be taken into account. Remote and rural communities need opportunities for more effective consultation and negotiation with learning institutions to ensure that learning is relevant to local needs. A visible local contact point is desirable; local learning brokers may assist institutions, individuals and communities to access appropriate learning (Kilpatrick, 1997).

Information and communications technologies

The growth of information and communications technologies will increase access to learning for people living in rural and remote areas. However, information and communications technologies have their own set of barriers which relate to cost, lack of confidence with new technology, and the physical provision of equipment and infrastructure.

Promoting and supporting lifelong learning and the development of learning communities

The Queensland Open Learning Network was established in 1990 by the Queensland Government and is now celebrating its 10th anniversary of meeting the learning needs of rural and remote communities. QOLN achieves this by providing and maintaining a technology infrastructure to ensure access to a wide range of learning opportunities. While it facilitates the provision to communities of formal accredited programmes from universities, colleges and other learning providers, it also offers its own programmes and services to encourage the development of lifelong learning in communities.

That is, to support lifelong learning and to contribute to the social and economic sustainability of rural and remote communities, QOLN provides:

- an access infrastructure;
- bridging and support programmes and services.

An access infrastructure

Effective and meaningful learning can only occur if both communities and learning providers are confident that they have access to the necessary technological infrastructure at reasonable cost. QOLN has established and manages and maintains a technology platform for mutual access by both communities and educational institutions. The technology platform provides easy access to a range of contemporary information and telecommunications technologies.

QOLN's infrastructure is centred on a network of over 40 Learning Centres located in regional, rural and remote communities. Centres are linked and supported by a sophisticated technology platform and a human support network of coordinators. Access to and use of the infrastructure is open to learners as well as education and trainer providers. Services are available to communities through local Open Learning Centres that are equipped with computers and modems for accessing services and communication facilities. Access to the platform for learning providers offers significant benefits. Providers searching for new support options for rural and remote learners can choose the most appropriate support technologies to suit the requirements of their clients. They can ensure services are provided at times and in ways that suit both their organizational objectives and the needs of communities. Consequently, services 'ebb and flow', becoming available only when they are required and delivered in ways that meet community expectations. Lastly, learning providers can avoid costly and, at times, risky investment in new technologies and concentrate their efforts on the core business. For rural and remote learners, QOLN establishes, maintains and manages facilities and services to facilitate their access to education and training opportunities, including information, learning programmes, learning support services and communication and information technologies.

Bridging and support programmes

QOLNs bridging and support courses are based on the principle of equitable access for all. The most obvious impediment to active participation in learning for rural and remote learners is distance. However, distance compounds other impediments such as socio-economic status, age, gender, employment status and prior educational experiences and opportunities. While QOLN's network of learning centres and its technology infrastructure provide both technical and human support to learners and communities, the problems of ensuring equitable access to learning opportunities is much more than just provision of technology, centres and centre coordinators. The challenge is to ensure that products and services are employed to help learners become autonomous, responsible people who control their own destiny and contribute to community development. QOLN's use of its infrastructure to achieve these outcomes is based on three key strategies:

● building learning foundation and opening pathways;
● using technology to encourage participation;
● developing lifelong learners who participate in and contribute to the communities in which they live and work.

Building learning foundations and opening pathways

QOLN's programmes and services focus on the development of core skills and competencies that provide the key foundations for continuous learning. Core skills and competencies include:

● learning to learn skills;
● literacy and numeracy skills (including Information and Communication Technology (ICT) literacy);
● understanding others and working in teams;
● information skills and problem solving;
● personal mastery and effective communication.

These core skills and competencies are underpinned by approaches that motivate learners, assist in developing a desire to learn, and facilitate the development of learner self-knowledge, self-esteem and personal confidence. The approaches are based on a strong commitment to continuous lifelong learning with its potential to transform the lives of individual learners and regenerate the communities in which learners live and work.

QOLN programmes and services aim to provide individual learners with the confidence and ability to pursue pathways to the achievement of personal goals, whether those goals are economic, educational, social or civic. They empower learners to seek employment, pursue further study, start a small business or participate in community organizations.

Using technology to encourage participation

Information and Communication Technologies make programmes and services accessible to rural and remote locations but their potential for learning is much broader than simply ensuring access to services. They have the potential, when used effectively, to empower individuals and advance lifelong learning.

To harness the power of new technologies QOLN's programmes firstly aim to ensure basic information literacy for everyone. Short, sharp, hands-on, introductory courses are provided to introduce new learners to computer and communications services. Access to more advanced courses is arranged as needed to meet the individual needs of learners. Secondly, by making modern technologies widely available in communities, learners are empowered to work independently to access products and services from anywhere, as they need them. Thirdly, new communication technologies give rural and remote learners a 'voice' with which they can: (a) seek support and assistance from experts, teachers or fellow learners; (b) learn collaboratively with other learners regardless of their location; (c) exercise choice and control over the scope and nature of learning products and services; and (d) communicate their requirements and needs to decision makers.

Lastly, rural and remote learners and communities are ultimately responsible for identifying their own learning requirements, although they may need assistance from other agencies. Such assistance may take many forms, including information, advice and/or consultancy services. Information and communication technologies facilitate open negotiation and discussion of learning issues and concerns that can be jointly addressed between community and the institution designing and providing learning services. Such strategies ensure both groups have accurate and reliable information on which to consider options available to them.

Developing lifelong learners who participate in and contribute to the communities in which they live and work

Human capital is being recognized as the key future resource for communities, especially rural and remote communities struggling with the effects of the globalization of national economies and the impact of new technologies on business imperatives and operations. Human capital is the combined knowledge, skills and abilities of the individuals within a community. By encouraging and facilitating lifelong learning for individuals, QOLN aims to contribute to the social cohesion and economic development of communities by fostering a learning culture to underpin economic activity and quality of life for all. Lifelong learners contribute to community development in many ways:

- Lifelong learners stimulate community experimentation and innovation by demonstrating personal qualities such as open communication, calculated risk-taking, and questioning.
- They promote collaboration and team building.
- They contribute real skills such as problem solving, organizational ability and information skills to community development activities.
- They promote and support the adoption and use of new technologies through promotion and demonstration.

Drawn from life – personal fulfilment and regeneration

QOLN recognizes that the development of lifelong learning is a long-term goal and the rewards for communities will evolve slowly. However, the rewards for individuals are already evident in comments from existing and past learners.

The following comment illustrates the self-esteem and confidence building outcomes of lifelong learning:

> The benefits I received from undertaking the course were more than I ever expected. My self-esteem improved dramatically, even to the point where I decided to join different groups to meet people. Through this decision I have found several wonderful friends.

Lifelong learning also contributes to the attainment of personal goals whether they are related to employment or further study:

> I believe the course has not only given me the opportunity to undertake university studies, but has given me the self-esteem and confidence to achieve my goals. I now have a job which I enjoy immensely and which has given me a position where I can help people to achieve.

Interestingly, attainment of personal goals is not always related to course completion:

> I sincerely appreciated the course even though I didn't finish it (having a job is wonderful) – it gave me a lot of confidence in my approach to work situations.

The key role of information and communication technologies in supporting lifelong learning is evident in the following comments:

> I bought a computer and have practised like mad, bought a printer as well, and now there is no stopping me.

> I am an 'over 50s' trying to unravel the mysteries of the computer. Being computer illiterate was an understatement in my case. Your Coordinator is always obliging and helpful and I feel comfortable and at ease in the centre. I can now see some light at the end of the computer tunnel and am even going to buy my own computer. I'm much more confident to go out there and purchase one without the fear of all the jargon doled out to me by the sales people. Thank you for being instrumental in adding an extra spark to my life.

All the features and outcomes of lifelong learning are obvious in the following extracts from letters from two students – motivation, confidence and self-esteem building, collaboration and teamwork, adaptability and a willingness to help others:

> Before I started the course, my self-esteem had really been down, I had held an executive position in my earlier career in advertising but that had been over 15 years ago. Since then I had spent the years at home surviving on one wage trying to raise my four children as best I could with an often absent husband, working part time in local takeaways and cleaning at a local youth camp – a far cry from my earlier days when I had my racy little sports car and money was not an issue.
>
> I did not wish for those earlier days back, but as my 40th birthday was approaching, I started feeling that I could be doing more with my life. I was overweight and thought because of this issue alone I was unemployable back in the type of career I wanted. How wrong could I be? One of the assignments was to write a fictitious Letter of Application to be sent with our updated résumés to fictitious employers. I applied for a position as advertising Executive in the Newspaper Industry. On returning my assignment my tutor suggested that I should use the letter and résumé if a real position was advertised.
>
> A few weeks later a position was advertised. I thought 'what have I got to lose?' So I sent in my application. That was three months ago and where am I now? I am Sales Executive for the local newspaper. Yes I'm still overweight and I've realized that is not even an issue. The issue is to believe in yourself and your ability and together with the skills you have acquired during your course, you can do anything you put your mind to, you just have to step outside that 'comfort barrier' as so many of us have and have a go.

> I am a tradesman (carpenter/joiner) who left school at Year 10 and commenced my apprenticeship. After years of hard work, I had worked my way up to obtain registration as an unrestricted domestic and commercial builder. By the time I had reached 37 years of age with the years of toil behind me, the direction the construction industry appeared to be heading no longer inspired me. I had become bored with my job and work became uninteresting. The poor attitude I had developed not only affected me, it was also having an effect on my family. I had simply reached the limit of my existing education and I decided that I had to do something about my situation. The simple solution was to change professions, thus I discovered something more challenging – re-education.
>
> Re-education for me meant that I had to obtain a senior certificate in Maths and demonstrate that I had a reasonable level of communication skill. This is where QOLN's courses played a major part in my re-education. The courses allowed me to obtain the necessary skills in less than a year. Once I had reached that goal, I then gained entry to university to study engineering. I felt that what I had achieved was worth the effort.

At the present time I work from home and now help out more with house and family duties. This has precipitated another benefit of my re-education which is that my wife has also taken up the challenges of undergraduate study (Bachelor of Information Technology). I am able to provide my wife with support around the house as well as help with her study. Now my entire family is hooked on learning as are some of the people who have come into contact with me.

Re-education, is it an affliction or a contagious desire for knowledge? I'm not sure, but I have come to realize that ongoing education is an absolute necessity.

Conclusion

Lifelong learning is a continuous process that motivates and empowers individuals – it assists them to acquire new knowledge, skills and understandings that can be applied confidently in new circumstances and environments. These flexible and adaptable people will be the key to empowering communities, especially rural and remote communities, as they face the challenges of the 21st century. The challenges, arising mainly from the shift from an industrial and service economy to a knowledge-based economy, require people who can adapt to change by learning new skills and acquiring new knowledge. Through its technology infrastructure and its learning programmes and services, QOLN is contributing to the future development of both individuals and the communities in which they live and work.

References

Butler, E and Lawrence, K (1996) *Access and Equity within Vocational Education and Training for People in Rural and Remote Australia*, Australian National Training Authority, Brisbane

Kearns, P, McDonald, R, Candy, P, Knights, S and Papadopoulos, G (1999) *Lifelong Learning VET in the Learning Age: The challenge of lifelong learning for all*, National Centre for Vocational Education Centre Ltd, Adelaide

Kilpatrick, S (1997) *Effective Delivery Methodologies for Eeucation and Training to Rural Australia*, Centre for Research and Learning in Rural Australia, University of Tasmania, Launceston

Kilpatrick, S and Bell, R (1998) *Vocational Education and Training in Rural and Remote Australia*, National Centre for Vocational Education Research (NCVER), Adelaide

OECD (Organization for Economic Cooperation and Development) (1996) *Lifelong Learning for All*, Report of the meeting of the Education Committee at Ministerial Level, Paris, 16–17 January

Sher, J and Rowe-Sher, K (1994) Beyond the conventional wisdom: rural development as if Australia's rural people really mattered, Background paper in *Issues Affecting Rural Communities*, ed D McSwan and M McShane, Proceedings of International Conference, Townsville

Further Reading

Bates, A W (1996) The impact of technological change on open and distance education, in *Open Learning Your Future Depends on It*, Conference proceedings of the Queensland Open Learning Conference, Brisbane

Kearns, P (1998) *Lifelong Learning: Implications for VET – A discussion paper*, Research Centre for Vocational Education and Training, University of Technology, Sydney

Mason, R (1997) *Advancing Opportunities for Enhancing Learning*, A keynote presentation to the NetWorking 97 ANTA Flexible Delivery Conference, Australian National Training Authority, Brisbane

Reinecke, I (1997) *The Emerging Telecommunication Environment: Opportunities for the VET sector*, A keynote presentation to the NetWorking 97 ANTA Flexible Delivery Conference, Australian National Training Authority, Brisbane

Chapter 11

Campus re-engineering

Stephen Brown

An electronic campus

In June 1997 a policy decision was taken by De Montfort University to develop a substantial body of Web-based teaching, learning and assessment materials that can be accessed readily on campus, plus learning support systems that encourage and facilitate peer group interaction and staff–student exchanges, independent of time and specific university location.

The driving forces behind this major policy decision were recognition of the need to:

1. enhance flexibility of access to learning provision and support;
2. develop a position that could lead to collaborative ventures with other organizations.

This is not distance learning. It is an attempt to exploit the properties of online technologies to enhance the availability and quality of traditional provision through mixed mode delivery. It is management led, not a grassroots, bottom–up innovation, and the intention has been that this should be a university-wide initiative, not a localized trial. This chapter describes the first phase of setting up and implementing a university-wide project and the current process of embedding it into established mainstream activities.

Flexibility of access

There is a growing belief that learning is the key to individual employability and corporate competitiveness and that it should continue beyond when we leave formal education (DfEE 1998a). Knowledge is rapidly outdated in a fast-changing world, employees need to enhance their attractiveness through periodic self-development and employers need to update the skills of their workforce in order to remain competitive (BCC, 1998; HMSO, 1998; IoM, 1998; DfEE, 1998a). Yet less than a quarter (23 per cent) of UK adults say they are currently learning, and the learning divide between the learning-rich and the learning-poor is growing (Sargant *et al,* 1997).

Current UK Government policy is to encourage lifelong learning, through financial initiatives such as the establishment of Lifelong Learning Accounts and through interventionist strategies such as the creation of the University for Industry (DfEE, 1998b). In an era of lifelong learning, increasing numbers will need flexible learning opportunities, fitting study around domestic and employment commitments.

Fixed lectures and limited opening hours for buildings create barriers to ready access for people with alternative, overriding, commitments. New ways have to be found of carrying out at least some of the functions of traditional universities and, in the absence of significant sums of new money to effect change, new methods will have to cost less.

In the UK, per capita spending on HE students declined by 20 per cent between 1991–2 and 1996–7 (THES, 1999), stimulating greater competition between universities for resources. Also, UK Higher Education providers are facing increased competition in traditional overseas markets where countries such as the USA, Canada and Australia are vigorously recruiting students who might otherwise have studied in the UK. Furthermore, many overseas governments are seeking to expand and enhance their local provision instead of sending such large proportions of undergraduates to study abroad, eg India, Singapore, Hong Kong, Indonesia, South Africa and Malaysia.

The convergence of different media into a single networked digital domain, and the rapidly increasing accessibility of such media, is tempting many HE institutions to develop an online presence. From the UK perspective the recent appearance of 'virtual', 'online' universities such as Western Governors' University (www.wgu.edu) and Colorado University's CU Online (www.cuonline.edu), with their potential to deliver globally, are cause for concern. Commercial organizations such as Phoenix University (www.uophx.edu/) or ZD University (www.zdu.com) operating in the same way are further indications of the possible shape of things to come.

Collaborative ventures

The costs of developing a virtual online presence are not yet fully understood but are considerable, and a traditional university making the transition to predominantly mixed mode delivery and support would have to run both systems concurrently. In a climate of diminishing resources, the necessary diversion of investment capital from existing functions would expose the organization to risk. Competing organizations need to be able to respond rapidly and flexibly to new market requirements and competitive threats. Yet quality learning resource materials and support systems take longer to develop than traditional teaching. The perceived benefits of collaboration are more rapid development at lower cost and with shared (and therefore reduced) risk.

Origins

The Electronic Campus had a number of precursors which were important rehearsals. De Montfort is a distributed university with 10 campuses spread over central, eastern England, with over 100 miles (160 km) between its farthest points. The aspiration is to offer, as far as possible, equality of learning opportunities across and between different campuses. Widespread bussing of staff or students to different campuses is not economically viable. Alternative ways have had to be found to provide students with comprehensive, consistent and quality learning experiences regardless of their locus of study. Over the past four years the university has launched a variety of related, but independent, initiatives, including:

- videoconferencing;
- computer-mediated communications;
- automated assignment marking via optical mark reader and computer-marked multiple-choice questions;
- digital library developments;
- resource based learning.

The university now has six dedicated professional-level videoconferencing suites used for teaching. Conferencing and e-mail software has been thoroughly tested on a variety of courses. Computer-based multiple-choice questions are a routine element of many courses. The university has established an International Institute for Electronic Library Research and is researching digital library provision as part of the IBM Global Campus project (http://www.hied.ibm.com/portfolio.html). Established media design and production teams have considerable experience of developing learning materials in a range of media, including print, video, audio, Interactive Video, CD ROM and the World Wide Web. In particular, in 1995 we launched a prototype Electronic Campus type course on Architecture and Urban

Design, using a combination of traditional teaching methods and telematics course delivery and support methods. Traditional architecture courses are resource hungry, needing large studios, model-making facilities and intensive tuition. The aim was to move away from conventional studio and lecture-based teaching to deliver and support teaching and learning through online multimedia resources and computer-mediated communications. The new course included:

- World Wide Web case study material, enabling students to study a large volume of material in different ways and to make links with other Internet resources;
- computer-based assessments submitted electronically for marking;
- electronic study support via e-mail and conferencing;
- electronic document delivery providing information about the course content, structure and staff and schedules of lectures, practical classes, assignments, etc.

Strategy

Although these initiatives provided more flexible access and support across the university, they were not part of a single coherent strategy and their impact was at times limited by internal incompatibilities and even conflicts. The goal of the Electronic Campus is to ensure a maximum and rapid return on investment of resources through integration of previously disparate strands of activity. To achieve this, five key policy decisions were taken at the start of the project which set the parameters for development:

1. single delivery medium: the World Wide Web;
2. software standards for authoring, assessment and conferencing;
3. local project management and determination;
4. central funding and project monitoring;
5. shared production of learning resources.

The Web was chosen because its rapid growth and cross-platform independence offer the potential of a virtually universal delivery capability. This in turn helped to simplify the decision-making and development process. It set priorities for infrastructure investment, software tools and staff development and defined useful functional parameters. Software standards are necessary to reduce costs and maximize integration, although some flexibility has been retained to allow for variations in requirements and to avoid the dangers associated with dependence on a single product or supplier. Readily available, easy-to-use development tools ensure that all staff have easy access to them and where necessary, training courses can be made available easily and cheaply. Faculties have been encouraged to develop project proposals based on their own needs and aspirations and to retain ownership of those projects. However, funding for the initiative has been made available centrally as an incentive, and central control of project budgets has been retained to ensure that agreed targets are met. Pump-priming funds make it easier for faculty staff to get involved and for resource managers to sanction their involvement. They also make it easier to buy in resources at the institutional rather than the faculty level, eg site licences for software packages adopted as standards. Adoption of a formal process of bidding for central resource has made the activities of the central teams more visible and accountable and has legitimized them to a degree not previously possible. Central control of project budgets has enabled close monitoring of expenditure against agreed schedules and deliverables. Design and production of new materials and support systems has been achieved through a combination of highly specialized but necessarily limited central resources and less skilled but more readily available faculty-based resources. The intention here has been to maximize outputs but to ensure that sophisticated design and production expertise are available where necessary.

Management

Electronic Campus development is controlled by a high-level policy committee chaired originally by the Pro Vice Chancellor responsible for Learning and Teaching development. The initiative is underpinned by the Division of Learning Development (DLD), a major central unit responsible for library services, digital library research and implementation, learning and teaching strategy, staff development, media design and production services, audio-visual and videoconferencing services and educational technology development.

Each faculty has been allocated a Learning Development Manager (LDM) from the DLD to work with them to:

● develop appropriate teaching, learning and assessment strategies;
● develop teaching and learning proposals for internal and external funding;
● identify and obtain resource-based learning materials produced elsewhere;
● develop and implement learning support strategies and systems;
● identify and meet staff development needs in relation to implementation of the Electronic Campus.

Successful project bids result in the formation of Project Teams within faculties. LDMs provide ongoing assistance and a link back to the central production resources (graphic design, courseware authoring, programming, desktop publishing, audio, video and photography, digitizing, print, etc). Progress is monitored fortnightly at LDM meetings and remedial action taken where necessary.

Funding

Pump-priming funds have been made available centrally for Faculties to bid against for Electronic Campus projects. A pro forma guides faculty staff through a set of questions designed to encourage them to consider key issues and address the selection criteria applied to proposals. In addition, the Electronic Campus initiative has created a focus for institutional coordination of bids for external funds. Learning Development Managers work with their faculty to identify appropriate funding sources and to prepare bids which are scrutinized centrally before submission. Cross-referral of bids between funding sources now occurs regularly.

Development

The Electronic Campus is employing a combination of three possible development strategies:

- in-house development;
- embedding of materials developed elsewhere;
- collaboration with other organizations to develop new materials jointly.

In-house development is important because it helps to overcome the 'not invented here' syndrome. It provides an opportunity to showcase strengths in particular disciplines, it may be cheaper than buying in material from elsewhere and it opens up opportunities for revenue generation. It is also an essential prerequisite for collaboration with other institutions since it demonstrates competence and generates products that can be traded. Faculty staff have been encouraged to use simple development tools such as Microsoft Word, Question Mark, FrontPage and Adobe Acrobat, supported where necessary by central DLD designers and programmers using more sophisticated tools. Some faculty staff have also experimented successfully with WebCT, which is now being adopted as the main authoring and delivery tool for the Electronic Campus.

The disadvantage of the in-house approach is the amount of time and resource required to establish a critical mass of material. The average cost of each internally funded project so far is around £33,000, split on a 60:40 ratio between Faculties and the centre, and a module has typically taken around a year to produce. Materials developed elsewhere are a possible short cut. In the UK there are a variety of sources of low-cost and/or high-quality learning materials at HE level, in particular the products of the TLTP and the CTI but also OLF and OU. At De Montfort more than 30 academic staff across all faculties have been involved in identifying relevant learning resource materials produced elsewhere and embedding these materials where appropriate. Although this approach is proving successful, issues that have emerged include the costs of reviewing, licensing, modification, distribution and installation of software packages produced elsewhere.

Although some collaborative development has taken place, funded mainly through the TLTP, direct collaboration between De Montfort University and other institutions to create Electronic Campus materials has not yet happened on a significant scale.

Learning support systems

In addition to developing or importing learning materials, the Electronic Campus is focused on providing learning support systems that encourage and facilitate peer group interaction and staff-student exchanges, independent of time and specific university location. First Class conferencing software had been used to support teaching and learning within the university for four years. The university now operates six professional-level videoconferencing suites across its main campuses and, after some experimentation with different systems, standardized on Picturetel equipment. In addition, Microsoft Netmeeting is being trialled to evaluate its potential for remote class rooms utilizing its desktop video and audio conferencing features, combined with application sharing. Web CT was successfully trialled on two projects to evaluate its effectiveness and has now been adopted as the university standard for a fully integrated online course development, delivery and support environment, including conferencing.

Promotion

Awareness of the Electronic Campus was raised through separate meetings with all Deans of Faculties, presentations to all Heads of Departments, publication of articles in the university in-house newsletter, direct liaison via the LDMs, a travelling 'roadshow' showcasing Electronic Campus developments which visited each of the main centres of the university, and a Web site (http://www.ecampus.dmu.ac.uk). The Web site describes what the Electronic Campus is, its goals, how it is managed and progress so far. It also provides information about funding opportunities, offers help and guidance on how to prepare proposals, develop online materials, use e-mail and conferencing effectively and provides links to relevant publications, conferences, professional associations, online discussion groups and sources of learning materials.

Impact

In the first 22 months, over 30 different Electronic Campus development projects were established, ranging across all Faculties and at all levels, including further education, undergraduate, postgraduate and continuing professional development. By the end of the first year of operation (1998), over 1,500 students had studied online, including lectures, seminars, tutorials, practical assignments and cognitive assessments. In most cases, projects have been based on resources already developed in the university, converted to pdf documents, HTML pages, Web-interfaced databases and image banks, plus computer and videoconferencing. Projects under way will generate video and audio files as well.

Business as usual

The Electronic Campus was set up as an organizational change project, led from the top but intended to encourage local ownership. Although conceived as an institution-wide initiative, it was established initially as a distinct project with separate management and development processes in order to minimize risk. This inevitably limits its impact in terms of its benefits to the organization as a whole, increases costs through duplication and imposes limits to its expansion and sustainability. Innovations of this kind frequently fade away because they are not taken on board by the organization as a whole and the individuals associated with them move on to other activities (Brown, 1997). The next phase now under way is the transformation of this initiative into 'business as usual' by embedding it into established mainstream activities.

Strategic development plans

The university strategy for learning and teaching stresses the importance of flexibility of provision and the key role of new technologies. In turn, each faculty is being required to develop an annual strategic development plan for learning and teaching which identifies their primary student target populations; their intended learning and teaching modes and methods; and their resourcing plans, including staff and student development requirements and infrastructure needs. Faculty plans are being developed jointly with teams from the Division of Learning Development through a top-down cascade process involving the University Senior Executive team, Deans, Faculty Executive teams and joint Divisional/ Faculty working parties. These plans will provide the basis for course planning and resourcing in future and will ensure parity of priorities in relation to other activities such as research and consultancy.

Quality assurance

The University Quality Assurance procedures have been rewritten to ensure that proposals for new or revised modules take account of changes in learning and teaching methods and that applications for Electronic Campus funds are not considered independently of normal quality approval procedures. Consultation with Division of Learning Development representatives, in particular the LDMs, is now formally built into the development process at key stages to ensure that faculty-based staff have the benefit of professional advice and guidance when considering issues such as teaching methods, assessment strategies, learning support methods, learning resource requirements (eg library provision, IT facilities), teaching resource requirements (eg AV/IT provision, videoconferencing) and staff development needs (eg media production and acquisition skills).

Staff development

Electronic Campus staff development has been a combination of formal training events and informal problem-based learning. For example, a programme of formal IT staff training courses has been restructured to provide basic technical authoring skills using Microsoft Office products and more advanced Internet training including HTML authoring, Web site development and management, Internet communications and information search techniques. Project teams are also offered short courses on the use of specific software applications used within the Electronic Campus. Informal development takes place through interaction with the LDM, beginning with the project proposal pro forma which encourages teaching staff to consider learning objectives, prerequisites, relationship with other courses, assessment strategies, teaching methods, learner characteristics and requirements. A new department within the Division of Learning Development, the Centre for Learning and Teaching (CLT), has been created to both lead and support this aspect of organizational change. The university has increased its investment in professional development via this centre which, in the first instance, is funding faculty staff release and development activities to facilitate the development of strategic development plans.

Rewards

Although the opportunities to reward staff in a university are limited, it has been possible to put in place a number of incentives to encourage involvement in Electronic Campus developments. In the first instance there are the pump-priming funds made available centrally for Faculties to bid against. This money can be used to buy equipment, software, travel, learning resources, staff development and staff time. In practice, 78 per cent of the project money allocated to Faculties has been used to buy out staff time to release staff from other duties, particularly teaching. Money is not enough, however, to ensure adequate commitment. In our experience the faculty staff taking a lead in Electronic Campus developments have typically been heavily committed to other key activities as well, such as student recruitment, research, university consultancy, administration, etc. It has been difficult therefore for such people to allocate as much time to Electronic Campus projects as they themselves would like. Other, complementary, changes need to be put in place not only to facilitate but to actually reward contributions. The university has now set up a Teacher Fellowship scheme and enhanced the promotion system to formally recognize and reward innovation and excellence in teaching.

Conclusions

We already have considerable experience of developing and using resource-based learning materials and a lot of the content of the Electronic Campus already existed in some electronic form, if only as word processed documents or PowerPoint slides. Without these foundations to build on, the process would have been more costly and lengthier than it was.

Simple, familiar and readily available tools enable faculty staff to engage with the process with minimum investment of effort in terms of their own skill development. The corollary of this is the need to have a small, highly skilled central team to provide the necessary staff development and more sophisticated design and production capability.

In the early stages, some choice and flexibility regarding development and delivery tools and environments helps to bring faculty staff into the fold. As the innovation gathers momentum and supporters, the need for greater coordination and agreement on standards can be allowed to emerge collectively.

Our various attempts at awareness raising have not been particularly successful. What seems to have worked best is the system of Learning Development Managers, each dedicated to developing a long-term relationship with a specific faculty.

Maintaining commitment in the face of competing demands for faculty staff time cannot be solved through money alone. There have to be other drivers operating to encourage individuals and their Heads of Departments to commit significant amounts of human resource to the initiative. It is hoped that the faculty learning and teaching strategic development plans and the increased recognition of the importance of teaching innovation and excellence will fulfil this function.

Bottom-up approaches tend to founder on the rocks of competing policies and standards central to different parts of the institution. Staff eventually move on to other things and business returns to usual practices.

On the other hand, a top-down, management-led, approach can be frustrated at the level of middle management where hard choices have to be made about resource allocations in the face of strong competing pressures. Without a strong sense of local ownership in the Faculties themselves, innovation is unlikely to be pursued wholeheartedly or sustained in the long term. Commitment is most likely to stem from local control over decision making, so the temptation to control everything from the centre needs to be resisted.

References

BCC (1998) *Small Firms Survey: Skills*, British Chamber of Commerce, London

Brown, S (1997) Curriculum or Culture change, in *Open and Distance Learning: Case studies from industry and education*, (ed) S Brown, Kogan Page, London

DfEE (1998a) *Towards a National Agenda: First report of the national skills task force*, Department for Education and Employment, HMSO, London

DfEE (1998b) *University for Industry, Pathfinder Prospectus*, Department for Education and Employment, HMSO, London

HMSO (1998) *The Learning Age*, UK Government Green Paper on Lifelong Learning, HMSO Cmnd 3790, London

IoM (1998) *UK Corporate Employment Strategies and Trends 1997/8*, Institute of Management, London

Sargant, N, Field, J, Francis, H, Schuller, T and Tuckett, A (1997) *The Learning Divide: A study of participation in adult learning in the United Kingdom*, National Institute of Adult Continuing Education

THES (1999) Spending sword with two edges, *The Times Higher Education Supplement*, 29 May, p6

Chapter 12

Student recruitment and retention in a self-financing university

Danny S N Wong and Todd C Y Ng

Introduction

Tertiary education has traditionally thrived on heavy government support, with institutions generally assured of the number of students every year. Unless government policy changes, they do not have to worry about the amount of funding every year.

In Hong Kong, the conventional tertiary institutions rely on government support for more than 80 per cent of their recurrent expenses. Today, the Hong Kong government, through the University Grants Committee (UGC), directly funds eight institutions, providing roughly 15,000 first-year, first-degree students. Around 70,000 Full–Time–Equivalent (FTE) sub-degree, undergraduate and postgraduate students study in these institutions. The total direct funding amounted to US $1.7 billion in the academic year 1997–98.

In contrast, the *Open University of Hong Kong*, although established by the government, was mandated to operate on a *self-financing* basis from its fourth year of operation. It has no assurance on how many students it can recruit every year because it recruits from the vast pool of working adults. Demand is unpredictable, and competition is intense. It is also facing the fluctuating student retention rate typical of distance learning institutions. Just like a commercial operation, it has to work on its revenue strategies – how to recruit and retain more students, how to improve its courses and how to get more income.

This chapter focuses on the key aspect of the revenue strategies adopted by the Open University of Hong Kong (OUHK) – *student recruitment and retention*. Student recruitment and retention has been a widely researched topic in higher education. However, most of the researches focus on the cognitive, social and psychological aspects; financial issues are seldom looked at. This in fact may be attributed to a general lack of attention to finance issues in higher education research. According to the ERIC Clearing House on Higher Education, finance is a relatively minor topic in its database, with only about 6.5 per cent of the literature addressing the subject in 1996. They described this as 'a surprise, given the rhetoric and discussion about controlling costs, rising tuition, and shrinking financial aid' (*ERIC Trends – Finance*, 1996: 1). The National Commission on the Cost of Higher Education (NCCHE) of the USA also wrote: 'the truth is that institutions prefer not to look too hard at these matters, both because a broad-based curriculum is a desirable thing in and of itself and because of a desire to base decisions on quality and not on costs' (NCCHE, 1998: 14).

For the OUHK, finance has been a key issue since it was established 10 years ago. The difficulty of being self-financing can be illustrated by a comment from the NCCHE, which asserted a 'basic fact about academic finance: Virtually no activity ... generates enough revenue to pay for itself' (NCCHE, 1998: 13). For the OUHK, student recruitment and retention *have* to generate enough revenue to pay for the operation of the whole organization. That alone should make it a unique case in higher education.

The Open University of Hong Kong and its operating environment

The Open University of Hong Kong was first established as the Open Learning Institute (OLI) of Hong Kong in 1989. The University is the only institution in Hong Kong dedicated solely to the provision of tertiary-level open and distance education. It is open to anyone over the age of 17. It is also the only degree-granting institution not funded by the UGC. It received funding from the government during its first three years of operation. Thereafter the government provided only funds for infrastructure and capital expenditures occasionally. The University has to be self-sufficient operationally. The government's rationale is that since the University serves mostly adult learners who may be in full-time employment, the University should be able to recover its costs through tuition fees.

An examination of the environment that the OUHK has been operating under is useful for understanding its student recruitment and retention strategies.

Advantage of distance learning

Hong Kong is a city with a dense population. Over 6 million people live in an area of 400 square miles. Lives are busy and hectic. It is not uncommon for young professionals to engage in work-related activities after office hours. Some of them may be required to take frequent overseas trips. The competitive advantage of distance learning in Hong Kong is not its capability to reach students separated by physical distance, but its flexibility in allowing students to study at their own convenience.

Tertiary education in demand

Education, particularly at tertiary level, is treasured in Hong Kong. In 1989, when the OLI was created, only 7 per cent of the relevant age groups (aged 17–20) were able to gain entry to first-degree programmes; it is now 18 per cent. It is well accepted that to survive in a competitive society like Hong Kong, continuous upgrading of one's professional skills is vital. Therefore, the demand for continuous and professional education is vast. The OUHK's open access policy means that it could tap into the adult education market without entry restriction on potential students.

Keen competition

The demand is vast, but the competition is just as keen. The competition faced by the OUHK in providing part-time degree courses comes from two sources.

Conventional institutions

Most of the eight conventional institutions offer part-time degree courses. They are heavily subsidized, and therefore this competition is not exactly on equal footing. In addition, some of them also operate extra-mural departments, offering short courses and degree and professional programmes in collaboration with overseas institutions.

Overseas institutions

Hong Kong is a free economy and that applies to the tertiary education market as well. For many years, more than 100 institutions from the UK, Australia, the USA and Mainland China have been offering part-time degree programmes in Hong Kong. The students have many choices, and the institutions have to compete on many fronts, including quality, pricing, services, etc. The total turnover of these overseas programmes is estimated to be over US $100 million.

Openness and its implications

When the OUHK was established, the concept of open learning was new, and its applicability in Hong Kong was uncertain. Openness could be perceived to mean that the quality of the OUHK students and hence its education was 'lower'. This could negatively impact on the institution's recruitment effort in a market with a strong 'brand name' mentality.

Product strategy

Strategic focus: quality

The OUHK's revenue strategies centre on one element: *quality*. It sounds obvious but in reality it is not. The University was a new institution established in 1989. It had to become self-financing in 1993. Competition was keen. All these factors pointed to a low–cost, low–price strategy rather than a strategy focusing on providing quality products, which could entail high costs and thus lead to high prices. However, the University believed that, as a proper academic institution, no compromise should be made in the quality of its courses and programmes. It also believed that the strategy would benefit the University in the long run in terms of building a reputation and producing quality graduates for the economy.

Therefore, the University adopted a *quality assurance system* that was as intricate as that of any reputable higher education institution. Courses and programmes have to go through multi-layers of approval by committees before they can be offered. Despite the open access policy, the demands on the students are the same as, if not more than, those made by other tertiary institutions. Exit standards are also comparable.

Product value enhancement

The NCCHE stated that 'higher education is a *product*, a *service* and a life-long *investment* bought and paid for, like others' (NCCHE, 1999: 3).

The OUHK's products are its courses and programmes. A programme consists of a combination of required and elective courses. Its customers, the students, pay for the courses and expect to get a good learning experience as an outcome. To fulfil such an expectation, over the years the University puts more and more features into its courses. Up to early 1999, an OUHK course consisted of a combination of the following deliverables to the students:

- study materials in print, electronic, video, audio cassette and/or CD ROM format;
- TV programmes;
- part-time tutorial sessions;
- telephone tutoring;
- assignment marking;
- day schools (special seminars on a certain subject in a course);

- surgeries (special sessions to tackle more difficult subjects in a course);
- laboratories;
- Internet account for access to electronic library and Internet use;
- examination.

These features came with costs. The tutorials, optional to the students, are one of the more costly elements that are not provided by many major distance learning universities. However, the University saw it as an important feature, as in effect it enhanced pure distance learning with face-to-face elements. This again is another example of how the University strives to maintain its academic vitality within the self-financing constraint.

Marketability

Marketability of the courses and programmes is a critical factor in the University's product strategies. Market surveys and student number projections are in fact part of the quality assurance system. The actual enrolment is monitored closely every semester. Student feedback is gathered regularly. After five years, a programme will undergo thorough revalidation. Programmes that are no longer marketable might have to be phased out.

Increasing the demand on existing courses

Every product has its product life cycle, and academic programmes are no different. Some programmes may not be able to sustain their marketability after several years. Enrolment in the courses that make up these programmes will suffer. However, a sizable amount of development cost has been incurred for these courses in the past. Therefore, to make the most of its assets, the University devised different ways to revitalize the marketability of its courses with minimal additional investment:

- *Repackaging of the courses to form new programmes.* Existing courses were combined with new courses to form new programmes so that different target groups might be attracted to take the courses.
- *Articulation.* Sub-degree programmes at certificate, diploma and higher diploma level consisting of existing courses were offered. These programmes articulate closely with the degree programme structure so that the students can earn the sub-degree qualifications and accumulate the credits for a degree at the same time. They are motivated to continue their study and therefore student retention will be improved.
- *Cross-discipline merging of courses.* Courses that belong to different disciplines were merged together to form 'hybrid' programmes. For example, western arts courses and social science courses were merged together to form an International Studies programme.

While these repackaging strategies might not have brought dramatic increases in enrolment, they did inject some new life into some courses and programmes with declining demand.

Widening the product line

Besides repackaging, the University has constantly to look for opportunities for offering brand-new programmes. While this entails more significant investment in course development, it is a critical factor in sustaining the growth of the University. Over the years, the University has added new programmes that differ from the basic first-degree programmes in the following dimensions: clientele, level and language:

- *Programmes for targeted clienteles*. While the open access philosophy is still very much intact, several programmes for professionals at honours-degree level with entry requirements have been offered in recent years. They were developed mainly in response to new government policies and historical societal needs. The two professional groups to benefit from these programmes are teachers and nurses. Enrolment results for these programmes have been successful.
- *Programmes at postgraduate level*. This may seem obvious but again it is not. Master's degree programmes are traditionally small-population programmes entailing high unit costs. On the surface it is risky for a self-financing institution to offer them. However, the target students of distance learning Master's degree programmes are usually more mature working adults who work long hours and consequently would prefer the flexibility of distance learning. Moreover, the Bachelor's degree graduates of the University are a prime source of potential students. In this way, these programmes could further improve student retention. This has indeed proven to be the case, as the University's MBA programme, offered in 1994, quickly became the biggest part-time MBA programme in Hong Kong by attracting new students and graduates alike. Another programme, the Master of Education, has also been enrolling students steadily.
- *Programmes in Chinese*. This again seems more obvious than the reality. Almost all the tertiary education courses in Hong Kong are conducted in English. A degree taught totally in Chinese is rare and not highly regarded. However, the demographics have been changing, with more new arrivals from mainland China every day. With Hong Kong returning to be part of China in 1997, the Chinese language took on higher importance in official and social contexts. There also exists a vast contingent of Chinese speakers in Asia and the rest of the world. Taking these factors into account, the University began to develop Chinese courses in the early 1990s. Two of the pioneering programmes, Chinese Humanities and Primary Education, met with success. In 1998, the University began to offer business programmes, including an MBA, in Chinese. More programmes in Chinese are being planned.

Pricing strategies

All the subsidized universities in Hong Kong use the same tuition fee scale set by the UGC. However, as a result of the self-financing mandate, the OUHK has autonomy in setting its own tuition fee level and structure. The myriad complexities and possibilities faced by the University in setting its pricing policy are no different from those faced by commercial entities.

Positioning against subsidized universities

In theory, it should be unrealistic for the self-financing OUHK to use the tuition fee level of subsidized universities as a yardstick. In the initial years, this was true, as the University's student population was not large enough for it to enjoy distance education's strength of economies of scale, although ironically it was receiving a certain amount of government seed money every year.

Table 12.1 *Fee scales of the OUHK compared with those of subsidized institutions*

(US$)	1993	1994	1995	1996	1997	1998	1999
OUHK's	$8,960	$10,530	$11,920	$13,100	$14,150	$14,610	$14,610
Inc %	+13.0%	+21.2%	+13.1%	+9.9%	+8.0%	+3.3%	0.0%
Subsidized fee	$6,530	$9,230	$11,820	$14,360	$16,190	$17,110	$18,190
Inc %	+46.6%	+41.2%	+28.1%	+21.5%	+12.7%	+5.7%	+6.3%
OUHK vs subsidized	+32.9%	+14.2%	+0.8%	−8.8%	−12.6%	−14.6%	−19.7%

Fortunately, because of the government's mandate to recover 18 per cent of the costs, universities in Hong Kong raised tuition fees dramatically from 1993 onward. This enabled the OUHK gradually to set its fee at comparable or even lower levels than those of subsidized universities. More importantly, it gave an opportunity for the University *to position itself against the conventional universities* in order to establish a reputation of being a proper and quality institution. Moreover, as the student population got bigger, the University could bank on the cost-effectiveness of distance education in setting competitive fees. The fee scales of an OUHK Bachelor's degree compared with the subsidized fees since 1993 are listed in Table 12.1.

The University went from a tuition fee that was 32.9 per cent above that of the subsidized university in 1993 to one that is almost 20 per cent *below* theirs now. The OUHK fee has become more competitive, and its reputation has been growing at the same time.

Positioning against overseas competitors for selected programmes

Since the University has taken the subsidized institutions' pricing as the reference point, the pricing charged by the overseas institutions operating in Hong Kong became of secondary consideration. There is no prominent overseas provider in the market, but many of them do take the OUHK as their major competitor and actually follow OUHK's pricing. Nevertheless, when the OUHK launches some new programmes such as the MBA, of which the market is mature and full of competitors, the OUHK will take into consideration the pricing of the overseas programmes as well as that of the subsidized institutions. For the MBA, the University began at the lower end of the pricing scale. As a result, it quickly gained a foothold in the market and became the biggest part-time MBA programme in Hong Kong after one year.

Credit-based pricing

The University adopts a credit system. All courses carry credits of 5, 10 or 20 depending on the study load. The students accumulate 120 credits for a Bachelor's degree or 160 credits for an Honours Bachelor's degree. The tuition fee is set on a per credit basis. The more credits a student takes, the more tuition fee he or she will pay. This system ensures that the students are paying for what they are getting, and the University is getting the tuition fee for what it is supplying. In contrast, all subsidized conventional universities in Hong Kong charge their students on a yearly basis.

Incremental fee system

Traditionally, college tuition fees have almost always been set independent of cost or even market considerations. The NCCHE observed among US institutions that, 'there are wide disparities in expenditure levels between and among different instructional levels and disciplines... Yet most institutions do not charge higher tuition for higher cost programs,... differences in tuition and fee levels for undergraduate and graduate courses of study generally do not reflect the true cost differential' (NCCHE, 1999: 14).

In contrast, it is critical for the OUHK to consider cost and market factors in setting its tuition fee. The University's courses are divided into several levels – Pre-foundation, Foundation, Middle, Higher, Honours and Master's level. Based on these levels, the University adopted an *incremental fee* system from the October 1994 semester onward. Under the system, lower fees are set for entry-level courses in order to attract new students. Once they get over the hurdle of the first semester and have proven to themselves that they are able to succeed at the OUHK, financial considerations become of less concern. Higher fees are set for the higher-level courses, which would help the University recover the higher costs incurred for developing and delivering the courses. The magnitude of the differentials varies between 5 and 10 per cent, and it is revised every year, depending on the enrolment results, student sentiment and costing considerations. The system has proven to be helpful in attracting more students and generating more income for the University.

Cost strategies

The lack of attention to cost control from the higher education community is illustrated by the following observation stated in *ERIC Trends – Finance*: 'There are a number of articles from the public, businesses, and boards that call for reducing costs and controlling expenses. In contrast, there is virtually no literature from the higher education community on controlling costs'(*ERIC Trends – Finance*, 1999: 2). Nevertheless, with declining federal aid and the formation of NCCHE in 1997, US institutions have to begin to pay more attention to the matter. Their focus has been on cost containment and fundraising rather than tuition to meet expenses.

For the OUHK, cost control is on the agenda from day one. It believes that successful pricing strategies must be accompanied by good cost strategies. It must keep the cost down to stay competitive at the pricing level.

Management of direct costs

In the distance learning mode of operation, the most important expense is the direct cost of teaching, which includes the cost of the learning materials and the cost of providing tutorials. The lower the direct cost, the higher will be the contribution margin and the lower will be the student numbers needed to break even.

During the earlier years of OUHK, learning materials were mostly supplied by overseas institutions, principally the UK Open University (UKOU). This approach enabled the University to start offering academic programmes faster, but it is costly in the long run. In addition to paying a royalty to the copyright holders, the University also incurred the expenses of adaptation; as a result the University gradually developed more and more of its own course materials. By the 1997–98 academic year, over 40 per cent of its courses used materials developed by OUHK itself.

Tutorials are the most important form of learning support to students. At OUHK students are divided into groups of 30, referred to as tutor groups. Each tutor group is led by a tutor, whose responsibility is to lead periodic tutorial sessions and answer students' enquiries by telephone. Tutors are all employed by the University on a part-time basis, and are hired on an as-needed basis. To ensure teaching quality they all undergo a series of training activities. The employment of tutors in this manner provides flexibility to the University and reduces personnel cost.

The careful management of materials and labour costs has enabled the OUHK to keep its direct costs below 30 per cent of tuition fee revenue.

Management of fixed costs

Since OUHK's capital resources such as the campus building, the electronic library, and computer systems are funded by ad hoc grants from the government, fixed costs incurred at the OUHK are mostly personnel costs. Through meticulous planning the University has been able to keep these under control.

The University has a lean structure. The total full-time staff establishment is just over 400 for the 1997–98 academic year. Less than a hundred of these are academics, who generally require higher compensation. The academic staff cost is about 56 per cent of the total staff cost. In areas where expertise is lacking, the University can appoint part-time consultants. This is particularly important for course material development, where senior academics in the specific discipline are preferred.

Distribution strategies

In business terminology, education is in effect a retail operation. A wide and convenient distribution channel for the students/customers to obtain information and purchase its products is essential to its success. While the University could not establish many distribution outlets for the students because of cost considerations, it adopts a variety of strategies to facilitate the students in making their purchasing decision.

During recruitment periods, potential students can obtain the basic information about the University and information on the available courses through the prospectus and courses supplement. Applicants can mail in the completed forms within a one-month period. On successful application, they can register for the courses by paying the tuition fee directly into the University's bank account through the branches of two major local banks. The banks provide this service to the University at no charge. This direct and simple method saves the University considerable operating costs for payment processing; it is also convenient to the students.

After the mail-in registration, some course places may still be available. A special walk-in registration is then held over a two-week period. Students come to the OUHK campus to apply, register and pay – all in a one-stop process.

Promotion strategies

With no assurance on demand, the OUHK relies a lot more on active promotion to help student recruitment than do conventional universities. The annual promotion budget, including advertising, direct marketing and public relations activities, is about US$ 1.3 million, or 2 per cent of the tuition fee income in 1999.

Advertising and publicity

Just like any commercial retail operation, the OUHK has to advertise a lot. The media used include newspapers, magazines, TV and even the Web. In addition to information advertisements about recruitment details, the University also puts out image advertisements to enhance general awareness. As the vast majority of the target students of OUHK speak and read Chinese as their first language, most of the advertisements are placed in Chinese-language media and presented in Chinese (see Figures 12.1 and 12.2).

The OUHK also engages in a variety of public relations activities to help promote the image of the university and indirectly help student recruitment and retention. These activities include issuing press releases, arranging celebratory events, seminars, etc.

Figure 12.1   *Image advertisement Apr/99 semester*

Figure 12.2 *Information Advertisement, April/99 Semester*

Direct marketing of inactive students

OUHK students who have not enrolled in any course in a semester are classified as *inactive students*, as opposed to *dropouts* for conventional institutions. In an open and distance learning system, they are an expectable phenomenon. The key issue is whether they will stay away from the system forever and become real dropouts, or whether they will come back and enrol for courses, thereby improving student retention. Every semester, the University will mail letters to inactive students, notifying them of the opportunity to re-register. Tele-marketing campaigns are also carried out, keeping in touch with inactive students in a warm and friendly way.

Corporate marketing

Most of the OUHK students are working adults. A lot of them need company sponsorship or approval before they can register for courses. The influence of the employers on the students' decision to study at the University is obvious. Therefore, the University has developed a scheme, called the Employer Support Scholarship Scheme, to establish relationships with employers all over Hong Kong. Through the scheme, the employers know a lot more about the University, which would facilitate their decision in supporting their employees to study.

Referrals

Just like any retail business, a major channel through which potential customers come to know about the OUHK is referral from their friends and relatives. Realizing this potential, the University initiated a student-get-student programme, encouraging students to refer their friends to enrol at the University. The programme has met with notable success.

Results

The student recruitment and retention strategies adopted by the University have led to impressive results. Since 1993, when the University began to operate on a self-financing basis, the number of active students has been rising consistently. The Key Performance Indicators (KPIs, a term coined in the book *Working Toward Strategic Change*, by Dolence, Rowley and Lujan, 1997) of the University since 1993 are as follows.

Student headcount

Table 12.2   *Student headcount of the OUHK, 1993–1998*

Student headcount(*)	1993	1994	1995	1996	1997	1998
New student	4,200	5,100	5,200	4,300	5,700	5,400
Old student	10,800	13,100	14,800	16,000	17,100	18,800
Total	15,000	18,300	20,000	20,400	22,900	24,300
Full-time equivalent	6,800	8,100	9,200	9,500	9,900	10,600

(*) As of the October semester of the year and rounded off to the nearest hundred. Rounding differences may occur.

The University recruits 4,000 to 5,000 new students every semester, or 8,000 to 10,000 per year. This stable new student recruitment rate has enabled the University to sustain its growth. The retention rate of old students has also been steady (see Table 12.2). The retention rate, indicated by the number of old students in a semester divided by the total number of students in the previous semester, has stayed consistently at around 80 per cent. The growth in student numbers has been achieved despite the economic downturn in recent years, which was commonly seen as a deterrent factor to part-time study in Hong Kong.

Study load

The students' study load can be reflected by two ratios: number of course places per student and number of credits per student (see Table 12.3). In general, both ratios showed slight decline in recent years due to the economic downturn. However, surveys showed that the majority of the students are very resilient in their study. Some of them actually study for *more* courses and credits in order to graduate earlier because of the unfavourable economic climate. The growth in the student headcount and the small decline in the study load of the students in a depressed economic climate are testaments to the quality of the education of the University.

Table 12.3   *No. of course places and credits per student, OUHK, Apr/95–Oct/98 semester*

	Apr/95	Oct/95	Apr/96	Oct/96	Apr/97	Oct/97	Apr/98	Oct/98
Course places per student	1.76	1.74	1.76	1.72	1.73	1.68	1.69	1.62
Credits per student	9.65	9.52	9.68	9.26	9.32	9.00	9.03	8.66

Conclusion

The Open University of Hong Kong is a unique case in the history of higher education. Never before has a higher educational institution established by the government been required to provide quality higher education on a self-financing basis. Throughout its 10–year history, the University has had to strike a balance between upholding academic values and injecting financial reality into its operation. Its student recruitment and retention strategy reflects this apparent paradox, as commercial practices are embedded in an academic framework. So far, the University has proven that academic and commercial culture together can indeed be synergistic.

References

Dolence, M G, Rowley, D J and Lujan, H D (1997) *Working Toward Strategic Change*, Jossey-Bass Publishers, San Francisco

Educational Resources Information Centre (ERIC) (1996) *ERIC Trends – Finance*, ERIC – Clearinghouse on Higher Education

The National Commission on the Cost of Higher Education. (1998) *Straight Talk About College Costs and Prices*, USA: ERIC – Clearinghouse on Higher Education, January

Further Reading

Daniel, Sir J (1996) *Mega-Universities and Knowledge Media*, Kogan Page, London

Educational Resources Information Centre (ERIC) (1999) *ERIC CRIB – Maintaining Financial Health: Tuition Strategies, Cost Containment, and Fundraising*, ERIC – Clearinghouse on Higher Education

Educational Resources Information Centre (ERIC) (1999) *ERIC Trends – Administration*, ERIC – Clearinghouse on Higher Education

Turoff, M (1997) *Alternative Futures of Distance Learning: The force and the dark side*, Keynote presentation at the UNESCO/OPEN UNIVERSITY International Colloquium, Open University, Milton Keynes, April

Chapter 13

Using networking tools to support online learning

Ron Oliver and Catherine McLoughlin

Challenges of online learning

As the World Wide Web extends learning beyond the classroom to learning communities, so must roles and concepts of learning and teaching be reconsidered. Web-based instruction involves creating an environment where learners are supported in developing independent learning skills. The Web provides many opportunities and advantages to teachers and learners in terms of its capacity to:

- provide access to information;
- support collaborative learning;
- enable communication between learners.

However, opportunities for learning must be created within a framework that recognizes the social, collaborative and interactive nature of learning so that technology based tools for learning are situated within a sound pedagogical framework (Davis, 1997; Reeves and Reeves, 1997). It is sometimes claimed that the World Wide Web can create cognitively powerful instructional strategies and environments and that these are superior to the traditional classroom where learning is individualized and teacher-centred (Thomas *et al*, 1998). Examples such as Computer Supported Interactive Learning Environments (CSILEs) and cognitive apprenticeships are innovative learning frameworks that are supported not only by technology, but also by strong theories of constructivist learning (Scardamalia and Bereiter, 1994; Collins, Brown and Newman, 1989). Socio-cultural and social constructivist theories of learning affirm that cognitive development must take place in the context of supportive environments, and that such support may be social, cultural, experiential or collaborative (Roschelle and Teasley, 1995). The implications of these theories for educational practice are that learners need to be assisted, supported and guided as they develop competence. Within a technology-supported environment, we can recast these findings as follows: *The learning environment must be designed to enable novice learners to gain knowledge within a supportive framework.* The chapter will address the question of how to achieve effective forms of support in online learning environments through use of the technology as a cognitive tool.

One of the major changes that confronts the online teacher is that the learners have access to the World Wide Web at all times, and can explore, investigate and research areas of knowledge according to personal preference and interest. This degree of self-direction is different to that of learners in face-to-face contexts, and so the forms of support that the teacher offers must also be different. Second, the role of the teacher changes in this environment, and becomes less directive and more facilitative.

Characterizing learning support environments

Many educators are hopeful that new technologies being developed and adopted in the schools will become integrated into the classroom, and will support inquiry, problem-solving skills and autonomous learning. These new technologies and the growth of Internet-based teaching and learning signal new directions for teachers, and require the creation of new forms of learner-centred pedagogy, supported by technology. Earlier forms of supportive learning environments were those where computer assisted learning (CAL) materials were used to provide a rich variety of instructional formats which individuals could engage with on an individual basis. Similarly, with computer assisted learning instruction (CAI), the adaptation of instruction to individual needs was not found to offer advantages over group work, as was first supposed (Maverech, 1993). Later research established quite conclusively that collaborative work around computers provided more social support, cognitive enrichment and task engagement through peer interaction than individual study with computers did (Hoyles, Healy and Pozzi, 1994; Nastasi and Clements, 1993). Studies of these environments found that peer dialogue, social interaction and collaboration were powerful supports for learning. Social constructivist theories of learning based on the work of Vygotsky have affirmed the central role of peers, adults and knowledgeable others in the development of cognition and understanding. While much of the research in the early 1980s focused on asymmetric interactions in classroom settings, later views of supportive learning relationships have explored other forms of support through peers (Azmitia and Montgomery, 1993.)

The repertoire of learning and teaching approaches has vastly increased via the World Wide Web, and offers teachers an array of innovative activities. The WWW provides a medium for collaboration, social dialogue, interaction and communication where learners can learn both formally and informally through interactions with others. Accessibility, flexibility and self-directed learning can lead to new forms of learning online. Yet these same possibilities open up significant questions for educators and designers. How can online environments be designed to ensure learning? What structures and forms of support will ensure that collaborative and meaningful dialogue will ensue between participants? What forms of teaching assistance are likely to create motivating contexts for learners? Although there are new tools for learning, we still need a framework in which to conceptualize learning support in networked learning environments.

Theoretical foundations of learning support

The term 'scaffolding' is increasingly used to describe certain kinds of support which learners receive in their interaction with experts, teachers and mentors as they develop new skills, concepts or levels of understanding. In this paper, it is proposed that online learning can be achieved through cognitive tools that support learning processes. (Later in this chapter, these tools are explained as WebFaq, RonSub and WebURL). Each of these Web-based tools supports or scaffolds learning in a unique way. The term scaffolding was originally coined by Wood, Bruner and Ross (1976) as a metaphor to describe the effective intervention by a peer, adult or competent person in the learning of another person. Bruner explicitly relates the term scaffolding to Vygotsky's concept of 'the zone of proximal development', that is, the actual developmental level of the learner compared with the level of potential development that can occur with guidance or collaboration with a more competent person. In Web-based learning environments, the metaphor of scaffolding is appealing in principle, yet elusive and problematic. The appeal of the concept lies in the fact that it directs attention to the role of the instructor or teacher in the learning process, and does so in a way that emphasizes that good teaching is necessarily responsive to the state of understanding achieved by learners.

In this chapter, the Web tools described can support the process of effective student–centred learning with technology by:

- providing peer support in the task that the learner is attempting;
- enabling learners to search for and share information and later perform these functions independently;
- enabling learners to articulate problems, share solutions and engage on collaborative problem solving.

In telelearning contexts, there is a need to redefine the term *scaffolding* and apply it to performance requiring an effective support environment. In conventional settings, teachers are usually the agents for scaffolding. Teachers, for example, have always assumed roles whereby they have monitored learning within their classrooms and have provided the forms of support required by the individual students. In the student-centred learning environments which are typical of most online and computer-based settings, teachers have a less visible role and have to plan for the provision of effective scaffolding for the learners. In instances where teachers have taken more central roles through technology-mediated communi-cation such as e-mail, high levels of personal communication can become unsus-tainable (eg McLachlan-Smith and Gunn, 2000).

More and more, educators are looking for various forms of technology to provide learner support, which previously was performed by teachers. In this book, for example, Morgan and Smit (2000) describe how mentoring processes can be used in open and distance education for this purpose. The forms of tech-nology that have been investigated have included intelligent tutoring systems (ITS) and intelligent agents (eg Giardina, 1998; Anderson, Boyle and Reiser, 1985). Intelligent systems have many design and development costs that usually preclude their adaptation in settings beyond their initial development. Few instructional settings have been developed where ITS can be used in flexible and scalable ways. As scaffolding devices, these products can only serve very narrow uses and purposes.

Electronic performance support systems (EPSS) represent another form of electronic scaffold which have been developed and trialled extensively to support student-centred learning. The EPSS is, once again, a specialist device which is able to provide just-in-time support and help at the request of a learner. Electronic support systems are usually designed with interactive features to provide learners and users with various forms of assistance in completing tasks requiring some form of expertise or knowledge. This interactive software is usually intended to both train and support the user in the performance of tasks (Wild, 1999). Successful EPSSs require a vast array of resources and supporting systems for users. These include: an information base (eg online reference and help facilities and case history databases); interactive and learning experiences; productivity software (often used with templates and forms); and an advisory system or coaching facility (Gery, 1995). As with ITS systems, the requirements for successful EPSS systems make them complex and expensive entities suited to narrow uses. While capable of providing a strong scaffolding role for learners, EPSS systems are not usually tools available for use by teachers and learners in immediate online settings.

One form of scaffolding that is extremely appropriate to online and flexible learning programmes is the support provided among the learners themselves. In most online environments, learners are connected through a variety of means and through astute planning and design of the learning activities, and can act in support of the learning of their peers by collaborating, giving comments and feedback on drafts, and by offering alternative perspectives. Designing learner-centred scaffolding features into online and Web-based courses can provide an effective means of supporting student learning that is both a cost-effective and efficient way to manage learning at a distance.

Online learning support tools

The forms of learner activity that have the capacity to provide scaffolding for peers include collaborative and cooperative activities, those involving discussion and dialogue, and more defined support activities, including peer assessment and peer-tutoring. The following sections describe several online tools that have been developed by the authors as learning tools in online settings which provide various forms of scaffolding and support for learners. We have chosen a range of tools to demonstrate the different forms of support and associated learner interactions that they are able to provide. The tools described demonstrate online support for learners in learning tasks which range from information access, through collaborative inquiry strategies to networked forms of communication.

Information access

We have developed several Web-based tools which have been used successfully to enhance students' access to information and resources. In all instances, the nature of the tools has been collaborative, encouraging learner participation and involvement in a way which provides a sustained form of support for the learning processes. In this section, we describe two such tools, WebURL and WebFAQ.

WebURL

The Internet and WWW are vast repositories of information and one of the major impediments for successful use is not so much finding information but establishing the credibility and veracity of the source. The task of identifying and documenting strong Web sites for units and courses will tax even the most enthusiastic teacher. Getting students to aid in this task provides opportunities and advantages for all. In our programmes we use a very simple tool to assist in this process. WebURL provides a simple interface to a database-driven program that enables learners to add details of useful Web sites across the course topics to a public bulletin board. This activity creates a dynamic list of resources for the learners and generates its own activity and usefulness. The tool requires those who post site information to provide some feedback on the utility of the site in the form of a description. (see Figure 13.1).

Theoretical support for the value of WebURL as a learning tool comes from several areas of research in computer-based and online learning:

● Use of the tool encourages learners who are using Web-based resources to be

Week 3
Interactive Multimedia Authoring Systems

The following URLs have been submitted...

---

http://www.macromedia.com/support/director/how/shock/contents/html
Interesting online tutorials on the authoring of Shockwave movies using Director as a source.
Check out web reviews for even more resources!
Submitted by Satch Kirkpatrick halc83@men.net.au on Mon Mar 1 13:22:39 1999

http://www.imago.com.au/imago/index/html
I M A G O Multimedia Centre – A Western Australian, cutting edge research centre in the
area of Multimedia. Also helps connect multimedia artists with companies with design
projects.
Submitted by: Drew Robinson verilla@iinet.net.au on Mon Mar 1 14:40:13 1999

http://grahicssoft.minigco.com.msubdirect.htm
macromedia director's web site
Submitted by: Rebecca Strickland rebeccas@student.ecu.edu.au on Mon Mar 1 14:51:08 1999

http://www.inproduction.com/interviews.htm
This site is really good if you have the right software. It has lots of interviews with a number
of companies about their corresponding authoring systems and also has links to most of the
company web sites.
Submitted by: Sarah Clough clough@wantree.com.au on Mon Mar 1 15:40:56 1999

http://www.blender.nl/
Blender is a freeware modelling, raytracing and rendering package. THE MOST totally
comprehensive I have ever seen or heard of. It runs under a few *nix-like operating systems,
such as Linux 1386, Sun Solaris, SGI IRIX and Linux Alpha. If you don't have Linux, you
have probably at least heard of it, and if you are a bit ambitious, a bit experimental, a bit 'on
the edge', you should get it!!
Submitted by: Drew Robinson verilla@iinet.net.au on Mon Mar 1 15:58:37 1999

http://www.tiac.net/users/jasiglar/MMASFAQ.HTML
Multimedia Authoring Systems FAQ (Frequently Asked Questions)
Submitted by: Paul Robinson probinso@student.cowan.edu.au on Mon Mar 1 16:07:55 1999

http://www.mcli.dist.maricopa.edu/authoring/index.html
A page dedicated to the subject to Multimedia Authoring
Submitted by: Paul Robinson probinso@student.cowan.edu.au on Mon Mar 1 16:11:59 1999

Figure 13.1 *WebURL, online resource sharing tool*

reflective users of Internet information. Those who find and post sites are
encouraged to establish the credibility of the information (eg Oliver and
Omari, 1999).

- Posting the sites becomes a collaborative activity among class members who
  are able to share in the successes (and failures) of others (Susman, 1998).

- The activity encourages learners to store details of useful Web sites and to
  share this information, activities which provide strong support for independent, self-regulated learning (Scardamalia and Bereiter, 1994).

WebFAQ

WebFAQ is a learning tool which was designed to support a variety of supports
and activities for the learners. In its simplest form, WebFAQ is a Web-based
database that enables students to share and collaborate in the task of designing and
developing computer-based products (see Figure 13.2). The tool was developed
to provide a means of supporting students enrolled in programming classes who
could benefit from a facility enabling them to share and pass products in an

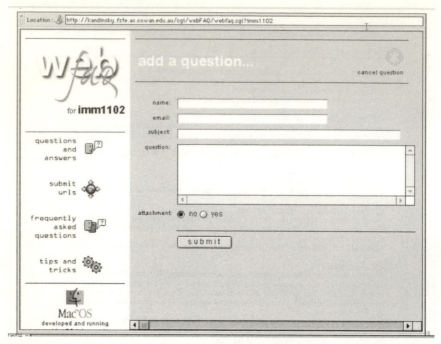

Figure 13.2   *WebFAQ, online resource sharing tool*

online format. WebFAQ was designed to enable students to post computer files to a bulletin board together with requests for assistance or as a means of offering files for others to use. The intention of the tool is to provide a system that would enable advanced students to support others requiring assistance and to provide some form of motivation and inducement for peer scaffolding to occur.

In its implementation, WebFAQ provided a series of supports for learners and required little teacher intervention in its operation. Students were encouraged to use the system and provided with a variety of inducements in the form of course credits to do so. Learners who acted in mentoring roles for others in the class were acknowledged through the allocation of credits for the tasks completed. These students extended their knowledge through their mentoring roles and provided others in the class with access to online support and help.

The system was built to enable the questions posed and solutions submitted in one semester to become items in the frequently-asked-question database for the next semester. The problems and their solutions grew as resources for new learners and the value of the system as a means of supporting and scaffolding student learning expanded. This system supported asynchronous forms of communication between learners and incorporated a form of interactivity whereby learners used reciprocity and active engagement in their interactions, activities characteristic of meaningful and effective dialogue in online learning settings (eg Hewson and Hughes, 2000).

Collaborative learning

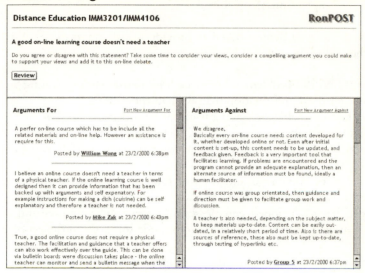

Figure 13.3   *RonSUB, online problem-based learning system*

The previous tools we have described were designed to enable learners to share resources and information in a cooperative fashion, in a manner which enabled their learning activities to be supported and scaffolded by the activities of others. A more purposeful tool for collaborative learning that we have developed is called RonSUB. RonSUB supports a problem–based learning environment in which learners collaborate in a Web-based learning environment to solve a series of problems (see Figure 13.3).

This Web-based system provides the infrastructure for a learning activity whereby learners are organized into small groups, within their larger class workshop cohort. In a course there may be many workshops and hence many groups. Our Web-based system provides the following functionalities:

- A series of weekly problems are presented and in each week students work in the Web-based environment to create a group solution.
- Once a group has posted its solution, it can view the solutions of other groups in that workshop.
- Each group is required to read the solutions of the others and to choose the best solutions (peer assessment).
- The class tutors add their marks to provide an overall mark for each problem solution.
- The best solutions from each workshop are displayed and students can review these.
- The system maintains a record of the marks obtained by each group and shows this in graphical form for each problem.

- At the end of the course, the system provides the marks for each student across the range of problems solved.

This activity has been demonstrated to provide many opportunities and advantages in the settings in which it has been used:

- Students find the problem-solving activities extremely motivating and have accessed far more information than we had anticipated.
- The activities enable on- and off-campus learners to be part of the same learning environment.
- Learners have been supporting each other through activities in the shared learning spaces.
- The activities encourage and support the development of strong skills in using the Web for information access.
- Students have developed generic skills in forming arguments and creating logical answers as they have sought to provide solutions to the problems.

Once again, there is sound theoretical support for the value of RonSub as a learning tool:

- The problem-based learning environment encourages learners to reflect on the information and ideas and to articulate their views (eg Oliver and Omari, 1999).
- The students learn from the communication and interaction with their peers in the problem-solving processes (eg Jonassen et al, 1999).
- The communication and collaboration provides for meaningful interactions and purposeful engagement (eg McLoughlin and Oliver, 1998a; Collis, 1997).

Enhanced communication

The use of many Web tools can be justified from a learning perspective purely through their capacity to support learner communication and interaction (McLoughlin and Oliver, 1998b). Many tools such as e-mail and chat rooms are used extensively by learners in support of their academic activities. We have developed several tools which provide deliberate form to Web-based communication in a manner that once again provides support to student learning.

One such tool supports the students in the conduct of an online debate (see Figure 13.4). The tool provides the learners with the capacity to take a stance on a topic which requires either a substantiating argument or a refutation. Learners can view the arguments of their peers and add their own in the form of submissions to a dynamic bulletin board displaying feedback in parallel frames representing the arguments presented.

> **IMM 1122 & IMM 4122**
>
> Workshop 1   [Back to Main]   Problem 4
> Group 2   HTML Versions?
>
> **Group 2 Problem 4 Submission**
>
> **HTML Versions?**
>
> You have been asked by a colleague to develop her personal Web Pages to be placed on the company Web site. What standard of HTML should you use HTML 2.0, 3.2 or 4.0?
>
> Aspects which need to be looked at is what type of company it is, who is it aimed at and what version of HTML it is using. As companies need to be competitive in web presentation on the web, it would be likely to be done in a recent version of HTML (probably 4.0). In using the same version as the rest of the company's site, she will be able to take advantage of some of the features. People are going to access her site though the company's so if it were technology based, it would have a specific target audience like people searching for the latest, hi-tech software, and so would probably use a higher version of HTML, like 4.0. If it was less technology oriented, it would have a larger target audience and would have to cater for many different browsers and HTML formats.
>
> Older versions of HTML, such as HTML 2.0 are very basic. If she wished to have a page without tables or frames and only basic layouts of text and graphics then 2.0 would suitable, though the presentation created by 2.0 can seem dull due to its lack of features. HTML 3.2 is presently the most common format used throughout the web. Supporting tables, frames, backgrounds and diverse colours, 3.2 can be viewed by almost any browser As well as the text, multimedia, and hyperlink features of the previous versions of HTML, HTML 4.0 supports more multimedia options,
>
> Contributing Students:
>
> ☑ Mark Tang
> ☑ Andy Chui
> ☑ Rebecca Webb
> ☑ Linda Fetherston

Figure 13.4   *Online debate, a communication and learning tool*

The online debating environment provides a very efficient setting to gather information on a topic through a process of student inquiry. The activity can be structured in a variety of forms to achieve particular learning outcomes. For example, the emphasis can be on the process of arguing and students can be encouraged and rewarded for their contributions to the argument. On the other hand, the emphasis might be on establishing the strength of the arguments, in which case students can be encouraged after the debate has finished to ascertain, from the arguments presented, the side with the most convincing points. All these activities can be supported online and represent significant tasks for the learners with minimal teacher intervention. Once again, the setting demonstrates the capacity of the online environment to provide support for student learning which in the main is generated through the various activities of the learners themselves.

Discussion and conclusion

Online and open learning can be an isolated and solitary experience for many learners. Contemporary practices in online learning tend to provide few meaningful and worthwhile opportunities for learners to interact and communicate with others in the learning process. Many teachers urge, some even compel, learners to participate in online chat sessions or to communicate with others through e-mail. Such activities, however, are often devoid of any explicit learning opportunity and tend to be included as a complementary rather than as a deliberate form of learning activity. In this chapter we have described several deliberate learning activities that encourage learners to communicate and collaborate in meaningful ways. The activities have been designed to provide a way for learners to communicate so that the involvement of others acts as a stimulus and support for learning.

The approaches we have described in this chapter have all involved deliberate roles for both teachers and students in the online environment. There may be a tendency to design online environments in ways which increase student-teacher communication through e-mail and bulletin boards. The implementation of this form of dialogue may result in volumes of communication which become time consuming and unproductive. In a sustainable online environment, teachers should be able to choose when and how they participate and the quality of learning should not be overly influenced by the times when the teacher chooses to stay offline. The design of online resources demonstrated in this chapter shows that by creating settings where learners communicate with peers, we can reduce the expectation of learners to communicate directly with the teacher while still maintaining the levels of support required for meaningful learning.

References

Anderson, J, Boyle, C and Reiser, B (1985) Intelligent tutoring systems, *Science*, **228** (6), pp 456–62

Azmitia, M and Montgomery, R (1993) Friendship, transitive dialogues, and the development of scientific reasoning, *Social Development*, **2** (3), pp 202–21

Collins, A, Brown, J S and Newman, S E (1989) Cognitive apprenticeship: Teaching the crafts of reading, writing and mathematics, in *Knowing, Learning and Instruction: Essays in honour of Robert Glaser*, ed L B Resnick, pp 453–94, Lawrence Erlbaum, Hillsdale, New Jersey

Collis, B (1997) Supporting project-based collaborative learning via World Wide Web environment, in *Web-based Instruction*, ed B Khan, pp 213–21, Educational Technology Publications, Englewood Cliffs, NJ

Davis, N (1997) Do electronic communications skills offer a new learning opportunity in education?, in *Using Information Technology Successfully in Teaching and Learning*, ed B Somekh and N Davis, pp 167–83, Routledge, London

Gery, G (1995) Attributes and behaviours of performance-centred systems, *Performance Improvement Quarterly*, 8 (1), pp 31–46

Giardina, M (1998) Integrating intelligent advisory strategies and student modelling procedures through the development of IPES, in *Proceedings of Ed-Media 1998*, ed T Ottman and I Tomek, pp 397–407

Hewson, L and Hughes, C (2000) Generic structures for online teaching and learning, in *Innovation in Open and Distance Learning*, ed F Lockwood and A Gooley, Kogan Page, London

Hoyles, C, Healy, L and Pozzi, S (1994) Groupwork with computers: an overview of findings, *Journal of Computer Assisted Learning*, **10**, pp 202–15

Jonassen, D, Prevish, T, Christy, D and Stravrulaki, E (1999) Learning to solve problems on the Web: Aggregate planning in a business management course, *Distance Education*, **20** (1), pp 9–57

Maverech, Z R (1993) Who benefits from cooperative computer-assisted instruction?, *Journal of Educational Computing Research*, **9** (4), pp 451–64

McLachlan-Smith, C and Gunn, C (2000) Promoting innovation and change in a 'traditional' university setting, in *Innovation in Open and Distance Learning*, ed F Lockwood and A Gooley, Kogan Page, London

McLoughlin, C and Oliver, R (1998a) Planning a telelearning environment to foster higher order thinking, *Journal of Distance Education*, **19** (2), pp 242–64

McLoughlin, C and Oliver, R (1998b) Maximising the language and learning link in computer learning environments, *British Journal of Educational Technology*, **29** (2), pp 125–36

Morgan, C and Smit, A (2000) Mentoring in open and distance learning, in *Innovation in Open and Distance Learning*, ed F Lockwood and A Gooley, Kogan page, London

Nastasi, B K and Clements, D H. (1993) Motivational and social outcomes of cooperative computer education environments, *Journal of Computing in Childhood Education*, **4** (1), pp 15–43

Oliver, R and Omari, A (1999) Using online technologies to support problem-based learning: Learners' responses and perceptions, *Australian Journal of Educational Technology*, **15** (1), pp 58–79

Reeves, T and Reeves, P (1997) Effective dimensions of interactive learning on the World Wide Web, in *Web-based instruction*, ed B Khan, pp 59–66, Educational Technology Publications, Englewood Cliffs, NJ

Roschelle, J and Teasley, S D (1995) The construction of shared knowledge in collaborative problem solving, in *Computer Supported Collaborative Learning*, ed C O'Malley, pp 69–100, Springer Verlag, Berlin

Scardamalia, M and Bereiter, C (1994) Computer support for knowledge building communities, *Journal of the Learning Sciences*, **3** (3), pp 265–83

Scardamalia, M, Bereiter, C, McLean, R S, Swallow, J and Woodruff, E (1989) Computer-supported intentional learning environments, *Journal of Educational Computing Research*, **5** (1), pp 51–68

Susman, E B (1998) Cooperative learning: A review of factors that increase the effectiveness of cooperative computer-based instruction, *Journal of Educational Computing Research*, **18** (4), pp 302–03

Thomas, P, Carswell, I, Price, B and Petre, M (1998) A holistic approach to supporting distance learning via the Internet: Transformation, not translation, *British Journal of Educational Technology*, **29** (2), pp 149–61

Wood, D, Bruner, J S and Ross, G (1976) The role of tutoring in problem solving, *Journal of Child Psychology and Psychiatry*, **17** (2), pp 89–100

Wild, M (1999) Finding an educational role for performance support systems, in *Proceedings of Ed-Media 1999*, ed B Collis and R Oliver, pp 1169–74

Chapter 14

Mentoring in open and distance learning

Chris Morgan and Andre Smit

Introduction

The term *mentoring* has become something of a buzzword in higher education of recent years, following trends of business and industry where mentoring schemes have flourished for many years. Mentoring in higher education mostly occurs in face-to-face settings and generally takes the form of either staff–staff mentoring, where experienced teachers provide support for new academic staff, or student–student schemes, where on-campus students provide support to new learners. This chapter focuses on the somewhat neglected area of mentoring in open and distance learning contexts, where opportunities can be created to enhance student interactions, learning and well-being. We initially discuss models and definitions of mentoring, and the confusion regarding terminology is clarified. We also briefly examine two applied case studies of mentoring at a distance. Evaluation of these case studies and issues emerging from their first few years of operation are also covered in some detail. Finally, we draw some tentative conclusions regarding the value of mentoring in open and distance contexts and suggestions for those interested in developing their own mentoring programmes.

Definitions and models of mentoring

Mentoring relationships have been commonly fostered in business to support the training and career development of inexperienced staff. Traditionally mentors were selected because they were more senior and had an appropriate track record, and the mentoree aspired to follow them. As organizational hierarchical structures are changing and being replaced by flatter and leaner structures, the traditional mentoring models may no longer be effective. The new organization is tending to be made up of a network of individuals participating in cooperative and coordinated ways (Limerick and Cunnington, 1993). Mentors will be seeking to be transformational rather than directional, aiming to facilitate growth in the mentoree rather than to pass on the lessons from their own experiences. Several terms have been used by Conway (1995), Barbuto (1992), Hagerty (1986) and Watts (1996) to describe the mentor in the one-to-one relationship: peer supporter; coach; teacher; guide; sponsor; boss; guru; and relative. This chapter uses the following model to describe and locate mentoring relationships. There are three dimensions to the model (see Figure 14.1), outlining the key factors that distinguish mentoring relationships, the level of involvement, and the degree of influence in the relationship.

The first dimension delineates the three key factors that distinguish mentoring relationships:

- the degree of *power* within the relationship that the mentor commands;
- the level of identification with the mentor in creating an open atmosphere which helps *learning*; and
- implementation of the programme determines the objectives of the programme, coordination and *involvement* of mentors and mentorees.

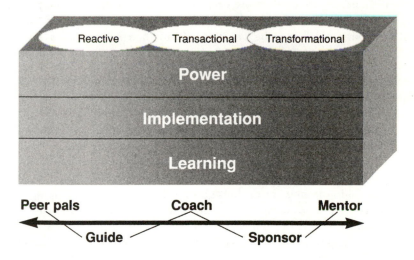

Source: Smit (1999: 9)

Figure 14.1   *Three dimensional mentoring model*

The second dimension suggests that the mentoring is not hierarchical but linear, and that a continuum exists with mentors and peer pals on the end points of that continuum. This does not mean that mentors are more important than peer pals. Mentors are positioned at one end and are the most 'involved', while sponsors, guides and coaches, who are less powerful than mentors in effecting change, are spread along the middle of the continuum. Depending on the objectives to be achieved through mentoring, the mentoring relationship may be at any point on the continuum.

The third dimension incorporates the degree of leadership influence in the mentor/mentoree relationship. Leadership is defined as the process of influencing the activities of individuals and groups towards goal achievement. Mentoring is transformational. Mentors provide leadership to inspire change and build new cultures. Coaches are transactional; they provide leadership to get the job done and attain set goals. Peer pals are reactive, peers supporting each other when the need arises.

Mentoring in open and distance learning

In the context of open and distance learning, mentoring is less frequently encountered or referred to in the literature. This is surprising given the opportunities which mentoring affords as well as the rich resources of people available in learners' workplaces and local communities (Race, 1994). To a degree, mentoring occurs in distance education on an informal basis when learners seek the support of colleagues in undertaking an assignment or working through a problem. Generally we don't know very much about our learners' support structures beyond that which is offered by the institution, nor do we help learners to harness support which may be available within their communities and workplaces. Opportunities for distance learners in mentoring programmes include:

● *Creating multiple discourses.* One of the often-cited problems with distance programmes is the tendency of course materials to focus on the one-way dissemination of content, and the views of course authors, thereby discouraging the active construction and exchange of meanings by learners (Evans and Nation, 1989; Morgan, 1993). Regular interactions with a mentor can create new sources of dialogue and can support learners to identify and critically engage with problematic issues. Work-based mentors may be particularly useful in offering practical insights on theoretical issues, helping learners to bridge the worlds of theory and practice. Moreover, traditional academic programmes frequently do not have the structure to access best industry practice and recent innovations, as well as the debates and concerns most relevant to contemporary practice.

● *Helping overcome isolation.* Whether a learner's isolation is a geographical or psychological issue, the well-timed support of a mentor can do much to encourage and motivate learners and help them to become familiar with the processes and culture of distance education. For learners who are reluctant to make contact with academic staff, mentoring provides another avenue for support, useful information and advice. Studies in student discontinuation in distance education regularly point to the importance of students being able to access timely, relevant support (Brown, 1996, for example). Although mentors do not replace the need for appropriate academic support, they offer learners another avenue to test their ideas and thinking in a 'safe', non–assessable context.

- *Enabling the development of work-based competences.* Mentoring can provide useful ways of teaching and assessing disciplinary skills at a distance. Although distance education has developed a variety of means to demonstrate skills to learners, it is much more difficult to monitor individual learners' progress, and to assess their level of achievement, unless residential schools are employed for the purpose. Mentoring enables learners to practise and develop specified skills in a real-life, 'safe' context. A mentor or coach provides supportive developmental feedback and may also act as a summative assessor, certifying to the educational institution that their learner has acquired certain skills to the specified level.
- *Providing higher levels of flexibility.* Mentoring provides learners with the opportunity for more choice, flexibility and self-direction in arranging their study programme and achieving programme objectives. Similarly, it provides educational institutions with new opportunities to offer programmes at a distance which would otherwise require significant components of face-to-face contact, and may exclude remote or heavily committed learners.
- *Creating dialogue between theory and practice.* Mentoring schemes tend to promote valuable dialogue between the worlds of work and academe. They have the potential to create benefits not only for the learner, but also for host workplaces, communities and educational institutions. Mentors themselves will often benefit from the relationship as a form of professional development, where their previously unarticulated values and practices are open to exploration and dialogue.

Types of mentoring relationships in distance education

Students mentoring students

Experienced learners who are willing to be mentors may be paired with new learners, ideally in the same discipline area. In this context, mentors have a general brief to offer relevant support and information exchange as needed by the learner, and often entails the sharing of study skills, time management, information retrieval, essay writing, and generally 'working the system'. Communication at a distance usually occurs by either phone or e-mail as negotiated by the pair. These mentoring relationships are 'reactive' in nature and can be positioned at the peer pal end of the continuum in the above model.

Coaches mentoring students in the workplace

Coaching is a form of mentoring aimed at teaching specific tasks and developmental needs. For example, learners may be required to develop certain skills which they must satisfactorily perform to a certain level to pass a subject. The learner will appoint a workplace mentor who is suitably qualified to teach the skills, and the coach may also certify that competence has been achieved. If the learner is new to the work environment, other roles may also include facilitating career development, personal growth and understanding the culture of practice in the discipline area. Within the three-dimensional model, coaching is defined as transactional. This view sees coaching as an interpersonal influence. A coach influences people on a face-to-face basis to achieve set goals by providing the resources necessary and rewarding performance by formal and informal means.

Mentors and students in a transformational learning environment

This is a form of mentoring which aims at deeper and more transformational forms of learning than coaching, where mentors may shape themselves more as role models and aim to facilitate growth in learners rather than to pass on the lessons from their own experiences. Mentors will therefore need a working knowledge of the processes of learning and change, such as the kind of transformation learning model outlined by Hay (1995) who describes transformational mentoring as about learning to learn. Ideally students not only experience a change in perspective, but also have an awareness of the process by which they are doing so. The student plays an equal part in analysing what is happening, so that mentor and student work in partnership to increase the student's openness to learning. Hay (1995) further points out that it is impossible to facilitate transformational learning in another person without accepting that we will learn from that person too.

In distance education, these kinds of mentoring arrangements are likely to occur in work-based, project learning, with a relatively high level of self-direction and also open-ended objectives and assessment. Learners may identify a particular project and select an appropriate mentor with whom they work in collaboration to identify learning goals and processes. Reflection by the learner upon processes and outcomes are likely to form a significant part of the assessment.

Case study 1 – Students mentoring students

The first case study considered here is a student-student mentoring scheme at Southern Cross University, Australia, which pairs new distance learners with experienced ones to provide support and information and to act as role models. Mentors are senior social sciences undergraduates who are studying the theory and practice of mentoring simultaneously with their mentoring activity. Thus the scheme has the dual aims of:

- decreasing the isolation of inexperienced distance learners and thus addressing the poor retention rates of first year distance students; and
- providing hands-on mentoring experience to learners pursing a career in human resource management and a particular interest in workplace mentoring.

During a semester of study, final year students undertaking this optional unit are required to enter a mentoring relationship with two volunteer first year students (mentorees), and develop a journal to reflect on their experiences. The mentorees are assigned to them by the unit coordinator, and the accompanying study materials introduce mentors to the theory and practice of mentoring. Mentors also learn about responsibilities in areas such as age, gender, confidentiality and privacy with academic supervision and share reflections with each other via a discussion list. Most of the mentoring contact is by phone or e-mail. However, where practical, and if participants are geographically close, they may wish to organize face-to-face meetings.

The unit coordinator acts as a mentoring coordinator, and is responsible for: matching of mentors and mentorees:

- implementing the 'no-fault' clause, which means that at any time during the mentoring relationship, either the mentor or the mentoree can request the unit assessor to terminate the relationship;
- facilitating the mentors' learning, by conducting action learning teletutorials and conducting a discussion list for mentors to exchange ideas about the mentoring process;
- evaluating the programme.

Evaluation

Reflective journals, teletutorials and e-mail transcripts were used as a strategy for data collection. Data indicated that the following facets of mentoring were important to mentors during the process:

- implementation;
- learning;
- power.

Within each of these facets, mentors reflected on concepts such as coordination, equity, involvement, age and gender, time, roles and status, knowledge, leadership and learning issues.

Implementation

The majority of mentoring literature appears to detail many potentially positive outcomes of mentoring. However Yoder (1990) argues that many mentoring programmes may be devised with rose-coloured glasses, and that potential pitfalls do exist. It may be argued that it is not necessary to look for everything mentoring can provide in a single relationship. Some of the commonly occurring issues raised by mentors in the implementation of the scheme include:

- initial concerns about adequacy;
  (After initial feelings of inadequacy, I felt comfortable that I have provided reassurance and offered some thoughts and encouraged the mentoree to develop some strategies around achieving goals and meeting needs not covered by the University course.)
- need to 'go with the flow';
  (I have not tried to deepen my relationship with my mentorees with formal contracts or challenges to their thinking − I really don't think that is what they want from me and would feel intrusive if I tried. I think that the literature is right − true mentoring is rare and cannot be 'forced' onto the situation, however well intentional the participants.)
- expectations.
  (This person turned out to be quite self-sufficient and required very little in the way of support or assistance from me as a mentor. Contact with this person was difficult due to her busy schedule and while we did keep in touch, our relationship remained characterized by very low levels of involvement.)

Learning

The theme of 'learning' had a significant influence on the mentoring relationship, as highlighted by the following comments:

- relating theory to practice;
  (The mentoring programme has provided me with an invaluable opportunity for the implementation of theoretical knowledge and skills acquired through my four years of university studies. The programme I felt raised my self-awareness and development in all areas, learning to reflect and analyse my own approach to mentoring, and then adjusting to address the specific needs and learning styles of individuals.)
- becoming a change agent;
  (I have consciously worked to build her sense of self-esteem with positive feedback and encouragement through listening to her concerns. I have also contributed, through various coaching activities, to the development of her skills in researching, synthesizing information, report-writing and technical aspects of academic writing and computer skills. I have also

encouraged her to be assertive by coaching her in expressing her needs explicitly and confidently within the university system.)

- learning about difference.
  (I learned from the mentorees about other ways of studying and coping with study and time. These were mature adults with mature adult skills for managing study, life and time.)

Power

The data from this study indicated that power relations had a significant influence on the mentoring relationship; the following comments highlight some of the issues:

- age and gender;
  (the mentoree indicated that he had no issues around our difference in gender; however he suggested that he may have found it difficult to relate to a mentor who was much younger than himself.)
- experience and age;
  (The first mentoree was a postgraduate student, 10 years older than myself. It is often assumed that the mentor is to be older than the mentoree, in order to be wiser. Initially, I felt very intimidated by the mentoree's age and greater knowledgeable power and experience of the real world. I felt obliged to prove myself as a potential source of knowledge in order to gain credibility and commitment from the mentoree.)
- value differences;
  (I was nervous about discovering a clash of values with the mentoree who was assigned to me; however, I found that by overcoming my internal self-judgements about being 'unconvincing as a mentor', I gained more self-confidence.)
- confidentiality.
  (My mentoree commented that she had taken confidentiality for granted and didn't think it necessary to sign a formal agreement about it. Later on in the relationship, she realized that it helped her to feel more secure about opening up about her personal issues with me.)

Case study 2 – Community and work-based mentoring

This is a mentoring model that enables distance learners to develop work-based skills or to be introduced to the culture of a disciplinary setting, while studying the theory and practice of the field. It is currently operating at Southern Cross University in diverse disciplines such as operating room nursing, counselling and acupuncture. The scheme enables learners to select an appropriate mentor from their own community or workplace with whom they gain exposure to the discipline, and practise specified skills in real-life settings. Mentors provide support and feedback to students as well as a report of their progress, and may also act as assessors, certifying learners' achievements to the educational institution. The scheme provides learners with the flexibility to be able to study subjects in their own settings, which otherwise would require long hours of face-to-face attendance at potentially far-flung institutions.

For example, the acupuncture programme enables nurses from around Australia to acquire this postgraduate qualification, provided they are able to be mentored by a suitably qualified practitioner in their local community. Students receive a range of study materials and tasks, including a mentor's brief, developed by the university to assist the mentor in facilitating activities which range from a general introduction and exposure to Chinese medicine, to specific skills such as needling, and to running a small business and interacting with clients. Face-to-face workshops and exams are conducted by the university to ensure that consistent standards are met, although the mentor's input also contributes significantly to formal assessment. Mentors do not participate in this programme for altruistic reasons alone. They find there are many benefits in terms of their own professional development and updating of their disciplinary knowledge, as well as the rewards of a mutually stimulating relationship. However, the university encourages potential mentors to think carefully about the responsibilities and pitfalls of the role, particularly regarding time commitments. Both mentors and learners are supported by an academic coordinator from the university, who is responsible for course materials, face-to-face workshops and assessment.

Although the term 'mentor' is used here in a general way, the role may be in many cases more akin to a coach. However, learners and mentors have considerable freedom to shape the relationship in the way they choose, over and above core assessment requirements, and it will depend to a large extent on the needs of the learner, the abilities of the mentor, and the developing dynamics of the relationship. In some nursing programmes where mentoring has flourished, nurse mentors have been trained by the university through a programme covering teaching, learning, mentoring and reflective practice. In these instances, mentors are more equipped and willing to take on a transformational role.

Evaluation

Evaluation of the scheme to date has focused on the experiences of learners and mentors through questionnaire data and follow-up interviews, exploring the nature of the mentoring relationships, as well as benefits and pitfalls (Stewart, Morgan and O'Reilly, 1996). On the positive side, most learners supported the scheme and found many valuable learning outcomes. Some learners reported that they were happy to limit their involvement with mentors to the structured development of specified skills. In other instances, a mutually rewarding relationship developed which has continued beyond the life of the specific subject.

Some commonly occurring issues or problems include:

- *Availability of mentors.* In rural or remote communities, learners often experienced considerable difficulty locating suitably qualified mentors. Depending on the nature of the programme, alternative arrangements can sometimes be made, which might also entail some travel. In most instances, mentors are required to have certain qualifications, such as 'registered practitioner with minimum five years' experience', although some discretion and flexibility may be employed in this regard.
- *Negotiating a mentoring relationship.* Learners are often inexperienced in approaching professionals to negotiate a mentorship. We have found it important to support learners by providing some basic protocols, and information for prospective mentors which outlines the nature of the role and some basic expectations and outcomes. We encourage learners to think carefully about what their own needs are in relation to the relationship as well as any needs or concerns that prospective mentors may wish to express. Clarity at this stage is vital to the foundation of a good relationship.
- *Role and time commitment of mentors.* Ambiguities regarding the mentoring role and the necessary time commitment by the mentor are two of the most common reasons for breakdown of relationships. In some instances, this results from unanticipated changes in the mentor's circumstances; in other instances, it is the result of inadequate early negotiations or support from the university. As discussed earlier, clarity in early negotiations, particularly regarding mutual expectations and time availability, is essential to the ongoing success of the relationship.
- *Support and training of mentors.* Although some prospective mentors are attracted to the role, they may feel ill equipped or uncertain about their capacity to fulfil the role. The university needs to encourage and foster relationships with mentors, providing detailed information about their role and welcoming contact with an academic coordinator to discuss problems. In some instances more formal training is appropriate, particularly where the mentor is likely to have ongoing relationships with many learners.
- *Validity and reliability of mentors' reports.* In some instances mentors are asked to assess learners' achievements, particularly when specified skills are being developed. Mentors will require detailed descriptions of competences and the level or standard of performance required to fulfil this role properly. To avoid problems of validity and reliability between assessors, learners receive a non-graded pass for this component of their assessment, providing mentors have reported satisfactory performance. Grades are usually derived from other written work, such as journals, essays and so forth, which are assessed solely by the university. Mentors will often require some support in conducting assessments, and may also experience some conflict between their formative mentoring role and their summative assessment role. Most mentoring programmes seek to avoid this by ensuring that all assessment is

supervised by the university, unless mentors have been specifically trained for the role.

- *Relationship breakdown.* Inevitably some relationships break down, most commonly as a result of changed circumstances, time constraints or, less frequently, incompatibility. In such event, it is important to acknowledge mentors' involvement, and support learners to clarify any issues or problems without attaching blame or fault (a mutual 'no fault' clause is a good idea in mentoring agreements).
- *Acknowledgement of mentors.* Mentoring is time consuming and a highly skilled activity, so it is important that mentors are acknowledged appropriately for their efforts. In most instances, payment is not possible or appropriate, but other acknowledgements such as certificates of appreciation can be issued by the university, detailing their involvement. It is a way of thanking mentors for their time and commitment, and also allows them to incorporate it as part of their professional portfolio.

Conclusion

Although mentoring schemes are by no means new in the workplace, nor in higher education in general, a great deal of their potential in distance education has yet to be tapped. These case studies reveal that mentoring can provide powerful learning experiences for distance learners, although clearly there are a range of logistics and pitfalls which must be addressed for any scheme to flourish. Issues of common concern in these case studies include:

- sufficient institutional and academic support to assure quality in the mentor/learner relationship;
- university staff who are committed to the sometimes labour-intensive work of ensuring that mentoring schemes are well administered and that meaningful dialogue and learning are fostered;
- programmes which are sufficiently flexible and self-directed in nature to maximize learning opportunities through mentoring;
- regular evaluation and updating to ensure that worthwhile learning outcomes are being achieved.

References

Barbuto, S (1992) The mentoring phenomenon – A brief historical view, *The Australian Journal of Advanced Nursing*, **2** (4), pp 1–12

Brown, K (1996) The role of internal and external factors in the discontinuation of off-campus students, *Distance Education*, **17** (1), pp 44–71

Conway, C (1995) Mentoring managers in organizations, *Equal Opportunities International Journal*, **14** (3–4), pp 1–52

Evans, T and Nation, D (1989) Dialogue in practice, research and theory in distance education, *Open Learning*, **4** (2), pp 37–41

Hagerty, B (1986) A second look at mentors, *Nursing Outlook*, **34** (1), pp 16–19

Hay, J (1995) *Transformational Mentoring: Creating developmental alliances for changing organizational cultures*, McGraw-Hill Book Company, London

Limerick, D and Cunnington, B (1993) *Managing The New Organization: A blueprint for networks and strategic alliances*, Business and Professional Printing, Chatswood, Australia

Morgan, A (1993) *Improving Your Students' Learning: Reflections on the experience of study*, Kogan Page, London.

Race, P (1994) *Open Learning Handbook*, Kogan Page, London

Smit, A (1999) *Mentoring in the Organisation*, Southern Cross University, Lismore, Australia

Stewart, J, Morgan, C and O'Reilly, M (1996) Shared learning resources: workplace learning, mentoring and assessment, *Access Through Open Learning: Occasional papers in open learning*, vol 6, December, Southern Cross University, Lismore, Australia

Watts, L. D (1996) *A Guide to Mentoring*, National Staff Development Committee for the Australian National Training Authority, Melbourne

Yoder, L (1990) Mentoring: A concept analysis, *Nursing Administration Quarterly*, **15** (1), pp 9–19

Chapter 15

Changing the pattern: towards flexible learning, learner support and mentoring

Santosh Panda and Tapan Jena

Introduction

Health and medical education for prospective doctors usually takes place in medical colleges and schools, following a four-stage learning process: learning from lectures and text books, demonstration of skills by teachers, performance of skills under the supervision of the teacher, and further practice of the skills on patients. The use of open and distance learning for practising doctors, whilst practised elsewhere in the world (see the Open University Joint Centre for Research in Medicine <http://iet.open.ac.uk/JCM/homepage.htm>) is innovative in India and requires sensitivity in its implementation and in learner support. This chapter describes these aspects in national and institutional contexts, and analyses the impact of such teaching and learning in continuing medical education in a decentralized and flexible framework. Our focus is a Postgraduate Diploma in Maternal and Child Health, for practising doctors working especially in rural areas, offered by the Indira Gandhi National Open University (IGNOU), India.

India has a population of about 1 billion with mothers and children constituting nearly 60 per cent of the population. Several indicators suggest a low health status of mother and child: infant mortality 71 per 1,000 live births, maternal mortality 4 per 1,000 live births, a severe protein energy malnutrition of 8 per cent and a low level of literacy (40 per cent) amongst women. The Government of India has implemented several measures to aid child survival and safe motherhood. One such measure has been the provision of numerous training and orientation programmes for medical and para-medical staff. The need is great since it is estimated that approximately 300,000 MBBS doctors need to be trained to meet maternal and child morbidity and mortality demands (SOHS, 1996). However, problems have arisen regarding the nature of these programmes and in particular the disruption of service in rural Primary Health Centres (PHC) and Community Health Centres (CHC) that such training courses cause.

A Postgraduate Diploma in Maternal and Child Health was therefore designed by the IGNOU in 1997, following the recommendation of the Government of India, and funded by the World Health Organization. The 32-credit one-year Diploma comprised 18 credit theory and 14 credit practical components (1 credit = 30 student study hours). The programme covers three specialized areas: Preventive & Social Medicine, Paediatrics, and Obstetrics & Gynaecology. To meet the requirement of 14 credit practical components, a student has to complete 43 skill demonstrations, five activities, 14 field visits and a project. The Diploma, with an enrolment of about 700 practising doctors annually, mainly from rural hospitals, aims at:

● improving the knowledge and skills in Maternal and Child Health (MCH);
● upgrading clinical competence for providing quality MCH care.

The innovative form of teaching and learning reported in this chapter focuses on the 14-credit practical components of the Diploma.

The pattern of teaching and learning

The multimedia teaching – learning package included self-instructional print materials, programme guides, practical manuals, assignments, logbooks, counselling provision, hands-on training, a project component, videos and teleconferencing. Within the package, only video and teleconferencing components were optional.

IGNOU has a networked operational system of headquarters, 26 regional/recognized regional centres and 558 study centres/work centres. The implementation of any health education programme within this framework is extremely difficult due to a combination of factors and numerous stakeholders. Public health is the responsibility of, and is regulated by, each of the 26 states in the country. It is based on union/government guidelines, health/medical education practices in medical colleges coordinated by the State Directorate of Medical Education, and health services (provided at government hospitals) coordinated by the State Directorate of Health Services. Furthermore, the infrastructure for Public Health varies from state to state, with each having somewhat different pedagogic/training needs and different resources. These factors, and a wide variation in cultural practices and health perceptions, represent a major challenge to implementing a commonly accredited national health education programme in 18 of the 26 states of India. Thus flexibility was needed if the proposed programme was to be successful in such a decentralized framework of health provision.

The conventional medical student studies the theory and gains practice at a medical college or school. The doctor (*student doctor*) following the Diploma would attend theory sessions and conduct practicals at the Programme Study Centre (PSC) (medical college). Practical skills would be refined with patients at a Skill Development Centre (SDC) (district hospital); they would obtain additional practice on patients at the workplace (WP) (rural primary health centre or personal clinic). This three-tier practice was undertaken three times (three spells) in a year. The total of 43 skills across three areas of specialization was almost equally distributed among the three spells. In addition, the student doctors undertook five activities, 14 field visits and project work at the workplace. Of the 14 credits or 420 hours, the student doctor was expected to devote 123 hours at the PSC, 89 hours at the SDC and 198 hours at the WP. Skills were practised in the work place during routine patient care through the year. Student doctors also refined their skills during the six days in each spell at the PSC and during the 2–3 weeks at SDC.

The Diploma was implemented through 23 PSCs in 18 states and about 140 SDCs (1 PSC: 6 SDC). At each PSC, there were two counsellors (medical professors) for each of the three specialized areas. Each counsellor was responsible for 4-5 student doctors and at each SDC there was one hospital doctor for each of two specialized areas (ie excluding preventive and social medicine); each hospital doctor was responsible for 4–6 student doctors. A student doctor maintained a logbook for all skills practised at the three centres; an assessment of the logbook by PSC and SDC counsellors contributed 10 per cent to the 30 per cent weighting given to continuous assessment.

The complex relationship between independent states and other professional bodies in the Public Health area made monitoring of the programme problematic and resulted in an alternative mechanism being developed. A regional consultant was identified, typically a senior retired health officer in the state, who provided liaison between medical college, district hospitals, state health departments, university regional centre and the headquarters. They supervised the functioning of the PSCs and SDCs and facilitated the mobilization of resources, especially at SDCs, to meet local needs. A Regional Health Sciences Advisory Committee, with members from each of the participating agencies, coordinated the overall implementation of the programme in each state.

The administrative arrangements and learner support were decentralized and flexible enough to take care of the support needs of each learning centre and the support needs of each student doctor. For the reinforcement and transfer of skills student doctors had to repeat the practice of each skill at all the three learning centres. At the PSC, each counsellor worked with small groups of 4–5 students each, and taught through practical demonstration of each skill on one or two patients. At the SDC, each counsellor worked in small groups of 4–5 students, and each student doctor practised the same skill on about five patients under the supervision of the counsellor. In the workplace, the student doctor practised the same skill on about 10 patients. During the practicals, the *counsellors at the PSC and SDC assessed the student doctor.* If performance was judged to be unacceptable, additional practice was required prior to the next spell. This procedure was followed over the three spells.

In addition to administrative flexibility and decentralization, flexibility was built into learner support at the SDC. At the SDC there were two specialized counsellors, one each for paediatrics and for obstetrics and gynaecology. While there was group learning of generic skills, individual negotiation and pacing were possible, all activities being recorded in the student doctor logbook. The logbook provided the counsellor with information upon which appropriate (based on local practices) academic, vocational, administrative and personal support was provided.

Mentoring

As part of course requirements each student doctor was allocated a counsellor at a medical college and district hospital; the counsellor provided academic, vocational and personal support. Informal interviews with the student doctors during the first year of the Diploma revealed that many of them needed additional support regarding study skills, approaches to study, motivation, and personal problems, and sought confidential support at a personal level. As a result, in the second year of operation an informal mentoring scheme was introduced at selective SDCs with willing counsellors and student doctors taking part. SDCs were judged to be appropriate venues because both counsellors and student doctors were involved in supervising and practising respectively a variety of skills on patients. Evidence from interviews with the first cohort of counsellors and student doctors indicated there was a close interaction. By working together and sharing experiences both counsellor and student doctor felt they had benefited. The counsellor, in his or her role as mentor, was considered to be a peer supporter, a teacher and guide (though considered superior by most of the student doctors) who could interact on a one-to-one basis at a deeper and more personal level.

Arrangements in the second cohort were more flexible. The student doctors were asked to nominate a mentor from their SDC – given the willingness of the counsellor to act as a mentor. The nature of the mentoring relationship was to be by negotiation but intended to enable students to facilitate learning, develop varied skills of application and grow as professionals in their fields of specialization. Most of the counsellors were not mentors and whilst counsellor-mentors counselled some student doctors, others combined counselling and mentoring roles. Since a student doctor chose only one mentor, counselling sessions were attended for the other area of specialization. In the process of skill development, both parties considered mentoring a process of negotiation of meaning and adoption of practices that were locally based and sometimes patient based. Both diagnosis and treatment were negotiated, and were tried out on a number of patients. In the process, the mentors could develop a culture of practice in those areas of specialized skills considered important from the viewpoint of the medical profession.

During the skill sessions at the SDC, the counsellor-mentor provided individual (academic, personal and vocational) mentoring support to the student doctors. Further individual support was extended through additional face-to-face meetings, by phone and by post. Although the logbook was used to record skill development sessions, mentoring activities were recorded by both the parties and, with their full consent, details of the nature of the activities shared with researchers.

The close relationship between counsellor-mentor and student doctor enabled the nature of practical activities to be negotiated. Such self-choice and self-direction were judged in no way to hinder assessment of skills and logbooks but to have a positive influence. Indeed, a comparison of the performance between those student doctors who did have a counsellor-mentor and those who did not, revealed that the performance of the former was superior in terms of depth of treatment, range of perspectives, and localization of diagnosis and treatment. It was judged that this was because the mentors and student doctors were involved in complex cases, a variety of local patients, a mix of modern medical and local treatment (based on prevalent cultural practices), and the psychological aspects of patients (so important for medical treatment). It was also evident that counsellor-mentors took greater interest in the practice of skills by individual student doctors at the workplace.

Evaluation and implications

Mentoring took the form of an informal, supportive arrangement between willing student doctors and counsellors. The evaluation was equally informal with no pretension that it represented a rigorous, carefully structured, statistically sound study. The insights provided can only be regarded as points for further investigation. A large number of mentors and student doctors were interviewed by the authors; mentoring records (reflective journals) were examined and attempts were made to determine where mentoring appeared to be effective, where it could be formalized and strengthened. Similarly, attempts were made to identify possible limitations and where its implementation was counter–productive. In this illuminative approach (Parlett and Hamilton, 1977) there were no preconceptions. The following were revealed as areas worthy of further investigation:

- The mentor's knowledge in the area of specialization (and the depth in areas of non–specialization), personal integrity, seniority and reputation influenced choice of mentor and mentoring relationship. It was dominated more by respect and less by friendship.
- Mentoring facilitated the practice of skills at SDC more times than prescribed.
- The informal mentoring situations were devoted more to application of skills in varied different ways, as negotiated by both mentor and student doctor.
- The process helped the mentors to learn to adjust to the individual learning styles and mindsets of student doctors, and to develop professionally through peer learning. The former also got to know more about effective treatment processes prevalent in rural areas.
- The mentor could help build confidence in student doctors to organize their study, practise skills and maintain logbooks; and above all, the mentor could sustain them throughout the programme.
- Since distance study for in–service professionals such as doctors involved combining study with work and with domestic, social and other commitments, both mentors and student doctors learnt from each other to deal more effectively with these demands.
- It was generally found that the combined role of counsellor-mentor was more effective and supportive than counsellor and mentor as separate roles.

During the course of our exploratory investigation several possible limitations were noted and could be considered further in any mentoring system:

- Student doctors were able to enter a mentoring relationship with any existing counsellor who was willing to extend their role to include that of mentor; this often restricted the area of specialization. The dominance of academic expectations over personal and motivational aspects caused some student doctors to withdraw from the relationship. A few mentors felt inadequate in terms of the demands made upon them and withdrew from the arrangement. However, in the majority of cases the mentoring relationship was sustained due to the voluntary choice of the mentor, and mutual commitment to continue the relationship.
- The majority of student doctors were in the age range 35–54 years. In some cases, student doctors had chosen mentors who were younger than themselves. In many of these cases the relationship was sustained but in some the student doctor withdrew. It appeared that this was a result of cultural and

social patterns rather than mentoring – where generally younger persons are expected to obey their elders.
- The lack of any coordination or dialogue between the PSC counsellor and the SDC mentor regarding assessment, grading and feedback on logbooks had an adverse effect on monitoring. Mentors in different specialized areas at the SDC compounded this, as they did not communicate between themselves.

In distance education for professionals, which combines skill training and workplace practice, effective mentoring would add pleasure and quality to the learning experience. A few suggestions from our experience may be of use:

- Mentoring needs to be built into the course design and be a compulsory part of programme implementation if it is to be effective. Further, some institutional mechanism to facilitate mentoring as a support strategy would increase its effectiveness.
- It would be useful if a mentor could specialize in more than one area of skill/subject.
- Whilst a flexible pattern of mentoring is desirable, proper coordination, monitoring, and communication between all parties is essential for effective and active learning.
- Mentors need to be provided with freedom and flexibility in choosing time, resources, styles, strategies, and even evaluation mechanisms so as to bring meaning into this personalized learning support system.

References

Parlett, M and Hamilton, D (1977) Evaluation as illumination: a new approach to the study of innovatory programmes, in *Beyond the Numbers Game*, ed D Hamilton, D Jenkins, C King, B MacDonald and M Parlett, Macmillan, London
SOHS (1996) *Background Material for MCH*, School of Health Sciences, Indira Gandhi National Open University, New Delhi

Chapter 16

Innovations in online assessment

Chris Morgan and Meg O'Reilly

Introduction

The range of innovations associated with distance and open learning in recent years is successfully overcoming one of its most significant hurdles: that of the physical separation of teachers and learners. Interaction is now readily mediated through desktop computer and network technology, and we have seen an explosion in the forms of interactions now available to distance learners who are able to be connected. Yet for all this innovation, summative assessment activities have remained relatively static in open and distance settings, and even perhaps a little conservative in comparison with assessment activities in face-to-face teaching contexts.

This is not to suggest that distance teachers are any less innovative or creative than their face-to-face counterparts. To the contrary, distance teachers and trainers face considerable challenges and a range of additional logistics in devising and facilitating sound, equitable and meaningful assessments. With the aid of computer-mediated communication, issues such as geographic dispersal of learners, inequitable access to resources, a multiplicity of contexts and work-based interests, as well as difficulties with interactions, and authentication of assessments, can be dealt with in a number of innovative ways. We refer to these strategies in our chapter as 'online learning' and 'online assessment'.

With the range of problems which distance educators face, it is not surprising that when it comes to assessment, with all its attendant pressures to ensure fairness and consistency, we opt for relatively safe and known methods such as written essays and invigilated examinations. These tried and true methods meet our immediate needs as assessors, as they are relatively equitable, and are easy to be 'processed' in educational environments where increasing enrolments and shrinking budgets seem to be the order of the day. Yet for open and distance learners these methods of assessment are quite narrow in their outcomes, and hardly reflect a commitment to openness or flexibility. If we accept that assessment drives and shapes student learning, then these methods when used as the primary forms of assessment in a programme will most likely lead to the neglect of important graduate qualities. The development of problem-solving skills, the ability to work in teams, self and peer evaluation, and a variety of communication skills such as discussion, debate, cross-cultural dialogue and the negotiation of shared meanings, have been often relegated to the 'too hard basket' by distance educators.

Practices are changing, however, and examples can be found of effective innovations in online assessment which benefit students in all study modes. The focus of this chapter is interactive assessment, which seeks to develop a broad range of abilities in distance learners, and engage them in collaborative and negotiated learning experiences. We present six case studies from Australia, the USA and The Netherlands. Each of the examples uses online learning not only as a means of enabling contact and dialogue between learners, but also to provide interactive assessment activities which add new dimensions to the learning encounter and develop important abilities in learners.

Case studies

1. Debating online with international peers (a collaborative project of University of South Australia and Governer's State University, USA)

The online assessment in this undergraduate media subject is an option students can choose if they are able to participate in an international debating team (across three universities and two continents). Teams are formed early in semester – three speakers on each side – and preparation is carried out in online areas which are private to team members. The topic (relating to the global media) is given and roles are chosen by participants. Students are not given their own choice of topic, nor do they self-select into teams. This removes the possibility for complacency and emphasizes the importance of the skills involved in developing argument, collaboration with unfamiliar team members and at times supporting contrary viewpoints to those held.

In the final two weeks of semester, the debate is carried out according to the standard protocols of formal debate, the elements of which include presentation of the affirmative and negative cases, rebuttals and summary. The event is held in an open forum asynchronously during the whole two-week period.

Debating teams are graded on two aspects:

- evidence of team interaction via private team discussion sites;
- individual contributions posted in the course of the debate.

Points are allocated for each speaker regarding the content of the argument, organization of the material and method of presentation. The winning team receives no additional marks for delivering the victorious argument; however, such success is intrinsic to students achieving high individual grades for their participation. Furthermore, marks are allocated for preparatory activities in order to assess consistent and sustained interaction throughout the semester and not just for debate performance.

The power of this assessment is the international collaboration by students on issues so inherently global in nature. Students also gain considerably from the teamwork, as they are collaboratively analysing texts, developing an argument, carrying out a formal debate in written format, engaging with multiple voices in an international arena, and are thus gaining insight first hand about globalization and the media.

2. Joining a volunteer online support service (Charles Sturt University, Australia and Syracuse University, USA)

Students in this subject are enrolled in a teacher librarian programme, and are given the option of undergoing online training for the 'KidsConnect' volunteer network. This is a question–answering, help and referral service for school children which helps them learn to navigate the Internet and supports teacher librarians to fulfil their role as providers of high-quality information services to school children. The training is provided in partnership with the Information Institute of Syracuse, Syracuse University.

Having been trained as volunteers, learners undertaking this subject complete a series of individual, customized digital reference responses to information and Internet location questions posed by school children from around the world. As a supplementary task, they also reflect upon the outcomes of their support in relation to children's needs and the implications for their role as teacher librarians.

Students are assessed according to predetermined criteria relating to their successful completion of the training programme, their preparation, research and communication of their question–answering activities, and their evaluation and reflections upon the effectiveness of the programme and of their own participation within it.

Benefits of this assessment task for learners include the opportunity to be part of a large global network of information providers and some first-hand experience in their teacher librarian role. Students are exposed to the online training of a 'real' digital reference service, which is far more developmental than completing a series of 'dummy' reference exercises set by the lecturer. They become part of a professional team, are provided with step-by-step instructions with a variety of examples on which to model their answers, and are provided with individual and immediate feedback as they compile each reply to their practice questions. As such, the assessment in this subject is very meaningful and authentic, and some learners continue their involvement well beyond the requirements of the assessment task.

3. Developing consultancy skills (Open University, The Netherlands)

This graduate subject places teams of students (four members per team) in a workplace context. The task of each team is to provide consultation to an organization or business upon an organizational problem. The problem is selected from among student nominations from their own workplace context, and is thus both an authentic issue and a scholarly question for learners to address. Students take six months to complete their placement. During this timeframe, the task of the consulting team is described as professional assistance in identifying, diagnosing and solving problems concerning various areas and aspects of management and business. An action learning cycle, in the form of orientation to the problem, action planning and implementation is the basic model within which students work towards their own learning outcomes.

Progress with the problem is undertaken and reported according to a 10-step consulting process structured in a logbook. Logbooks are available through the subject-specific Web site. Each student submits this logbook electronically and this is marked online, with formative feedback being provided in response to each submission. Through this incremental logbook process and the action learning cycle, client organizations are also empowered to learn from the experiences of students, academic staff and workplace-based managers involved in the projects.

Final submission by student teams must provide recommendations and advice to the client organization. The student also completes a self-assessment sheet which is included in the final grade. The action learning loop is completed when graded assessment for each individual student is formed from a combination of marks contributed by the client organization, fellow students in the team, the academic coach and the examiner.

4. Practising legal discourse (Macquarie University, Australia)

Communication skills within the legal profession rely on clarity and precision in both written and spoken forms. Thus the building of a substantial vocabulary of legal terms and development of appropriate skills in reasoning and argument requires consistent practice over time.

To support the development of these abilities in the course of this undergraduate subject, students are required to submit a formal written critique of 300 words every week and to contribute to a weekly informal discussion. The formal critiques are valued at 50 per cent of the final grade and the informal discussion at 10 per cent. As all critiques and contributions to discussions are assessable, the participation is regular and enthusiastic.

At the beginning of each week individual students are assigned different extracts from the study materials concerning discrimination and the law. They must post their critiques to a listserv discussion list and all other students in the cohort must comment on these. Discussion is moderated by tutors, therefore with formative feedback being regularly and quickly provided, the development of skills in legal discourse can be supported incrementally.

Students are marked according to the following criteria. Having read a piece of work and drawn out the argument, students are expected to:

- explain how the author has built the argument, what evidence was used, and how the counter-arguments were presented;
- articulate why the author's argument was convincing or unconvincing;
- make explicit the assumptions behind their own opinions and justify those assumptions;
- draw conclusions about the likely consequences or implications of their stand.

The regularity and consistency of contribution required in response to the applied questions set results in a high level of spontaneity of discussion and a considerable depth of understanding along with a willingness to support student peers. This relatively 'low-tech' application of computer-mediated communication ensures a low level of technical frustration for end-users and consequently a high level of learner control, collaboration and negotiation.

5. Solving problems and making decisions collaboratively (University of Southern Queensland, Australia)

The nursing profession by its very nature demands skills in collaboration and teamwork, the abilities to adopt a problem-solving approach and to make sound decisions based on observed and reported evidence. In this example, regular guest lecturers present authentic case studies for consideration by the student group via an online classroom. These hypothetical case studies relate to questions of law, ethics and nursing practice thus providing rich stimuli for computer-mediated discussion and the negotiation of understanding among students.

There are three 1,000-word items of assessment, one for each of the domains – law, ethics and nursing practice. In order to develop their written work, students are required to participate online by articulating their understanding of the issues in question and by reflecting and reviewing the perceptions of their peers. Through further negotiation of solutions to the problem cases presented in the online classroom, students achieve a level of critical analysis in their submitted work which incorporates:

- nature of the problem;
- issues surrounding the problem;
- alternative perceptions of the problem;
- implications of the various perceptions for nursing practice;
- evidence in the form of data and its sources;
- final position of group or individual regarding the problem case.

Once again this relatively 'low-tech' approach to supporting online dialogue fosters a context where knowledge can be shared and collaboratively constructed, and learning can be applied with direct relevance to the workplace.

6. Developing a Web site and science conference (University of Melbourne, Australia)

The development of a variety of communication skills using an increasing array of media has become an essential ability within traditional science subjects. In this agricultural science subject, students experience task-based online communication, Web-publishing and public speaking (including computer-based presentations such as Powerpoint or live on the Internet).

Each student develops a Web page in the first two weeks of semester as their personal Web-based communication springboard. They then collaborate with their peers to select a popular and contemporary discipline-based theme, instigate and organize a conference around this theme and invite keynote speakers from industry to add practical substance to the programme.

The development of a Web site also occurs throughout semester in support of the live conference event scheduled for the end of semester. The conference programme is published, registrations are taken, abstracts are published and peer reviewed and finally the full papers are published as conference proceedings – all online. Each of these steps carries a weighting towards assessment.

Papers may be co-authored, with each student working with up to two co-authors. After papers are published on the Internet and presented at the conference, they are assessed by two appointed peers and a staff member. The instrument for this component of assessment is designed by students. The final component of assessment requires students to submit a self-evaluation of the value of their own contribution to their community of peers.

This scheme involves continuous assessment throughout the semester enabling the provision of extensive formative feedback. Marks are made available on the Internet, further facilitating a rapid review by students of their ongoing work. Final grades are determined through a synthesis of input by staff, student peers and self-assessment.

Discussion

Each of these case studies presents innovations which push the boundaries of the traditional paper-based distance learning experience. Where distance learners have traditionally worked individually, and perhaps in some isolation, with little or no interaction with their student peers, learning in these cases consists of social, participatory encounters. Assessment events are no longer viewed as an add-on to the teaching and learning materials. Rather, they are integral to the design and structure of the subject, capitalizing on the knowledge that it will drive and shape learning outcomes more effectively than the volumes of directed study materials traditionally offered in distance education. These assessments encourage purposeful dialogue, multiple discourses, collaboration, peer and self-evaluation, and contribute to a sense of community and shared purpose amongst distance learners, in contrast to the individualism that characterizes much of the traditional distance education experience. Some of these elements are considered in more detail below:

- *Purposeful dialogue.* There is little doubt that the principal advantage of online learning for distance learners is the expanded opportunity for interaction and dialogue with teachers and peers. In many instances this is reflected by the development of discussion lists which encourage learners to contribute comments and interact with their peers in relatively unstructured ways. As valuable as this is as a form of interaction, these case studies exemplify ways in which dialogue can be employed more purposefully to create rich collaborative processes and products such as an international debate, negotiated problem solving, provision of professional services, peer evaluation, and so forth. In these instances the challenges for teachers lie in their capacity to facilitate and manage these potentially complex encounters effectively, as well as to develop and communicate appropriate criteria upon which students are to be assessed for their interactive and collaborative efforts. For distance learners, particularly those who are used to 'going it alone', there will be new challenges presented by learning that is participatory and more paced than former print-based experiences.
- *Multiple voices.* Case study 6, the Web site and conference, provides us with an excellent metaphor for the potential richness of online discourse. Although print-based materials provide learners with varieties of guided conversation, the voice of the teacher or course writer has been the dominant, and perhaps overwhelming, voice in the encounter. This can lead to learners adopting an uncritical stance in relation to the subject matter and a tendency to adopt surface or reproductive learning strategies. These case studies provide examples of attempts to broaden this discourse to admit a variety of new voices, such as student peers, practitioners, international colleagues, guest presenters and so forth. Ideally the teacher's views sit side by side with a range of others, jostling for attention by persuasiveness of argu-

ment. In such instances learners are exposed to the subject matter in a more problematic and critical light, and are encouraged to engage more deeply with issues.

● *Authentic tasks*. Authentic assessment tasks are ones that encourage learners to apply their learning in 'real life' settings, often requiring a complex blend of higher-order knowledge and skills. Authentic tasks such as applied teamwork and collaborative decision making, for example, are often required in many vocational and professional settings, yet are rarely assessed in distance education programmes, due to obvious difficulties. Online technologies have significantly increased the opportunities for authentic assessments, and hence we see some interesting examples in these case studies, such as the provision of consultancy by learners to real organizations, supplying online support to children learning to navigate the Internet, or collaboratively publishing in a professional journal. These assessments draw together a range of knowledge and skills to address often complex and ill-structured issues and problems that are more reflective of the working world. As authentic tasks are often complex with potentially many variables, judgement of student achievement is more likely to be open to interpretation than that of smaller, discrete tasks. The challenge is for teachers to devise marking criteria that are sufficiently broad to cover most situations, yet detailed enough that they are useful and provide guidance to students.

● *Cross-cultural dialogue*. New learning opportunities for international dialogue and collaboration have also emerged from Internet technology. Learners in some of these case studies have enjoyed opportunities to learn directly about other cultures through shared learning tasks. Discipline areas such as medicine, science, arts, politics, media and business have long-established global information and discussion networks and many contemporary issues of international relevance. In case study 1, for example, learners undertake an online debate with participants from three universities spanning two countries, requiring learners to develop a broader contextual perspective upon the issues. Cross-cultural dialogue may also challenge learners to develop more advanced skills in intercultural communication, to negotiate difference, and to confront cultural and racial stereotypes.

● *Peer and self-assessment*. The capacity to reflect upon and evaluate one's own work and that of one's peers is an important ability of any adult learner. Unless residential schools are facilitated for this purpose, distance learners have traditionally had little opportunity for this kind of assessment. As Boud (1986) notes, self-assessment is as much a learning process as it is an assessment process. Self and peer assessment helps learners to make judgements, to become more self-sufficient in their work, to take responsibility for their learning, and encourages learners to engage with others about their work (Gibbs, 1995). It is greatly assisted by the use of guidelines, criteria or standards that support the development of this ability. Through computer-mediated communications, distance learners now have the opportunity to preview or review the work of their student peers, and in addition to this, the online medium can also efficiently support the iterative and confidential process which peer and self-review usually requires.

- *Wider development of abilities.* Traditionally, open and distance learning has relied heavily on 'pen and paper' assessments such as essays, journals, projects and invigilated exams. Distance learners undoubtedly become very adept over time at structured written communications. But what of other skills such as problem solving, collaborative skills, oral communications, group facilitation and decision making, peer evaluation and support, to name but a few of the skills and abilities which society and employers have come to expect of its graduates? These cases represent a significantly broader repertoire of assessment methods which promote skills development for distance learners in a range of new directions. These skills and abilities are highly relevant to their discipline areas and are developed in applied contexts to provide added meaning and purpose to the exercise.

Despite the exciting range of new opportunities which online assessment presents, our enthusiasm should be tempered by some caution, to ensure that we are not undermining some of the existing strengths of traditional open and distance learning. For example, if the online medium becomes the principal or sole vehicle for learning and assessment, we may be denying access to learners in remote and non-technologically serviced areas, or to people who are unable to make the necessary investment in computing facilities, or to those who do not have the kind of technological literacy or confidence to master this medium of learning. Another strength which may be undermined is the relative flexibility and autonomy which distance learners have traditionally enjoyed. Distance learners now engaged in interactive and collaborative assessments will be more paced and structured in their studies, more akin to scheduled weekly classes. This may present tensions for learners who prefer to 'go it alone', particularly if they are already juggling a range of work and family commitments. Interactive and collaborative opportunities may also be resisted by distance learners if they seem tangential to their core purposes of study.

Conclusion

The successful creation of a community of learners is perhaps the central achievement in these case studies. Learners have the opportunity to express and debate ideas, to expand their thinking and understanding of subject matter, to collaborate with others, and to deepen their approach to assessment. The idea of a virtual community is only limited by one's imagination, and can be created to include not only teachers and learners, but participants in related programmes, resource experts, vocational or professional representatives, community and interest groups, international scholars and the like.

It has been necessary for innovators in these case studies to reconceptualize their teaching and learning activities to exploit the online medium effectively. There is a new learning context (an interconnected community rather than a series of individual learners), a new medium to explore (the World Wide Web, listservs, e-mail, course delivery tools), and new ways in which learners go about their learning (higher levels of interaction and collaboration). This rethink includes a consideration of subject aims and objectives, learners' needs and interests, approaches to the provision of course content and materials, facilitation of the teaching and learning environment and the most appropriate forms of assessment to promote and support these new objectives and learning arrangements. If distance teaching and assessment practices are not reconceptualized in this way, we are not likely to gain the benefits of the medium, nor are we likely to persuade learners to make the leap to online learning, when there are no tangible benefits or enhanced opportunities compared to print-based learning.

Acknowledgements

The authors wish to acknowledge gratefully the generous contribution of case study details by Ingrid Day (University of South Australia), Lyn Hay (Charles Sturt University), Kathleen Schlusmans and Jos Rikers (Open University, The Netherlands), Archana Parashar and Robyn Phillip (Macquarie University), Mary Oliver (University of Southern Queensland) and Glyn Rimmington (Melbourne University). The cases reported are taken from the work of Morgan and O'Reilly (1999).

References

Boud, D (1986) *Implementing Student Self-Assessment*, HERDSA Green Guide No. 5, Canberra ACT
Gibbs, G (1995) *Assessing Student Centred Courses*, Oxford Centre for Staff Development, Oxford Brookes University, Oxford
Morgan, C and O'Reilly, M (1999) *Assessing Open and Distance Learners*, Kogan Page, London

Chapter 17

VESOL: cost-effective video production to support distance learners

Patrick McGhee and Christopher O'Hagan

Introduction

VESOL is a set of online video–editing systems which enable lecturers to record and edit their presentations during delivery without the need for any technical assistance or post-production editing (O'Hagan, 1995a, 1995b). Videotapes produced with the system can be viewed by students at home, in study resource centres or in collaborative study groups as resource-based learning materials or revision aids. While the VESOL system requires little initial training for either academics or students to get started, the system is designed to support progressively more sophisticated uses, both technically in terms of the incorporation of multiple inputs such as data display and Internet connection, and pedagogically in terms of delivery structure, pace, cross-reference and timings. The system is flexible, robust and cost-effective but most importantly it maximizes academic autonomy in the production of video-based learning resources. The system is equally well suited for the production of learning resources in traditional, open or distance delivery contexts. A basic system can cost as little as $12,000.

While we have described and evaluated the actual and potential uses of VESOL in traditional contexts elsewhere (O'Hagan, 1995a; McGhee, 1998) this paper will review the use of VESOL in open and distance learning contexts. We will illustrate how VESOL enables the re-examination of some common assumptions about the efficacy of open and distance learning.

The identified need

VESOL was developed in recognition of the difficulties faced by academics in the production of video learning resources. The two conventional options are either to buy off-the-shelf commercially distributed videos or to produce videos in-house. Both of these possibilities present significant difficulties.

Purchasing videos produced externally has the advantage usually (but not always) of high production values, reviews of previous users and ease of acquisition, which should lead to appropriate and effective choices to fit the curriculum and a range of playback options. In practice these advantages are not always realized, however, for several reasons. High production values for educational video usually mean that a very wide audience is anticipated to generate sales to cover the high costs. This often leads to a dilution and 'popularization' of the educational content and thus the production of what is sometimes termed edutainment – too facile and too generic. Even the best programmes can compress too much material into a short time. These difficulties can make it hard for the tutor to use such video material for focused learning experiences, linked to specific outcomes.

Educational video is probably at its most effective when it provides a 'first-order' record of *phenomena* which while not educational in themselves, provide the raw material for subsequent exploitation by the academic tutor to demonstrate key *concepts*. Examples of such 'first-order' material might be archive footage of modern historical events, natural history footage of species in their natural habitat or an illustration of technical processes. Such archival or technical resources are not in themselves educational. They need to be rendered educational through focused work by tutors.

However, a further problem for commercial videos is copyright restrictions, which limit the options to edit the material to make it more educationally relevant, or to convert it to other formats, or to make it available to large numbers of students, without incurring substantial additional costs.

Consequently, educational institutions have often sought to produce their own material, because it can be precisely tailored to needs and copyright is in-house. Contracting out is usually a prohibitively expensive option, but equally in-house production incurs substantial capital and staffing costs. Standard video production commissioned by academic institutions for educational use can cost up to £25,000 per hour once sound recordist, camera persons, scripting, academic's time, pre-production, and post-production costs are included. Costs are not the only problem. The human and technical resources required are significant and complex to coordinate and the individual academic has little or no control over these resources. Additionally, unlike the production of say a new brochure for a conference or new course where university systems and practices are likely to be well established, recognized and costed, the production of video requires extensive negotiations across academic, administrative and technical boundaries. Thus any academic seeking to produce relevant educational videos for his or her students is likely to lose control over the project very quickly – always assuming that he or she manages to secure the resources required in the first place.

There are simpler ways of producing video resources from 'found' materials where copyright restrictions allow (as under the Educational Recording Agency licence in the UK) (O'Hagan, 1994). However, many distance learning providers would like to have easy access to a facility for producing an integrated learning package on videocassette incorporating the lecturer as a talking head, print and electronic data inputs and high-quality reproduction of standard acetates and whiteboards. VESOL provides such a facility and avoids many of the logistical, economic and pedagogical problems inherent in alternative systems for the provision of video-based learning packages.

Making videos of lectures in lecture theatres (as opposed to recording studios) by bringing cameras in on an *ad hoc* basis is much cheaper and easier to organize. However, the results are often disappointing, usually amounting to a fixed-shot of the lecturer sometimes with inaudible sound and often with illegible overheads. Technicians have to be booked and students briefed in advance. Further, if after viewing the tape the result is considered unsatisfactory then, given that the rebooking of technicians and the equipment is difficult, the lecturer is likely to abandon the project and is unlikely to attempt to repeat it. As a consequence there is typically no development of skill or confidence. While taping lectures can be successful with dedicated technical staff, enthusiastic lecturers, patient students and a great deal of luck, it has to be recognized that aspirations to *routine* in-house cost-effective production of lectures *in situ* are unrealistic.

In relation to distance learning the production of videocassettes for mailing to students is an oft-mooted but seldom tried project simply because access to and control of technical resources are limited. The UK Open University does use this method as well as broadcasting, but has access to massive resources, including those of the BBC. Their success in using video and television has ironically hindered those without such resources because it has set a kind of standard. Until VESOL challenged it, there was an assumption that video programmes in education had to be to 'broadcast standards'. This may be true for entertainment, and for 'art', but it need not be the case for learning resources. A comparison with print media in education would confirm such a view – a very wide range of different qualities is used. The development of VESOL and its offshoots was partly motivated by the notion of fitness-for-purpose with which we are quite familiar in print-based media.

The VESOL system

The VESOL system has been designed to overcome many of these problems and misguided expectations associated with the routine production of video learning materials based around taught sessions.

The basic VESOL system involves four cameras linked to a single control unit on a standard lecture theatre lectern. Camera 1 is a motorized camera usually fixed to the rear wall of the lecture theatre which, although normally set to a close-up of the lecturer, can zoom in and out, or pan and tilt around the room. Camera 2 is set to a wide-angle shot of the whole of the front of the lecture theatre. Camera 3 gives a fixed image of a standard whiteboard/slide projection screen or equivalent. Camera 4 is a rostrum camera, with motorized zoom, fixed to the ceiling located directly above the lectern itself, capable of imaging text and figures on paper or overhead transparencies. This rostrum arrangement is more secure and flexible than a standard bought-in document presenter. Output from one of the cameras is chosen as required by pressing one of four large buttons on the lectern, and the selected image is sent to the video recorder (VCR). A fifth button allows input from a computer or VCR. When the rostrum camera is selected it sends a shot of any documents, objects or demonstrations on the lectern to the master tape and *simultaneously* sends the same image, via a video projector, to the main screen of the lecture theatre. The house lights are automatically dimmed to a suitable pre-set level, in order to facilitate viewing by a live audience, if there is one. The system incorporates a small clip-on radio microphone which sends an audio signal to the master tape. The output from the system is an immediate online edited tape of the lecture with high-quality sound, smooth edits and a range of camera angles. The lecturer needs to do no more than press Start, Stop and the five output buttons. The audio track is crucial in maintaining continuity across cuts between cameras. O'Hagan (1995b) provides a description of the process from the moment the lecturer arrives in the lecture theatre.

Videos can be made of scheduled lectures with students present in order to facilitate revision by students or to present the same lecture to several groups of students. Alternatively lectures can be recorded without students present in order to maximize staff and student availability on part-time or modular courses. However, the system supports a myriad of other uses in traditional contexts, including staff development for inexperienced lectures, self-assessment for trainee teachers and preparation for students working on class presentations.

Other versions of the system include VELAB and MiniVESOL. The former is designed for recording laboratory or workshop-based sessions. These venues have permanent cabling, and the cameras are mounted when required. The editing and recording equipment is built into a portable trolley which also stores the cameras when not in use. Video recordings can be made of complex, expensive and audience-inaccessible demonstrations (O'Hagan, 1995c), The use of VELAB highlights an important advantage of in-house video production over commercially available videos. With VELAB specific health, safety and operational information relevant to local laboratories, procedures and personnel can be made (and updated as necessary).

MiniVESOL is a system built into a small room, approximately 3m by 3m, with just one fully motorized camera for the presenter, a rostrum camera with motorized zoom, and a computer with remote screen–control enabling overlays and dissolve with another input, plus ability to move and zoom around the screen image. This is a state-of-the-art system which allows the methodical production of videos in private. Presenters can practise until they get it right, whereas the lecture theatre systems are really 'warts and all'.

Applicability of VESOL to open and distance learning environments

VESOL lends itself particularly well to the production of open and distance learning materials:

- Video records of normal scheduled lecture series can be held in resource centres along with accompanying notes. These can support student revision, consolidation of earlier work within the same academic programme, access to taught sessions in related modules from other programmes of study, and access to taught sessions missed due to student illness or personal circumstances (O'Hagan, 1997). If multiple copies are made for loan or postal distribution, they enable access by part-time students or distance learners to material normally only available to full-time students.
- Short, focused videotaped tutorials which address a specific topic or teaching need are readily made. Students would not normally be present while such sessions are being recorded, perhaps using a MiniVESOL system. Examples of this use might be the making of a tape on research ethics in a social science discipline which is relevant to all years of study for all social science students, or the production of 'learning to learn' programmes for all beginning students. Instructions and guides for courses, modules, key topics, assignments etc in distance programmes are also easily produced.
- VESOL enables the production of short clips of teaching points which can be digitized and incorporated into multimedia packages or Internet open or distance learning resources. In fact, it is relatively easy to convert whole tutorials, because there is a base 'track' of both sound and image for the courseware developer to work from – no need for complex discussions between intellectual authors and technical authors.
- Videotaped feedback on coursework can be provided for the student with the tutor going through the script under the document camera while talking through the strengths, weaknesses and areas for development. MiniVESOL was invented with this use in mind. It is widely recognized that critical written feedback can come across as more negative than intended, because

the usual tone of voice and facial expression cues are missing. Not only does VESOL reinstate these crucial contextual signals, but the quality and quantity of feedback that can be given is also much greater. More can be spoken in the time it usually takes to write simple comments, and it is easier to qualify statements in some detail. Specific examples from the script can be highlighted on screen. A student can replay the tape and its comments as often as is required.

● Students can put not just faces, but personalities, to names – which facilitates greater approachability of teaching staff by telephone, e-mail or paper correspondence. VESOL tapes can be particularly beneficial for induction and orientation purposes where traditionally new students on distance learning programmes are inundated with forms and booklets. When VESOL is used as part of the initial introduction to a programme of distance study, the tutor can hold up a copy of each document as it is being referred to, helping the student to find their way through extensive mailings. While this might sound trivial, demystifying the bureaucracy of distance learning for remote learners is probably one of the more unexamined problems in the area of distance learning.

The key feature of VESOL in distance learning contexts is that it enables the production of video for learning even when student numbers are small, time schedules are tight and material requires regular updating. Traditional studio-based production is only economically justifiable when numbers are higher, extensive forward planning is possible and the material has a long shelf life.

Over the past four decades extensive studies have been made into the use of television and video in distance learning contexts. There is no convincing evidence that these media do not facilitate learning as effectively as any other method, provided they are used appropriately and with careful attention to learning outcomes. A useful summary of these studies can be found in Russell (1999). VESOL enables such careful customization of video to specific outcomes.

Illustrations

VESOL for open learning – child psychology

As part of the original evaluation programme of VESOL, student performance in a University of Derby Child Psychology module presented in traditional format was compared with the same module delivered through open learning using VESOL the following year. The lectures in the first year were recorded on VESOL and used the following year as resource-based learning materials (with no live lectures being given). Statistical analysis of student performance indicated that there were no significant differences overall between module grades in each mode (McGhee, 1998).

VESOL for generic skills development

The Educational Development Unit (EDU) at the University of Central England made a series of 20-minute programmes on Learning to Learn. These were used by normal subject lecturers to introduce new students to both research on learning styles and practical skills. They were also accessible by students independently. From the first release they were in great demand and half a dozen copies were soon in regular use. Within three months it was estimated that well over 1,000 students had seen them – many more than had been able to attend sessions previously provided by EDU staff.

VESOL for distance learning – postgraduate social science

Bolton Institute runs an MSc in Critical Psychology by distance learning. VESOL has been used to produce a critical review of American Psychology Association and British Psychological Society ethics codes. A distinctive feature of this programme is the opportunity to show the actual printed publications on camera and draw students' attention to significant features, which would not have been as simple using any other medium. Feedback on students' essays have also been provided using VESOL with each student getting customized feedback on video sent to their home address.

Implications of VESOL for distance learning

Interactivity and deep learning

One of the arguments against the use of linear video programmes is that they are not 'interactive', and it is then argued that interactivity is necessary for deep learning. This challenge itself has a narrow understanding of interactivity and of the relation between activity/interactivity and deep learning. Firstly, many conventional lectures have little interactivity between teacher and learners, partly because the learners are nervous of exposing their 'ignorance' in front of both their teacher (who may also be an assessor) and their peers. In a study of the impact of VESOL at Derby one student commented that he found the video-tapes 'more interactive': we understood him to be saying that he had control of his pace of learning with the tape, because he could review sections until fully grasped. Thus it might be argued that videotapes of lectures replace one form of interactivity with another form, potentially more significant, because student control of the pace of learning is more likely to assist engagement with the material than the occasional question. Secondly, one of the most constructive interactions is between learners, because it is a dialogue between equals seeking understanding, and this is readily stimulated between two or more students watching a video (without a tutor's presence), again promoting engagement with the material.

In fact it is this engagement, not the interactivity which may or may not promote it, that is the key to deep learning. All learning is linear in time, and arguing that linear video is 'less interactive' than non-linear video is as absurd as arguing that because a book is written linearly its argument is linear. The interactivity between mind and material comes from the way the author stimulates the viewer/reader to engage and think about the material and the way the argument is structured in relation to what the student already knows. Non-linear systems like hypermedia easily lose the learner because of the loosely structured context, and thus may confuse rather than engage.

How VESOL addresses the challenges to deep learning in distance learning

Encouraging deep rather than surface learning is a challenge to the designer of any learning materials. VESOL provides a means to address these problems by capitalizing on (1) its distinctive customisability of tapes, (2) high visual impact, (3) student control of pace of learning, and (4) the ability to direct student tasks from the screen, or the accompanying materials.

While there are many elaborations of methods of promoting deep, as opposed to surface, learning based on a constructivist understanding of learning, the model articulated in the Macfarlane report (Committee of Scottish University Principals, 1994) is one of the most useful in applied contexts, particularly where learning technologies are concerned. Drawing upon a range of educational research the Macfarlane report argued that deep learning, considered as a thorough conceptual understanding, required a set a seven phases of tutor input. These phases provide an analytical framework for drawing useful distinctions between the functions of different kinds of teaching inputs. The seven phases identified are Orientating, Motivating, Presenting, Clarifying, Elaborating, Consolidating and Confirming. While each of these phases provides challenges for all modes of delivery they involve particular challenges for tutors working in distance learning modes. While print or Internet-based distance learning programmes can and do address some of these challenges, we seek to identify in Table 17.1 the distinctive ways in which these challenges can be addressed by VESOL.

Distance and immediacy

Pedagogically the least interesting thing about distance learning is the distance itself. To describe learning as 'open' or 'at a distance' is not to describe it at all. Both these terms are attempts to describe the *absences* in new forms of learning when compared to a traditional model. (Where precisely is the learning that is 'closed' or 'proximate'?) The important issues of open and distance learning are not the openness or distance but the relationship of learning process to *time* and, specifically, the temporal structure of tutor–student interaction. What underpins learning in *any* mode is the conversational structure or learning dialogue that

Table 17.1 *Challenges addressed by VESOL*

Phases of teaching associated with support for deep conceptual understanding	Phases involve	Particular challenges for distance learning delivery	VESOL offers
Orientating	Setting the scene	Students are anxious and have no prior experience	Human embodiment of welcoming and orientating material. High impact initial presentation
Motivating	Pointing up relevance, evoking and sustaining interest	Students studying in isolation with other distractions can't focus on relevance	Enthusiasm can be conveyed with more immediacy – local features can be harnessed
Presenting	Introducing new knowledge within a clear supportive structure	Student has limited or no access to supporting materials or learning events	Detailed information can be annotated through voice-over and student can replay tape as required
Clarifying	Explaining with examples and providing remedial support	Limited range of examples which can be presented in print. Examples become dated	Examples can be 3-dimensional and dynamic – and regularly updated
Elaborating	Introducing additional material to develop more detailed knowledge	Student has to pursue cross reference to original material	Original material (or footage) can be incorporated in new 'elaborating phase' and/or student can review earlier 'presenting' tape as required
Consolidating	Providing opportunities to develop and test personal understanding	Distance learning materials difficult to customise	Tutor can direct student to take time out of watching tape to pursue linked activity with personal relevance
Confirming	Ensuring the adequacy of the knowledge and understanding reached	Difficult to motivate students to check their own learning as material in 'self test boxes' has limited reference points and illustrative material	Built–in self assessments are routinely available and student can control own pace through material. Motivation for self-assessment is high as test materials may have high visual impact

occurs between tutor and student (Laurillard, 1993). Learning based around resources does not face the challenge of being effective in the absence of interactivity, as we argued earlier, but the challenge to the tutor, as manifested in the resources, to engage the learner in a dialogue between mind and resources. We will here deconstruct this further.

It is easy to forget the preconditions and assumptions of learning that are embedded in the traditional modes of delivery – the architecture and dramaturgy of the lecture theatre, the ritual of small-group seminars, the etiquette of tutorials. The social organization of university teaching and learning draws upon and reproduces the social structures and role relationships of the society in which it is located. There is nothing 'essential' about the kinds of communicative exchanges that occur within such learning settings. An active learner is a learner who actively engages cognitively with information, not a learner who asks 'appropriate and interesting' questions in seminars.

Much thinking about distance learning assumes the taken-for-granted nature of institutional campus learning, and seeks to measure effective distance learning by the extent it *reproduces* the learning experiences of campus students, in the mistaken belief that what are in fact social constructions are intrinsic and necessary properties of effective learning.

VESOL may on the surface look as though it seeks to reproduce the learning events traditionally associated with campus-based learning. In fact it enables us to rethink and reinvent many of the learning events as learning conversations. Both the lecturer and the student can control the passage of time as embodied in the video in a way that is not possible in face-to-face communication. The lecturer can stop and start again in order to better gather her thoughts as she makes a video. The student can stop or start the tutor's input at will to reflect his own learning style or learning environment. Most importantly the lecturer can invite the student to suspend time by taking 'time out' of the session and pursuing a related activity, returning to the tape when the activity is complete. The interactivity made possible by VESOL draws on the elasticity of time inherent in video resources and deconstructs the apparent lack of interactivity implied by the geographical distance between lecturer and student.

VESOL provides distance learners and their tutors with the opportunity to incorporate psychological salience, immediacy and personal relevance in ways that print or commercial video cannot.

We would emphasize that VESOL does not draw upon an essentially 'better' or more robust form of interactivity than that offered by print, commercial video, traditional lecture or seminar formats or any other mode. Interactivity in general and interactivity for learning in particular must be contextualized in relation to learners' resources for interpreting, decoding and thinking through different formats of information presentation.

Comparison of VESOL with the problems of interactivity of the World Wide Web is interesting in this regard. The unstructured nature makes it very difficult for students to acquire effective models for structuring information into knowledge, and if courseware developers introduce too many hyperlinks the student may end up 'lost in hyperspace'. By contrast the effectiveness of VESOL is precisely that, like a book, it is linear in format and thus easy to use, but can put forward information in non-linear, branched ways which are clear to the student.

Of course there is scope for combining video-based learning and Web-based learning in interesting and effective ways. We consider now the potential role for VESOL in supporting distance learning in Internet contexts.

VESOL, bandwidths and bottlenecks

Much discussion on the current and potential use of the Internet for learning revolves around a cluster of technical issues centring on the availability of bandwidth. Technological optimists argue that progress will lead to progressively greater bandwidths enabling multimedia applications to be accessed and explored routinely by all. Pessimists argue that demand will always outstrip supply as, for example, 3D and virtual reality applications grow increasingly more demanding, and more and more users send more and more documents around hyperspace. None of the solutions to these technological problems is education-driven. The future of bandwidth depends on whether the Internet is dominated by electronic entertainment (which requires high bandwidth) or by e-commerce (which doesn't).

But the problems facing educational developers relate more to getting the material produced in the first place than to piping it through the Internet. The issue as to whether the Internet can cope with video communication for learning is irrelevant if good quality, cost-effective and customized educational video materials cannot be produced in the first place. VESOL provides the means by which learning materials can be produced in a manner that reflects the learners' needs in specified learning contexts.

Summary

VESOL is an innovative and robust video production system which enables good quality, cost-effective educational video to be created by academics in ways that reflect local circumstances and support identified learning outcomes. The system is well suited to distance delivery contexts and offers fresh approaches to addressing some of the distinctive challenges of remote learning.

References

Committee of Scottish University Principals (1994) *Macfarland Report*
Laurillard, D (1993) *Rethinking University Teaching: A framework for the effective use of educational technology*, Routledge, London ISBN 0415092892

McGhee P (1997) Resource based learning as a management issue, in *Flexible Learning in Action – Case studies in higher education*, ed R Hudson, S E Maslin Prothero and L Oates, Kogan Page, London, ISBN 07494 239 19

McGhee P (1998) Producing video resources for the psychology curriculum: an exploration in lecturer autonomy, in *Innovations in Teaching Psychology*, ed J Radford, J Rowe and D van Laar, SEDA Publications, Birmingham, ISBN 1 902435 01 X

O'Hagan, C M (1994) The use and abuse of video recordings in education, in *Aspects of Educational and Training Technology XXVII: Designing for learning*, ed R Hoey, pp 220–25, Kogan Page, London, ISBN 0 7494 11147

O'Hagan, C M (1995a) Video auto-editing system for open learning (VESOL), in *Aspects of Educational and Training Technology XXVIII: Computer assisted and open access education*, ed F Percival, R Land and D Edgar-Nevill, pp 236–42, Kogan Page, London, ISBN 0 7494 1414 6

O'Hagan, C M (1995b) Custom videos for flexible learning, *Innovations in Education and Training International*, **32** (2), May, pp 131–38, ISSN 1355 8005

O'Hagan, C M (1995c) Video Enhanced Laboratory (VELAB), in *Empowering Teachers and Learners Through Technology*, ed C M O'Hagan, pp 91–97, SEDA Publications, Birmingham, ISBN 0 946815 14 3

O'Hagan, C M (1997) Adapting existing content using VESOL, in *Online Educa 1997*, pp 173–75, International Where and How, Germany, ISBN 3 925144 09 9

Russell T L (1999) *The No Significant Difference Phenomenon: a comparative research bibliography on technology for distance education*, North Carolina State University, North Carolina, ISBN 0 9668936 0 3

Chapter 18

Supporting effective reading of pictorial materials in visually oriented learning environments

Ric Lowe

This chapter deals with approaches for helping learners to 'read' sophisticated visual displays that are normally difficult for the uninitiated to interpret. The context of the innovation described here is a multimedia-based training package for chemical process industries. The target audience for this package is trainees lacking background in the highly specialized form of pictorial representation used to portray process control systems on computer screens. Trainees need to be able to use these complex, abstract types of diagrammatic information as a tool for learning how to become process control operators. The approach in this innovation is based on (a) challenging prevailing notions about the role that pictorial information plays in learning and (b) questioning assumptions about the extent to which pictures can be expected to be self-explanatory. It was assumed that the package would need to develop trainees' domain-specific picture-reading skills before they could use process control diagrams presented during training as effective resources for learning about process control itself. The presentation strategies used took account of what trainees (who were novices in the content domain) would be likely to do when first faced with an unfamiliar, abstract pictorial representation. From that starting point, the strategies helped trainees to build up an interpretation of the depicted content using approaches designed to keep the cognitive processing load within reasonable bounds. Subsequent development of trainees' reading skills involved a 'considerate' exposition of the content using extensive aural and visual support to address learner needs typically not considered by subject matter experts.

Need for this innovation

Conventional wisdom is that pictorial representations in general have an intrinsic instructional effectiveness as a way of presenting unfamiliar or difficult subject matter. However, until quite recently, publishers of instructional resources tended to use pictures very sparingly because of their high cost relative to alternative means of presenting information (particularly text). In the past few years, technological advances have essentially eliminated this cost differential while also making it far easier to produce and use pictures for publications. The result has been a rapidly increasing reliance on pictorial representation to carry the responsibility for dealing with various types of instructional content. This shift has occurred both in traditional print materials and in the newer forms of electronic publishing. In the latter case, new technologies have provided powerful ways to manipulate visual information that open up the vast instructional potential of dynamic, interactive pictures. However, for such potential to be realized, this application of technology to pictorial presentation needs to be done well. Producers of training materials have wasted no time in adopting this technology so that highly pictorial approaches to presenting subject matter are now the rule rather than an exception. Unfortunately, much of this swing toward more pictorial treatments has not been informed by a principled understanding of how people learn (or fail to learn) from pictures. Rather, it seems to be driven largely by a mixture of naive intuitions about the instructional efficacy of pictures and the technical capacity to include them cheaply and easily.

In recent years there has been a growth in research activity dealing with how people process explanatory pictures (eg Schnotz and Kulhavy, 1994). The findings from this research should make instructional designers wary of simplistic, generalized assumptions about the instructional efficacy of pictures. In particular, it is now clear that people do not always find that pictures act simply as facilitators of learning. Indeed, the reverse may be true. For example, learners can find it particularly challenging to interpret the specialized or technical pictures (such as diagrams) found across a wide range of subject disciplines. These types of pictures are typically included by authors of instruction with the aim of making the content more accessible. However, many of these explanatory visuals can be so impenetrable to those who are not immersed in the content domain that they instead act as barriers to learning. In this sense, the visuals themselves (as opposed to what they depict) actually become part of the to-be-learned content. Unless learners are taught the specialized knowledge and skills required to interpret these visuals satisfactorily, the information they depict can remain inaccessible as a resource for learning. Unfortunately, the prevailing view is that pictures in general function as instructional solutions (rather than as a potential source of instructional problems). The fact that *some* pictures can have a powerful facilitative effect on learning is over-generalized to apply to pictures that in fact can pose considerable interpretative challenges. This undiscriminating attitude has meant that until very recently, important aspects of what is required to learn effectively from visual materials have been largely neglected by educational researchers. Consequently, even if instructional designers do accept that some visuals can be problematic, there is no extensive body of readily available guidance as to how this situation might be tackled. The development discussed in this chapter is presented as a first step in providing such guidance. It offers some possible approaches for supporting the learning of specialized visual reading capacities that are both principled in their origins and generalizable in their application.

Reading process control diagrams

Distributed Control Systems are widespread in the chemical and similar industries. They are a means by which an operator situated remotely from the equipment in a processing plant can both monitor and control the operation of that equipment. The process operator situated in the control room works from a computer screen that diagrammatically displays important summary information about equipment status and processes. Due to the complexity of processing plants, the screen display can only ever represent a small fraction of the full situation in a plant. By interacting with this display in real time, the remote operator can make adjustments necessary to maintain optimum product output and ensure plant safety.

Figure 18.1 is an example of the type of display that these operators work with and shows the abstract manner used to depict items of plant equipment and relevant associated information. It depicts a pump (top) connected by a pipe to a water tank (middle) which in turn is connected to a control valve (bottom). Although Figure 18.1 is shown as a static representation, in reality the operator's display is continually changing. Because process control displays are a moment-to-moment representation of the many interactive changes that occur as the plant operates, operators must deal with a continually varying set of visual information. A full appreciation of the complex demands these displays make on operators needs to take account of this highly dynamic nature. A large part of this complexity comes about because the diagrammatic representations that depict the process being controlled are interactive as well as dynamic. As the display

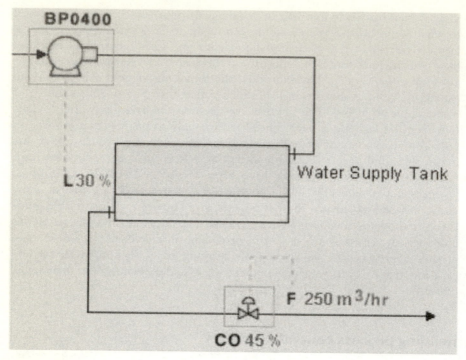

Figure 18.1 *Example of display*

changes, the operator must interact with it to control the process and this interaction results in additional changes that show up in multiple locations across the
display. Further, there is far more to these displays than immediately meets the
eye. This is because they contain hidden levels of information that appear only
when called up by the operator as needed. As a consequence, these displays have
an embedded complexity that is not initially apparent. For example, in the case
of Figure 18.1, additional information about the pump (symbol near the top left
labelled BP0400) can be obtained by mouse-clicking it. This action brings up a
further sub-panel that specifies and controls the mode of the pump (manual or
automatic) as well as its current operational status (on or off).

With so much happening in the display at once, it is essential that the operator
is able to 'read' the display efficiently and quickly to make sense of information
that is most relevant at any given moment. Extracting this relevant information
from such rich and complex displays is a highly demanding process, especially if
they are dynamic (see Lowe, 1999). It requires a highly strategic approach that
goes beyond merely recognizing the individual diagrammatic symbols. Many
different types of relationships are involved that concern both the graphic material on the display screen and the functioning equipment systems depicted by
the diagrammatic representation. To prepare would-be process control operators
properly, training resources should ideally address (albeit in a simplified way) the

types of demands that they will encounter in their working environment. This means that the dynamic, interactive character of process control displays needs to be a feature of the training materials. The *Smart Operator*™ multimedia training resource that is the subject of this chapter (Lowe and Neilsen, 1998; http://www.cbt.com.au/index.html) was designed with this ideal in mind and includes elementary process control simulation exercises guided by an embedded expert system-based mentoring facility as part of the instruction. *Smart Operator*™ targets an audience of non-specialist personnel whose only previous experience in process control has been with the specifics of the physical equipment in their employer's plant (not with the underlying engineering principles and abstractions upon which the plant was based).

The innovation

In order to learn how to become effective process control operators, it was assumed that trainees would have to go beyond the information depicted on the display in diagrammatic form and develop a mental model of the actual referent situation. In other words, they would have to think as directly as possible about the plant's operation rather than being preoccupied by the set of symbols before them. Such a mental model would be necessary as a basis for making and implementing control decisions about information extracted from the process monitoring facilities available in the display. However, in order to build a mental model of plant equipment and processes abstractly represented in the display, trainees would need to read the display appropriately.

The reading of visual information is a two-way process. It involves both (a) the graphic elements comprising the visual material (external to the reader) and (b) what the viewer already knows about the subject matter depicted (internal to the reader). For the external component, reading is influenced bottom-up by basic perceptual characteristics (such as the size, shape, colour and arrangements of the display constituents). For the internal component, reading is influenced top-down by the knowledge a viewer brings to the reading experience (such as the knowledge that the colour of the symbol for a pump is green when running and orange when stopped). A key assumption underlying the approach used in the *Smart Operator*™ resource is that learners who are novices in a domain lack the specialized strategic knowledge required for productive reading of domain-related visuals (see Lowe, 1997). Therefore they are deficient in the top-down aspect of reading necessary to interpret this type of display effectively. In particular, they may not know:

- precisely which regions of the display deserve their attention (for example, is it most important initially to attend to the state of the pump, water supply tank, or control valve in Figure 18.1?);
- how to break up the display into appropriate components (for example,

should the various markings clustered in the bottom of Figure 18.1 be treated as essentially all parts of the same component or as if they are different components?);

● what sequence to follow when exploring the visual information in the display (for example, should the display simply be 'read' from top left down to bottom right, as would be done for text?);

● how to connect the various components of the display together to form meaningful relationships (for example, in what ways is the level in the water supply tank related to the state of the pump and the control valve which are the other two main display components?).

In the absence of such knowledge, trainee operators would have a very limited basis for initiating the interpretative processes involved in reading the displays used in *Smart Operator*™. By default, their 'reading' would be confined to exploration that was driven by little more than highly generalized fundamental perception. Without relevant knowledge, trainees would only be capable of seeing the display as a graphic pattern rather than reading it as a meaningful portrayal of the situation it represents. Therefore as part of their training they need to be given explicit support to compensate for their lack of strategic knowledge. In effect, there was an additional task to be considered in the instructional design; that of teaching the trainees how to read the display. This aspect must deal with aspects of reading a process control display that are no longer of conscious interest to subject matter experts whose perspective is necessarily very different from that brought to the display by novices in the domain.

Once the main instructional content of the multimedia training had been authored, a decision was made to precede it with a demonstration segment that taught trainees how to read process control displays effectively. This segment was produced as a narrated animation in which the explanatory information about the display was delivered by the spoken word so that trainees could dedicate their visual processing resources entirely to the graphic display (without having to split their attention between graphics and on-screen explanatory text). The demonstration segment was presented in the form of a 'walk-through' of a display screen that showed a simple control system for a water supply (Figure 18.2).

An important feature of this animated demonstration was that it actually *removed* many of the dynamic aspects that would be present in a fully functioning process control display. Animation was used highly selectively and only in order to make specific instructional points. A highly realistic ('literal') simulation of a process control display can be extremely complex visually because of the variety and pace of dynamic changes involved. The *Smart Operator*™ demonstration animation did not present the rich, continuous representation of all the changes that could occur in a real display because that would have imposed an overwhelming information processing load on the trainee. By using animation very sparingly and strategically, key material was presented to the trainee in ways designed to maximize instructional effectiveness while minimizing extraneous

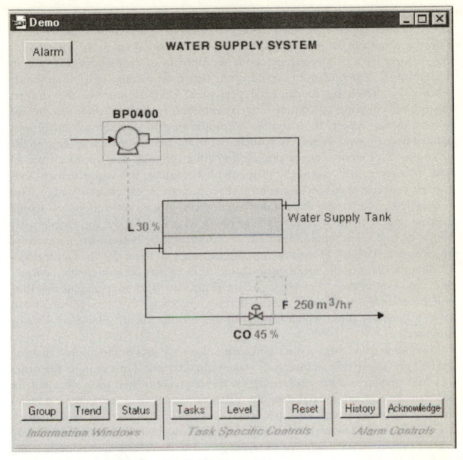

Figure 18.2   *'Walk through' of a display screen*

perceptual and cognitive demands. Note that this approach to the use of animation is novel in that it runs counter to the common practice of using the powerful technology available today to make animations as realistic as possible. Instead, priority was given to capacities of the learners (rather than to capacities of the technology).

The approach used in this demonstration was to begin working through the display information in a manner consistent with trainees' actual initial state when their instruction commenced (that is, a minimal starting level of domain-specific knowledge). This contrasts with the usual situation in which material is presented as offered by an engineer or experienced process control operator so that it is overwhelmingly dominated by a concern with content rather than being presented in a way that is centred upon a learner-based strategy or rationale for treatment of the information. This is not to imply any reduction in the importance of accuracy and completeness in the presentation of *Smart*

Operator's™content. Rather, it acknowledges that visual material provided by a subject matter expert may need to be extensively reworked and supplemented before it is suitable for presentation to beginners in the domain. It was assumed that trainees' lack of knowledge about the domain of process control (and its diagrammatic representation) would mean that their reading behaviour should initially be driven by fundamental perceptual characteristics of the display. Instead of following a 'content-driven' explanatory path as provided by the subject matter expert, the narrative accompanying the demonstration process control diagram was extensively reorganized in the first instance according to the visuo-spatial properties of the displayed graphic material. The approach was to start with perceptually compelling aspects of the display, not with the high-level abstract concepts about process control that characterize expert knowledge. This acknowledged the reality that for domain novices, process control displays would initially appear to be a relatively 'meaningless' graphic array and hence early efforts to read them would inevitably be dominated by bottom-up, generalized processing behaviour. However, it is also necessary to allow for the fact that not all salient features of the visual information in the display are sufficiently conspicuous (in terms of their perceptual characteristics) for us to be confident that they will be attended to by the viewer without direction. For this reason, clear, explicit guidance about which features of the information are salient needs to be provided.

In addition to relying on basic perceptual characteristics of the display, existing learned processing routines were also taken into account. For example, the order in which graphic entities comprising the display were treated took advantage of habituated, domain-general reading patterns rather than expecting trainees initially to struggle with the specialized and unfamiliar ways of reading such displays that would be used by domain experts (Lowe, 1993). The intention here was to keep the total cognitive processing load within reasonable bounds while gradually moving trainees to a basic understanding of the nature of process control diagrams.

The narrative accompanying the demonstration was supported visually by judiciously manipulating the amount and salience of information presented in the process control diagram. Initially the peripheral regions around the border of the diagram (containing buttons and labels) were removed so that only the central area largely comprised of diagrammatic information remained. Within this cut-down area, trainees were given support for selectively attending to individual graphic entities under discussion by visually de-emphasizing the remaining material to make currently non-salient information perceptually less conspicuous. These approaches can be seen in Figure 18.3 (an early frame in the animation) in which the starting point for explanation in the cut-down display is the water tank. This is both the central entity in the display area as well as the largest. The 'natural' perceptual conspicuity of the water tank was enhanced by modulating the relative display saliences to direct attention to this entity (by greying-out and blurring the rest of the display).

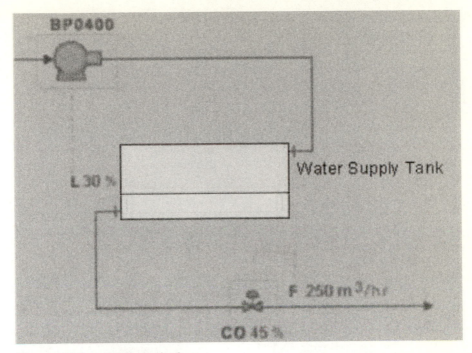

Figure 18.3 *Cut-down display*

The water tank element shown in Figure 18.3 was established as the initial reference entity for subsequent development of the explanatory path along which
trainees were guided during exploration of the display. The exposition continued
by carefully building away from this initial entity while considering perceptual
salience, proximity, habituated reading direction, and conceptual relatedness.
Consequently, the next two items introduced were the water pump at the top
left of the display and then the valve at the bottom right (Figure 18.4). Once
again, conspicuity was manipulated using the greying-out/blurring approach to
direct attention to the relevant elements.

With the introduction of these two further entities, the main components of
the water supply system represented by the diagram had been established so that
work could begin on relating the depiction to its real-life referents. In other
words, interpretation of the display in terms of the functions and behaviour of
the equipment represented was introduced as early as practicable so that a foundation for the development of situational meaning could be set down. An important aspect of developing such meaning is an appreciation of the key operational
relationships between the system's different components. It is these relationships
that link the individual pieces of information together into meaningful patterns.
Once the basic entities had been covered, key relationships were made explicit.
For example, the pipes leading from the pump to the water tank and then away
to the valve were identified in terms of their functional relations and the water

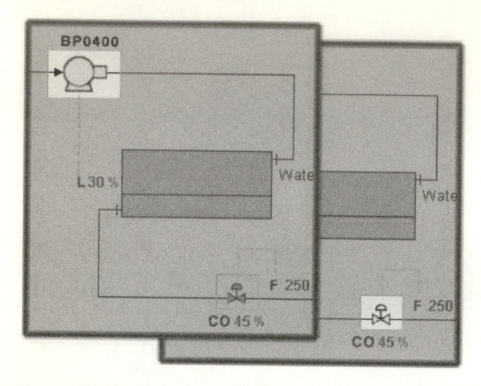

Figure 18.4 *Development of explanatory path*

flow between these items shown by an animated red dot moving along the pipe as these functional relations were explained. Later, more visually subtle relations were introduced, such as that between the physical water level in the tank and its numeric representation as a percentage (Figure 18.5).

Superficially, the water supply process control diagram appears relatively simple in graphic terms (for example, it contains few items). However, there are embedded rules which govern its dynamic behaviour and multiple levels of information that need to be 'unfolded' by the operator during process control activity. These hidden characteristics have the potential to overwhelm trainees if presented directly and exhaustively without considering the need to limit cognitive load. For this reason, another principle adopted for this development was to deal with the inherent complexity of process control display information by using multiple passes through the content. This entailed an approach of first providing a solid foundation then building up layers of information by progressive elaboration of that initial structure.

Experienced process control operators work on the basis of abstractions about the systems they deal with and this gives them the capacity to cope with a range of specific situations that arise. However, introducing such abstractions to trainees directly (as is the usual case with much instruction) is likely to be coun-

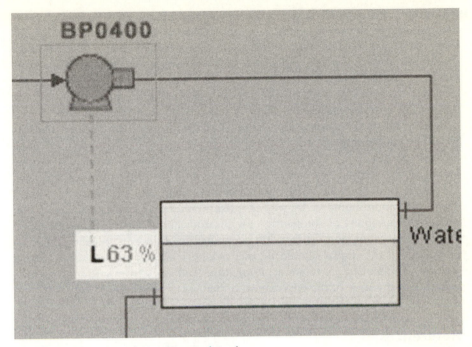

Figure 18.5   *Key relationships explained*

terproductive if there is no base of domain-specific knowledge to give them
meaning. In *Smart Operator*™, the approach used was to help users develop the
necessary abstractions from specific instances.

Implications

The approaches used in the project described in this chapter draw a clear distinction between the type of explanatory treatment of a visual display that would be
provided by a subject matter expert and the explanatory pathway likely to be
most appropriate for a student beginning in the subject domain. Because domain
novices lack the relevant knowledge necessary to guide productive and appropriate exploration of specialist visual displays, their initial processing is likely to be
driven largely by the perceptual characteristics of a display and habituated generalized visual processing routines. Rather than effectively ignoring these funda-
mentals and imposing expert-like treatments of the subject matter from the
outset, instructional designers would probably be wise to acknowledge and then
build upon these primary processing tendencies. The following discussion
suggests some ways in which this might be done.

When unfamiliar visualizations of content are first introduced to learners, the
initial presentation could follow a sequence expected for processing that was

determined largely by the perceptual properties of the display. This would mean beginning with the most perceptually compelling aspects of the display (those that were largest, boldest, most central, etc), even if these were not considered by the subject matter expert to be the most suitable starting point for an explanation. Design decisions about how to progress to other aspects of the display during the explanation would be made on the basis of minimizing the processing load for the learner by following a well-defined and orderly route that used the initial entities as a base for gradual elaboration. Excursions from the starting material would be limited at first so that a rich and coherent network of associations could be built up between various aspects of the display. Explicit explanation of the nature of the relationships between entities would be used with each of these excursions in order to help the learner combine them into a meaningful whole. This explanation should be by way of spoken rather than visual text in order to reduce the possibility of competition for a learner's limited processing resources. However, visual support via cues and manipulation of the perceptual conspicuity of regions of the display should be used where it directly guides the learner's attention to thematically relevant information (and away from current information that at any stage of the explanation is thematically irrelevant).

References

Lowe, R K (1993) Constructing a mental representation from an abstract technical diagram, *Learning and Instruction*, 3, pp 157–79

Lowe, R K (1997) *How Much are Pictures Worth?*, Proceedings of the Putting you in the picture workshop, University of Newcastle, pp 29–34

Lowe, R K (1999) Extracting information from an animation during complex visual learning, *European Journal of Psychology of Education*, **14**, pp 225–44

Lowe, R K and Neilsen, T E (1998) *Design and Development of an Intelligent Simulation Training System for Process Control Operators*, Proceedings of Ed-Media/Ed-Telecom 98 conference, Association for the Advancement of Computing in Education, USA, June, pp 839–44

Schnotz, W and Kulhavy, R (1994) *Comprehension of Graphics*, North Holland, Amsterdam

Chapter 19

Professional development in distance education – a successful experiment and future directions

Ulrich Bernath and Eugene Rubin

The Virtual Seminar in Distance Education is an online, World Wide Web-based asynchronous discussion forum that was designed to provide university faculty and administrators with professional development in the field of distance education. In 1996/7 it was a granted project within the Global Distance Learning Initiative sponsored by the AT&T Foundation and The International Council for Open and Distance Education (ICDE). In 1998 two further Virtual Seminars were run on a self-supporting basis.

Formal and informal evaluations of the Virtual Seminars took place externally as well as internally. During the course of the Virtual Seminars evaluation reports and experiences were published in various articles (Fritsch, 1998; Bernath and Rubin, 1998a, 1998b). A Final Report and Documentation of the first Virtual Seminar for Professional Development in Distance Education has also been published (Bernath and Rubin, 1999a).

This chapter presents data and experiences that compare the three Virtual Seminars and provide some general evaluation of and conclusion to the overall project.

Table 19.1   *Comparative data of three virtual seminars*

	1997	1998 I	1998 II
Number of participants of the Seminar	43	43	41
Number of participants of the final evaluation	33	27	22
Response rate	76.74	62.79	53.66
Participation in the final evaluation	required	voluntary	voluntary
Seminar fee	non	US$ 580	US$ 580
Special fee for group participation	non	non	yes

Table 19.1 shows that the three Virtual Seminars were similar in size in terms of numbers of participants. It was assumed that 40+ participants would form a group large enough to guarantee online activity in the Virtual Seminar and also to allow scalability. The first seminar was supported by the grant and was offered free of charge. One of the goals of the first seminar was a design that would be self-supporting and toward that end, a fee of US $580 was introduced for the second seminar. In the third seminar, a special rate for groups from one institution was implemented to try to encourage more group participation and thus encourage a synergy that would penetrate beyond the participants and into their institutions.

The evaluation process in the first Virtual Seminar was externally conducted by Helmut Fritsch, the director of the Central Institute for Distance Education Research of the German distance teaching university, the FernUniversität. One of the participation requirements in the first seminar was to participate in the evaluation. This explains the relatively high response rate in the final evaluation in the first Virtual Seminar. In both following Virtual Seminars in 1998, participation in the Pre-Seminar Survey as well as in the Final Questionnaire was voluntary.

Participants of the virtual seminars

The Virtual Seminars invited participation from anywhere. The endeavour was primarily marketed through ICDE as well as other professional networks. From the Pre-seminar Survey results we learned that there was a growing importance of the Internet as well as of collegial networks for the marketing of the Virtual Seminars.

For experimental reasons the first Virtual Seminar was open to a maximum of 45 participants; 15 places were reserved for potential German participants, 15 for

Maryland and 15 for various participants from around the world. The design was chosen to allow a face-to-face meeting for evaluation within the geographical area of each Seminar Leader.

The second Virtual Seminar was open without any restrictions, and participants were accepted on a first come, first served basis. In the third Virtual Seminar, 21 individual participants and 20 group participants from four institutions (one in Mexico and three in the USA) formed the seminar group.

The three Virtual Seminars attracted 127 faculty and distance education administrators from 24 different countries. A detailed breakdown of the participants' countries of origin can be found in Bernath and Rubin (1999b).

The syllabi of the Virtual Seminars

The curriculum of the Virtual Seminars was conceived as being a mix of both theory and practice. The concept of 'theory' was a broad one, which encompassed the foundations of distance education (its history and formal educational theories), a broad conceptual look at national, cultural and institutional structures, and an overview of the effect of technology on the field. These were broad categories of discussion, and represented an attempt to get new distance educators as well as programme directors in distance education to appreciate how distance education evolved and to identify the important influences and issues of the present.

The idea was to ask top experts within the field of distance education to act as an expert mentor in each of the four areas of 'theory' (see the curriculum below). It was argued that the presence of such a distinguished mentor would act not only as a direct source of information and opinion within each topic area, but it would also act as a 'motivator' for the continuing involvement of the participants. It was assumed that participating faculty and administrators would need a strong reason to continue in the Seminar and it was thought that the presence of these top 'name' experts would be such a motivator. Our four experts were Börje Holmberg for the foundations, Otto Peters for the theories, Gary Miller for the institutional models as well as organizational trends and Tony Bates for the technology in distance education module of the Virtual Seminars. We learned that the involvement of our distinguished experts in the discussions (with their readings and their live participation) was the key ingredient of the seminar, and had the most relevance to achieving the goal of both the students and the organizers of the Virtual Seminar.

The seminar experience

At the core of the seminar was an asynchronous online discussion among the participants, the seminar leaders and the experts. These discussions, which

Table 19.2   *The syllabi of three Virtual Seminars*

	1997	1998	1999
Pre-Seminar week	n.a.	Introduction and practice with the conferencing system	Introduction to our conferencing system
Week 1	Introduction and practice with the conferencing system	Foundations of Distance Education	Foundations of Distance Education
Week 2	Foundations of Distance Education		
Week 3	Institutional Models of Distance Education	Institutional Models of Distance Education	Theories in Distance Education
Week 4	Theories in Distance Education		
Week 5	Technology of Distance Education	Theories in Distance Education	Technology of Distance Education
Week 6	Introduction to DE. Applications and Projects		
Week 7	Student Support	Technology of Distance Education	Organizational Trends in Distance Education
Week 8	Instructional Design		
Week 9	Technologies	Distance Education Applications	Distance Education Applications
Week 10	Summary and Conclusion, Project reports	Summary and Conclusion	Summary and Conclusion
Open Forum week 1–10	n.a.	Discussion of Seminar Experiences	Discussion of Seminar Experiences

centred around the topics in Table 19.2, were structured to allow the participants and the experts to interact in a systematic manner. While there is a variety of software on the market which facilitates these kinds of discussions, we used HyperNews, which is a threaded conferencing environment, meaning that each comment submitted by a participant shows up in an outline which allows readers to follow the 'thread' of the conversation. HyperNews was installed on the UMUC Web site, and all worldwide participants had to access that site in order to read and contribute to the discussion.

Team approach

The seminar was managed and taught using a team approach. This meant that the Seminar Leaders jointly developed and delivered their instruction as well as any other inputs for moderating and facilitating the discussion process. Thus they were in constant touch via e-mail and telephone to agree on their postings. Occasional face-to-face meetings took place between the seminars for evaluation and revisions of the syllabi.

A typical seminar week usually started out the weekend before with an introduction to the coming week being drafted and sent to the other leader. The introductions usually outlined a structure for the discussion. After additions and revisions, these well-thought-out pre-prepared contributions by the leaders were then posted to the appropriate HyperNews conferences. During the week, as various comments were made in the discussions, the leaders would either individually respond to the various participant inputs, or an e-mail or telephone consultation regarding an appropriate response would occur, resulting in a joint response. At the end of each week, a summary would be drafted and revised between the two leaders, and this too would be posted on Thursday evening so that all participants could read it on Friday regardless of where they were located. When a module ended, over the weekend the main page of the Web site would be updated with new announcements. In addition, access to the new readings was provided online in our password-protected environment and the next module's discussions would be enabled.

The experts were also crucial members of the instructional team. In the first seminar, the participants put forth comments for the first day or two and then the experts came into the discussion. This resulted in considerable interaction between the expert and individual participants and less among the participants themselves. In the second and third seminars, the participants commented on and discussed the readings for the first week of the module, and the expert came into the discussion at the beginning of the second week. The move from one-week modules to two-week modules seemed to accomplish several goals. First, it encouraged more extensive discussions *among* the participants that were often fairly elaborate. Second, when the expert came in, there was already a considerable amount of discussion and this allowed the expert to respond to broad issues rather than individual comments. Third, it allowed the expert to have more interaction time in the module, and thus have more elaborated and detailed discussion of issues. As a member of the team, the expert was in e-mail and telephone contact with the leaders before the start of their module and sometimes during their module.

The cross-cultural dimension and the global aspect of the Virtual Seminars

One of the goals of the seminar was to enable a cross-cultural sharing of experiences, ideas and opinions. This was deemed to be a potential positive outcome because:

- distance education occurs in some manner in almost all countries of the world and in a wide variety of ways, and using a variety of levels of technology;
- distance education is increasingly becoming a world–wide enterprise in that courses are now capable of being delivered almost anywhere in the world; and
- the cultural and regional bias that each participant brought to the discussion would result in a broader and deeper learning.

Our three seminar experiences definitely supported the above supposition that the cross-cultural aspects of the seminar would result in positive outcomes. Not only was a broad variety of opinion expressed, but often these opinions prompted discussion that reflected a more comprehensive analysis and understanding of critical issues. This was particularly true of technology–related discussions, where participants from nations that were not highly technology enabled often came up with innovative and useful solutions to problems that did not occur to participants from high-technology countries.

By being globally accessible via the Internet, the content and interaction allowed participants to differentiate and generalize across cultural borders and among the diverse practices within the field of distance education. It gave depth to the learning and forced the participants to think beyond their own cultural and environmental constraints.

The seminars were offered only in English and this inhibited some of the participants from fully engaging in the seminar. There was some evidence that a few participants were hesitant to contribute to the discussions because of their lack of confidence in their English skills. The Final Questionnaire results on the item 'I had some language problems' indicate that only very few stated 'I fully agree' (3.33 per cent, 3.70 per cent, 0.00 per cent in each seminar respectively), but a reasonable amount stated 'I partly agree' (33.33 per cent, 18.52 per cent, 22.73 per cent). On the other hand, if the seminar was only offered in each participant's native language, this would have diminished the benefits of the cross-cultural environment.

A knowledge building community

One of our experts, Otto Peters, observed that the seminar appeared to be a virtual *knowledge building community* (Peters, 1998). While this is not a new concept in the literature about computer-mediated communication, Professor Peters' observation summed up quite well the experience of most of the people involved in the seminars. Each seminar was a community in that the participants met, talked, agreed, sometimes strongly disagreed, sympathized, empathized, and formed relationships (several of which have lasted beyond the end of the seminars). And like other types of communities, each seminar was different from the others. Each had its own 'feel', its own pace, group dynamics and its own emphases on content matters. It was clear that the individual personalities of the participants and their backgrounds played a role in how the community functioned.

It is certainly true that our community was a knowledge building community. Both the experts and the participants built public as well as private knowledge structures from the discussions and readings. The open discussions forced people to think and rethink their ideas as well as sometimes to defend them. This kind of collaborative enterprise is being recognized as a critical component of online learning in the literature and needs to continue to be explored in a systematic manner.

The experts also gave positive reports regarding their own experience in the Virtual Seminars. They too felt stimulated by the discussion and enjoyed the give and take of ideas. The seminar experience became a milestone for significant research and programme developments in the field of online education and training.

The witness learner

Our formal evaluator for the first seminar, Helmut Fritsch, looked at the on-screen participation in the seminar as well as the questionnaire data and the face-to-face interviews with the participants. What struck him was the discrepancy between measurable, visible participation (appearing on the screen with a comment during the discussions) and the self-report of many of the participants that they were 'active', only they did not 'say' anything. In other words, many of the participants reported that they regularly read the discussion (sometimes every day) but for a variety of reasons chose not to actively submit a written contribution. It was clear that if one only looked at the written contributions, the participation rate appeared to be only about 50 per cent (and even then, not at all times). Yet, it also seemed clear that many of those whom we thought were functional dropouts were not. At the end of the seminar these non-contributors reported that they learnt a considerable amount from the seminar. Fritsch coined the term *witness learning*, to indicate that these 'passive' participants were in fact active learners, and that they appeared to learn from witnessing the interactions among the 'active' participants, leaders and experts. This is probably not unlike what happens in a face-to-face class where only a few students 'speak up' while the other students appear passive, and just listen. This was a kind of revelation to the seminar leaders, who often thought that what they saw on the screen was the total reality. It turned out not to be so. Other online seminars and classes would benefit from using software that tracked student 'reading' behaviour (whether they looked at a particular comment) versus their 'saying' behaviour (submitting a comment), thus giving a more accurate measure of dropout. There are software packages available on the market today that supply this capability.

As Fritsch has observed, the idea of witness learning was not previously prominent in distance education. This is because the one-to-one relation (Holmberg,
1995) that characterized correspondence education did not allow for multiple
participants in the interactions. Helmut Fritsch related the setting of the Virtual
Seminar and the notion of witness learning to distance education using online
tutorials. Such new settings allow the limitations of the one-to-one relation
between the tutor and the student in traditional correspondence education to be
overcome (Fritsch, 1998).

The ripple effect

It was also observed (by Ulrich Bernath) that the asynchronous mode of
computer conferencing allowed the reader to think over the dialogue for a
while, rethink it later or even sleep over the messages, before responding. It
seemed to be much like throwing a stone into the water (the incoming messages)
and seeing the ripples expand outward (the pondering on the content of the
message). In direct modes of communication one usually wouldn't wait and
ponder before answering. In asynchronous discussion processes one can 'work'
on the answer to be given. This pondering allows one to go in-depth and to raise
new ideas and notions to the surface. Furthermore, the written contributions to
the discussions remain and have effect on later discussions. As we moved from
topic to topic, things we discussed earlier – still available in their written form –
could be cited and therefore arose again and again in later discussions. With the
ripple effect in asynchronous dialogues we gain the power of reflection which
may substitute for some lack of spontaneity.

Participation

The participation data from the three seminars reveals interesting patterns. The
data from the first seminar showed that the average length of a comment posted
by a participant to the discussions with the experts was 187 words (with a range
of 76 to 477 words). To give an idea of how much this represents, a typical
single-spaced typewritten page holds about 350 words. This means that the
average contribution was about one half of a typewritten page. The 43 participants of the first seminar posted 250 comments and produced a total of 46,739
words over the five weeks with the experts. This represents a total of 133 typewritten pages. When added to the 56 comments and 11,796 words in the
distance education application modules in weeks seven to ten, the total was
58,535 words or over 167 typewritten pages of discussion over a period of eight
weeks. This did not include two weeks that dealt with introductions, administrative issues, etc, and represents only the discussion that was contributed by the
participants. The experts and seminar leaders contributed almost an equal volume
of discussion (61,178 words which equals 174 typewritten pages). Thus, any
active participant had to read the assigned online readings (not included in the

above data), and then read 340+ (167 + 174) pages of discussion. By almost any standard, the sheer volume of this task was formidable and thus the rate of participation is quite impressive.

Participation data can be quite deceptive. If one is told that a typical participant contributed an average of six comments over the course of eight weeks, each of which averaged 187 words, this seems to represent only a very small amount of activity. Yet these modest averages, when multiplied by 43 participants, results in over 46,000 words and the equivalent of more than 167 typewritten pages. The *volume* of participation actually increased across the three seminars from a total of 192 participants' contributions in 1997 up to 323 in 1998(I) and finally up to 375 in 1998(II). Thus, in the third seminar a participant (and leader) had to read an estimated 500+ pages of text.

This data clearly shows how the sheer volume of online activity can be overwhelming to both the teacher and the student, and why the workload of online faculty is often reported as significantly higher than face-to-face teaching. Our data certainly suggests that 40+ participants may be too many for the type of course structure and style of interaction of this seminar. It also suggests that similar systematic analyses of participant contributions should be done for other courses offered in the online environment to understand the effect on participation and workload. The data also suggests that the scalability of the seminar (the potential for reaching large numbers of faculty and administrators) is somewhat limited because the number of participants in each seminar needs to be limited to control the high volume of reading (at least for this interactive seminar model). Thus, while the seminar potentially can be offered many times online, each seminar would need to be staffed and could only be offered to, say, 25–30 participants at a time.

This will work fine on a limited scale (eg within a particular institution), but is difficult to implement on a large scale (eg thousands of participants).

The compiled data on participation shows that on average 50 per cent of all participants contributed to the discussions and that these contributors were responsible for 60 per cent of the total contributions. This translates into over 52 per cent of the total words written to the virtual seminar. This data suggest that in online professional development there can be significant involvement by the participants. The data we collected was helpful in allowing us to analyse the various aspects of participation. The data was less helpful to analyse adequately the phenomenon of non–participation. More detailed information about comparative participation data of three Virtual Seminars can be found in Bernath and Rubin (1999b).

The results of the final evaluation questionnaire

Participants were asked to complete a questionnaire at the end of each seminar. As can be seen in Table 19.1, the response rates for the three seminars were 77, 63 and 54 per cent respectively. While there were some differences between the seminars, the overall trends were quite similar. Participants were asked how important certain specific goals were for them, and whether or not they felt they achieved them. In summary, participants felt they had achieved most of their personal (professional and scholarly) goals as a result of the seminar.

When asked which elements contributed most to their personal success, participants indicated the seminar readings, their active participation in the discussion and witnessing other discussions. When asked to rate their behaviour in the seminar, participants were fairly positive. For example, when asked about the statement: *I think I reached the cognitive learning objectives of the seminar*, 48 per cent of the participants in the first seminar said they fully agreed and 42 per cent said they partially agreed, for a total of 90 per cent that indicated a positive outcome for this statement. The participants in the second (92 per cent) and third seminars (91 per cent) also indicated positive agreement. When asked about the statement: *I would be able to formulate my own position on DE theory*, 85 per cent, 81 per cent and 91 per cent, respectively, indicated a positive outcome.

Conclusions

One of the more intriguing outcomes of the Virtual Seminar is the joint decision of the two Seminar Leaders and their respective institutions (University of Maryland University College and Carl von Ossietzky University of Oldenburg) to pursue the design, development and delivery of a Master of Distance Education degree. This decision came directly from the original intent to develop a means to train faculty and administrators in the area of distance education. While pursuing this goal, the Seminar Leaders began to see that, in fact, there was a broad range of content and skills that needed to be addressed, and that there was a serious need for more comprehensive education/training for those who manage and direct the distance education enterprise. The new Master of Distance Education programme started in January 2000.

There are other similar Masters programmes, for example the Open University of the UK, Athabasca University in Canada and the University of Southern Queensland in Australia, but it was apparent to the authors that the demand for such training was rapidly increasing and the providers were few and far between.

It is this first course on Foundations of Distance Education in the new Masters programme that is the direct evolution of the Virtual Seminar, and the syllabus and teaching methods of this first course will be directly based on the syllabus and methods of the Virtual Seminar. As it stands, the Virtual Seminar is an ideal model for a broad look at distance education and would serve as an effective introduction to the field for beginning graduate students. We plan to continue the team teaching model and to continue to use a somewhat modified expert guided structure. For us, the Seminar Leaders, this was the perfect logical outcome of the Virtual Seminar.

It is worthwhile to mention that the seminar experience has proven to be applicable to the participants in other contexts. We learned this from participants who are now using HyperNews for their own teaching and from others who are applying the seminar concept and the experience to run their own computer conferences, virtual seminars and virtual tutorials.

We are glad that our participants in the experimental first Virtual Seminar agreed to allow a complete documentation of the virtual seminar process (Bernath and Rubin, 1999a). This documentation allows a deeper insight into the microstructure of our Virtual Seminar for Professional Development in Distance Education.

References

Bernath, U and Rubin, E (1998a) A virtual seminar for international professional development in distance education, in *INFORMATIK FORUM*, **12** (1), March, pp 18–23

Bernath, U and Rubin, E (1998b) Virtual Seminars for University Faculty and Administrators 'Professional Development in Distance Education' – A comparative approach to evaluation, in *ONLINE EDUCA BERLIN*, 4th International Conference on Technology Supported Learning, Book of Abstracts, 2–4 December, International WHERE + HOW, Bonn, pp 287 ff

Bernath, U and Rubin, E (eds) (1999a) Final Report and Documentation of the Virtual Seminar for Professional Development in Distance Education, A project within the AT&T Global Distance Learning Initiative sponsored by the AT&T Foundation and the International Council for Open and Distance Education (ICDE), BIS-Verlag, Oldenberg

Bernath, U and Rubin, E (1999b) *An International Virtual Seminar for University Faculty and Administrators: Professional development in distance education*, Paper presented to the 19th ICDE World Conference in Vienna, 23 June, 1999, available at http://www.uni-oldenburg.de/zef/literat/vienna2.htm

Fritsch, H (1998) Witness-learning. Pedagogical implications of net-based teaching and learning, in *media@uni-mulit.media? Entwicklung – Gestaltung – Evaluation neuer Medien*, ed M Hauff, pp 123 ff, Waxmann, Berlin (Medien in der Wissenschaft; Bd. 6)

Holmberg, B (1995) The evolution of the character and practice of distance education, in *Open Learning*, June, pp. 47–53

Peters, O (1998) *Learning and Teaching in Distance Education. Analyses and interpretations from an international perspective*, Kogan Page, London, pp 146 ff

Index